CHAIRMAN'S BOOK PRIZE
presented to

CARLY BLACK

for placing Third in Grade 9

STRATHCONA-TWEEDSMUIR SCHOOL

50 LEADERS WHO CHANGED HISTORY

50 LEADERS WHO CHANGED HISTORY

FROM CAESAR TO CHURCHILL, LEARN FROM THE MASTERS

CHARLES PHILLIPS

NEW BURLINGTON

NEW BURLINGTON

This book was designed, conceived, and produced by
Quantum Books Ltd
6 Blundell Street
London N7 9BH
United Kingdom

© 2015 Quantum Books Ltd

QUMLEAD

Publisher: Kerry Enzor
Senior Editor: Philippa Davis
Copyeditor: Donna Gregory
Proofreader: Josh Ireland
Indexer: Diana LeCore
Production Manager: Rohana Yusof
Design: Amazing 15
Cover Design: Jason Anscomb

ISBN: 978-1-84573-590-6

2 4 6 8 10 9 7 5 3 1

Printed in China by Toppan Leefung

CONTENTS

INTRODUCTION

As Commander-in-Chief of the Continental Army in the American Revolutionary War of 1775–83 and then as the first president of the United States in 1789–97, George Washington is often seen as the archetypal leader.

A great general in war, an authoritative head of state in peacetime, and a man who commanded the love of his people, Washington is often held up as the example against which we can judge all other leaders. He combined moral character, great energy, bravery, self-discipline, a strong sense of duty, and an ability to connect with and inspire those he led. Many of these qualities characterize other great men and women covered in this survey of history's 50 greatest leaders. But our investigation—which examines the achievements of diverse leaders including William Shakespeare, Mother Teresa, and Steve Jobs—also uncovers other, quite different characteristics such as an eye for opportunity, profound conviction, and a focus on simplicity.

What can we learn from these distinguished women and men if we are seeking to be leaders today? The examples of these great leaders—spanning centuries, continents, and fields from politics to commerce, culture and arts to military— demonstrate the myriad leadership styles that have been successfully developed and adopted. In many ways these articles highlight the individuality of the leader: As Vince Lombardi believed, leaders achieve success by their own hard work and determination. Leadership is about determining your own style, ideals, and aims, and setting out to achieve your goal.

Yet by pulling out core leadership styles across the 50 chapters, we also highlight sometimes surprising similarities: Karl Marx, William Shakespeare, and Steve Jobs are united by their innovative thinking that introduced new ideas and products to the world. Baseball manager John McGraw is set next to empire-builders Charlemagne and Frederick the Great, all three examples of ambitious leaders who aimed for only the best. It is these key characteristics that can span such disparate contexts that highlight the essential qualities we can use and adapt as leaders of all stripes today.

George Washington is held up as an exemplary leader. This equine statue celebrating the founding father stands in the Public Garden in Boston.

BE BOLD AND DETERMINED

Bold and decisive action is a recurring theme across all the stories in this book. Embodied by leaders from Roman general Julius Caesar to British Prime Minister Winston Churchill who made his defiant stand against Nazi Germany in World War II; leaders need to be bold to pursue their aims even in the face of challenges.

Such steadfastness is demonstrated not just by military leaders but by a whole spectrum of inspirational men and women whose absolute commitment to their cause enabled them to overcome setbacks and persevere. Jesus of Nazareth, Saint Peter, Mohandas Gandhi, Nelson Mandela, and Martin Luther King, Jr all weathered persecution and imprisonment in the name of their beliefs but proved steadfast in their commitment to their cause.

THE LEADER AS HEALER

All of these leaders were committed to healing divisions and promoting compassion and unity. As modern leaders we may be able to use our leadership gifts to find solutions to seemingly intractable problems, to bring opponents together, and to affect meaningful change; a positive outlook and a determination to defy the impossible can mark a leader out in any age. Think of Nelson Mandela and his commitment to healing the wounds of the apartheid era in South Africa or Daniel Barenboim, whose West-Eastern Divan Orchestra brings together Arab and Israeli musicians to help them find common ground in musical expression.

In order to bring meaningful change leaders need not only to have a strength of conviction in their own ideas but also to inspire others and to lead people to implement their vision. According to Ancient Greek biographer Plutarch, Alexander the Great made his soldiers feel as if they were unbeatable, leading them to successive victories on the battlefield. This ability to instil confidence is a key aspect of leadership. It is also seen in great sports leaders such as John McGraw and football coach Vince Lombardi.

Being a team leader may also involve having an eye for talent: Not only McGraw and Lombardi, but also the great Hollywood producer Samuel Goldwyn and computer pioneer Steve Jobs possessed this gift. Once a leader has talent in his or her team, he or she needs to be able to manage the team members so that they are happy to work alongside each other in a cooperative spirit. British prime minister Clement Attlee, who oversaw a period of great change immediately after World War II, and US presidents Abraham Lincoln and Franklin D. Roosevelt all possessed this capacity.

LISTENING AND PERSUADING

To work a team effectively leaders also need an ability to listen. Genghis Khan, famous for his utterly ruthless and bloody waging of war, might not seem an obvious example of this, but he paid attention to his advisors when they suggested he preserve the villages and craftsmen of the territories he conquered so he could levy taxes on their produce over the years. He was persuaded to take the long view. Leaders need to be able to listen to others and heed advice; they also need to listen to their own inner voice and trust their intuition to guide them in often difficult decisions. Napoleon relied on intuitive decision-making in the heat of battle, while Steve Jobs used his intuition in making million-dollar business choices.

A leader who knows what he or she wants to achieve must still convince others to follow. Arguably, the ability to persuade is the most essential of leadership qualities. Some leaders choose to embody the change they promote: Mohandas Gandhi or Mother Teresa made their way of living their message, while Siddhārtha Gautama demonstrated the effects of his teachings in his own life. Others possess the ability to speak with great persuasiveness, using rhetoric and impassioned delivery to convince: Those such as Winston Churchill, Martin Luther King, Jr, Abraham Lincoln, and the great orator Pericles, all famed for their delivery of seminal speeches. Such leaders engage not only their contemporary listeners, but also generations afterward, and their words still ring out today to inspire us.

HOW TO USE THIS BOOK

Organized by date of birth, the chapters in this book have been carefully designed for ease of reference. Each of the chapters in the book is color coded according to the type of leader being discussed (see key right). An information panel at the start of each article provides a quick summary of the key details, and a leadership analysis panel sums up the take-away lessons from each story—including the leadership type typified by that example (see key right). Time lines with key events are also featured with the key turning points indicated by the larger circle next to that specific entry.

KEY TO SECTIONS

 Arts and Culture

 Military

 Politics and Society

Religion

KEY TO LEADER ICONS

 Innovator   Defiant

 Combative   Reformer

 Leader by example   Persuasive

 Ambitious   Collaborative

 Unifier   Talent-promoter

 Strategist   Ruthless

 Paternalistic   Proud

 Inspiring   Revolutionary

1 MOSES

ORIGINAL FREEDOM FIGHTER WHO LED THE ISRAELITES' EXODUS FROM EGYPT

NATIONALITY: *Israelite*
ACHIEVEMENT: *Led Israelites from slavery to the brink of the Promised Land, establishing the Jewish faith*
WHEN: *Fourteenth century BC*

Generations have been inspired by the biblical narrative of Moses leading the Israelites out of slavery in Egypt—an account of an initially self-doubting man who took on the might of a great empire and convinced his people to follow him to freedom.

Moses is revered as the archetype of a prophetic leader—one who establishes laws and norms of behavior for the people he leads, while fostering an inspiring vision of what the future holds. According to the biblical narrative, Moses was an Egyptian-born Israelite warrior chosen by God to free his people from slavery and lead them toward their Promised Land of Canaan. In this tradition, Moses saved the Israelites from being subsumed in the melting pot of Egyptian society, and after their exodus, at Mount Sinai, established their enduring religious traditions.

The behavior Moses is said to have showed as leader of the Israelites has been a source of inspiration for many leaders. In the United States Martin Luther King, Jr, took on the mantle of a Moses in inspiring African-Americans in the civil rights struggle of the 1960s. King convinced people to adopt his strategy of civil disobedience in challenging racial injustice—and to follow him toward a brighter future (see page 206). He declared in a speech on April 2 1968, "I've seen the Promised Land ... I want you to know tonight that we, as a people, will get to the Promised Land."

For centuries many people who drew strength from the narrative of Moses believed implicitly in the story. Modern scholarship, however, suggests that the events of the story probably did not take place as told in the Bible. Nonetheless the narrative retains immense power for the force of the example it sets. People who seek inspiration from Moses outside of a religious context generally choose to focus more on the human and spiritual truth of the story than on whether it is historic.

Whether or not the events happened as described in the Bible, the story of a people being set free from slavery has many resonances for our lives—as does the account of Moses coming of age as a leader, forging his character in the most challenging of circumstances and then proving himself a man of faith and steadfast character.

CONVICTION—AND OVERCOMING DOUBT

In the biblical narrative Moses was called to his role as leader when he heard God's voice issuing from a bush on the slopes of Mount Sinai. According to the Book of Exodus

THE TEN COMMANDMENTS

1 You shall have no other gods before me
2 You shall not make idols
3 You shall not misuse the name of the Lord your God
4 Remember the Sabbath day by keeping it holy
5 Honor your father and your mother

6 You shall not murder
7 You shall not commit adultery
8 You shall not steal
9 You shall not bear false witness against your neighbor
10 You shall not covet.

Moses was living in exile at this time, having fled Egypt after he killed an Egyptian he found beating an Israelite. The voice of God told Moses he must return to his native Egypt and liberate his people, the Israelites, from slavery—then lead them to freedom.

Initially Moses did not believe he was up to the task, concerned that as a stammerer he was not well equipped to confront the Egyptian pharaoh. God—while stressing that divine power would go with him—conceded that Moses could involve his brother Aaron, a more confident speaker. A good deal of the power of the Moses narrative stems from this: The Bible shows him as a flawed leader, one lacking in self-confidence, doubtful of his ability to succeed in the monumental task set before him. We might interpret the command of God as the voice of Moses's inner conviction, his strong sense of what he should do, and Moses's lack of faith in his own ability as the inner voice of self-doubt that, from time to time, plagues leaders of all stripes. In his decision to take his brother with him to negotiate with the pharaoh Moses displayed impressive self-knowledge. He knew his strengths—and took steps to manage his weaknesses.

Another key aspect was his toughness. One of the most celebrated parts of the narrative is when Moses and Aaron confront the pharaoh with God's command "Let my people go!" And, after the pharaoh refuses, they hit Egypt with ten plagues, ranging from the turning of the waters of the Nile into blood, through infestations of frogs, lice and locusts to God's threat to kill the firstborn child of every family in Egypt. This account showed Moses to be immensely forceful—willing to take negotiations to the very brink. Leaders may often need to call on their determination to overcome opposition and drive on in the face of resistance.

INSPIRING FAITH IN OTHERS

According to the Bible, following the devastating plagues the pharaoh finally allowed the Israelites to depart. However, almost immediately he suffered a change of heart and

TIME LINE

The events below probably took place in the thirteenth century BC.

- Moses is born to Israelites Jochebed and Amram of the tribe of Levi.

- Abandoned as a child to escape being killed under a royal decree.

- Found by the pharaoh's daughter and raised at court.

- Kills an Egyptian and escapes to Midian.

- In Midian, on Mount Sinai, God calls him to return to Egypt and free the Israelites.

- Through Ten Plagues of increasing severity God and Moses force the pharaoh's hand.

- The Israelites make their exodus from Egypt.

- The pharaoh has a change of heart and pursues them.

- The waters of the Red Sea open, allowing the Israelites to escape, then close once more—drowning the pursuing Egyptians.

- On Mount Sinai Moses receives the Ten Commandments and founds the key traditions of Jewish faith.

- The Israelites wander for 40 years.

- Moses dies within sight of the Promised Land, passing leadership to Joshua.

set off in pursuit to reclaim his slaves. In a powerful part of the narrative, divine power held back the waters of the Red Sea to allow the Israelites to escape, then released the floods to drown the Egyptians who came after. Modern scholars have debated whether such a phenomenon could be explained by natural causes. One theory is that Moses relied on his knowledge of local tidal patterns: He knew when the tide was low enough to cross and when the water would pour back on his pursuers; another is that a strong wind cleared shallow waters to reveal a reed bed that the Israelites were able to cross. However, regardless of the historicism of the account, the message of the story is in Moses's able handling of the Israelites' dramatic escape. Like many a later leader,

HISTORY AND MEMORY

Some scholars argue that the events portrayed in the Moses story did take place, even if they have been modified in the telling. One theory is that the Exodus from Egypt took place in the thirteenth century BC when Ramses II (c.1304–c.1237 BC) was in power. Others suggest that the biblical account may derive from a folk memory of military campaigns by Egyptian pharaoh Ahmose in c.1530 BC in which he drove Levantine peoples out of the Nile Delta. Yet another theory posits that the story of Moses has roots in the life of Egyptian pharaoh Akhenaton (reigned 1353–1336 BC) who attempted to take Egyptian religion in a new direction, when he declared that there was only one god, the sun disc (Aten), and closed all rival deities' temples.

Moses offered a prayer to God after what he believed was a divine miracle—the parting of the Red Sea.

Moses needed to convince his followers to trust him at a moment of great crisis.

LAWGIVER

Bringing the Israelites out of Egypt was by no means the end of Moses's task: In the traditional narrative, he returned to Mount Sinai, where he established the basic elements of the Jewish faith. Moses achieved this by laying out the Covenant under which the Israelites worshipped God in return for his care and protection; receiving the Ten Commandments; creating the priesthood under the sons of his brother Aaron, and establishing the tradition under which God was present with the wandering Israelites in the portable Tabernacle (dwelling place).

For all this Moses is celebrated by the Jews as the Great Lawgiver of Israel, as Moshe Rabbenu (Moses, Our Teacher). Traditionally he is identified as the author of the first five books of the Bible— Genesis, Exodus, Leviticus, Numbers, and Deuteronomy. His narrative also explains the origin of the central Jewish festival: The final plague of the ten he visited on the pharaoh was the occasion of the Jewish Passover celebrated to this day.

Christians and Muslims alike honor Moses as a prophet, a messenger of God. From a secular perspective, meanwhile, he stands tall as one of the greatest leaders in all religious and philosophical traditions—a brave and steadfast man who inspired faith in his followers, led them in overcoming the gravest hardships, and established the religious and civic traditions by which they would live for thousands of years. A leader who developed inner strength through difficult experience and exemplified the strength and passion his followers needed.

LEADERSHIP ANALYSIS

LEADER TYPE: *Paternalistic*
KEY QUALITIES: *Brave, steadfast, faithful*
LIKEMINDED LEADERS: *Prophet Muhammad, Jesus of Nazareth, Mohandas Gandhi*
FACT: *According to the biblical tradition, Moses died on his 120th birthday.*

2 PERICLES

GREAT GENERAL WHO NURTURED GREEK DEMOCRACY AND ESTABLISHED AN ATHENIAN EMPIRE

Greek statesman and general Pericles led the Greek city of Athens to greatness and fostered the city's democratic institutions. He is celebrated above all as an orator who delivered clear-headed and superbly structured speeches.

NATIONALITY: *Greek*
ACHIEVEMENT: *Founded democracy in Athens*
WHEN: *c.450 BC*

In 431 BC Pericles delivered a funeral oration to honor the Athenian soldiers who had died in the first year of the Peloponnesian War. The stirring address was described by the ancient historian Thucydides in his account of the Peloponnesian War between Athens and Sparta (431–404 BC). It is said that in this speech Pericles demonstrated the peerless rhetoric and persuasive delivery for which he has been praised for centuries, elevating the greatness of Athens as a city "open … to the world" whose laws afforded "equal justice to all," a city that offered a shining example—an "education"—to all of Greece.

It was an established custom in Athens to hold a public funeral at the year's end for those who had died in battle: One of the foremost citizens of the city would deliver a funeral oration. Pericles's speech, however, departed from custom, focusing initially not on Athenian ancestors and recently killed warriors but on the greatness of the city of Athens herself. The people of Athens, he proclaimed, lived exactly as they pleased and yet were ready to face danger; perhaps nowhere in the world were there citizens so self-dependent, so ready to deal with emergencies, and so versatile. Pericles concluded his impassioned address by encouraging the living to be fired in battle by the values of their city as established by their ancestors: For "to be happy means to live in freedom, and to be free means to act bravely."

CLEAR-THINKING PERSUADER

Pericles came to power through his gift for persuasion. He was a clear thinker, a student of philosophy who was a good decision-maker; but his essential leadership strength was his ability to speak convincingly in appealing to reason in others.

He drew his authority from his capacity to convince his audience of a course of action. This is a quality required by all who seek to be leaders: Without the ability to convince others, any leader will struggle to put her or his ideas into action. Pericles had the rhetorical power to which great public speakers aspire. In particular, historians have compared Pericles's funeral oration of 431 BC (as immortalised by Thucydides) to

▲ *Pericles's finest hour—his stirring funeral oration in honor of the war dead of 431 BC—is imagined on this Greek banknote of 1955.*

President Lincoln's Gettysburg Address of November 19 1863, another famous speech that honored the dead while praising the values for which they had been fighting.

PHILOSOPHER AND SUPPORTER OF REFORM

Pericles came from a wealthy and well-connected family and took a great interest in education. He spent time with and learned from the philosophers Protagoras, Zeno of Elea (famous for his paradoxes and said by fellow-philosopher Aristotle to be the inventor of dialectics), and Anaxagoras, from whom Pericles particularly learned to remain unruffled in the face of trouble. He was a patron of the playwright Aeschylus and gave his support to the democratic reforms of Ephialtes, who introduced the popular assembly (Ecclesia), council, and law courts to counter the political power of the aristocrats. It was in the wake of Ephialtes's assassination in 461 BC that Pericles rose to prominence in political life.

According to Greek biographer Plutarch, who wrote a life of Pericles in c. AD 100, Pericles was extremely hard-working: He gave all his time to public office and none to the management of his own estates and reputedly only ever once attended a social occasion—from which he departed early. He managed the democratic institutions of Athens very skillfully and was renowned for remaining calm and clearheaded in the face of any apparent difficulty.

BUILDER OF THE PARTHENON

Pericles's most enduring physical legacy was the Parthenon temple and the buildings of the Acropolis in Athens. He oversaw the building of the Parthenon, which started in 447 BC, and a magnificent monumental gateway, the Propylaea, begun in 437 BC. The plan to rebuild the temples destroyed by the Persians (who had sacked Athens in 480 BC) was debated at a conference of Greek states called by Pericles. Such lavish expenditure, funded by annual tribute paid by the other states in the Athenian-led alliance, was challenged by Thucydides, (a different Thucydides to the historian who would write

TIME LINE

c.495 BC
Born.

492 BC
Persian War begins.

480 BC
Persians sack Athens.

478 BC
Athens is leading state in Greek alliance.

472 BC
Pericles pays for Aeschylus's Persian trilogy of plays.

461 BC
Enters public life after assassination of Ephialtes.

460 BC
War among Greek states.

454 BC
Leads defeat of Achaea.

447 BC
Building of the Acropolis begins.

445 BC
Peace with Sparta.

443 BC
Unchallenged leader of Athens after exile of Thucydides.

440 BC
Defeats rebellion by Samos.

431 BC
Delivers celebrated funeral oration.

429 BC
Dies, in Athens.

c.404 BC
Thucydides writes history of Peloponnesian War.

AD c.100
Plutarch writes Life of Pericles.

Pericles's life). Pericles's defense—on the grounds that the allies' tribute bought protection and as long as Athens provided this she could spend the money as she pleased—won the day and Thucydides was exiled. Having secured victory with his powers of persuasion, Pericles became the unchallenged leader of Athens after 443 BC.

COMBATIVE STANCE IN WAR

The war among the Greek states that began in 460 BC had been halted in 445 BC by the Thirty Years Peace between Athens and Sparta. Thereafter both sides maintained largely peaceful relations, but in the late 430s war began to seem more and more inevitable. Athens imposed a

PICTURING THE FUTURE

One of Pericles's great strengths as a public speaker was his ability to deliver compelling pictures of the future. The future he described was attainable, he promised, if those listening accepted his analysis of the present—and made the decision he was backing. Conceptualizing the future and describing it engagingly is a key aspect of a leader's vision-building role. Leaders must describe where a company or department is heading and what the benefits of following a particular direction will be. This can involve picturing the future that your company will create. An innovator such as Steve Jobs at Apple, Inc. built his success on a vision that wed technology to creativity (see page 215). He said: "It is in Apple's DNA that technology alone is not enough—it's technology married with [...] the humanities."

PERICLES'S PARTHENON

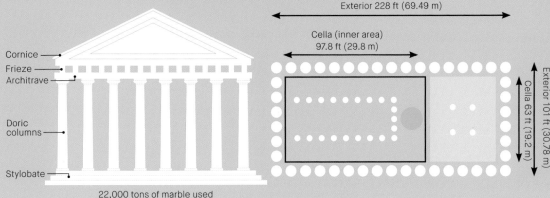

Cornice
Frieze
Architrave
Doric columns
Stylobate

22,000 tons of marble used

Exterior 228 ft (69.49 m)

Cella (inner area) 97.8 ft (29.8 m)

Exterior 101 ft (30.78 m)
Cella 63 ft (19.2 m)

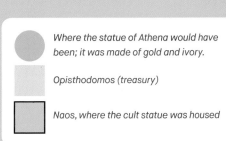

Where the statue of Athena would have been; it was made of gold and ivory.

Opisthodomos (treasury)

Naos, where the cult statue was housed

ban on produce from Megara (an ally of Sparta) through its empire, and allied with Corcyra (a colony of Corinth). When Sparta insisted that Athens back down on the Megaran trade ban and threatened war, Pericles insisted that Athens should not compromise but stand firm. His argument: Though the matter might seem small, to back down on this point might open the way to greater demands from Sparta in the future. The Peloponnesian War began in 431 BC. Pericles drew up an essentially defensive strategy based on Athenian naval strength.

The conflict proved to be a disaster for Athens—in large part because Pericles was not there to lead the city. He was struck down by a plague that ravaged Athens in 430–429 BC, and his successors were unable to prevent defeat at the hands of Sparta and its allies in 404 BC. This did not detract from Pericles's reputation—and over centuries since he has held a prime place as establisher of democracy and the Golden Age of philosophy in Athens, the man responsible for the building of the Parthenon, that globally celebrated symbol of classical Greece. He was, according to his great admirer Thucydides, "the first citizen of Athens" in its most glorious hour.

LEADERSHIP ANALYSIS

LEADER TYPE: *Persuasive*
KEY QUALITIES: *Great orator, credible*
LIKEMINDED LEADERS: *Winston Churchill, Martin Luther King, Jr*
FACT: *Pericles was always represented wearing a helmet because he was an Athenian general.*

3 SIDDHĀRTHA GAUTAMA

NEPALESE PRINCE WHO BECAME AN EXEMPLAR OF BUDDHIST LIFE

NATIONALITY: *Nepalese*
ACHIEVEMENT: *Founded philosophical religion of Buddhism*
WHEN: *Fifth century BC*

Abandoning his life of luxury Siddhārtha Gautama became an enlightened teacher and founded the philosophical and religious system of Buddhism in the fifth century BC. He led a growing band of followers with modesty, directness, and natural authority.

Remembered as one of history's greatest communicators, the Buddha swept away abstruse philosophy and delivered direct and compelling guidance on how to manage human desires and live a happy and fulfilling life from day to day. As followers gathered around him, he proved himself a leader who favored simplicity, eschewed conflict, and managed people's expectations and behavior with engaging honesty.

Central to the Buddha's teachings was the notion that, through concentrated effort, he had been able to achieve a state of mind that allowed him to see the simple truths that he considered to be hidden beneath the swirling confusion and difficulties inherent in human life. The term Buddha means "a person who is awake": He was a philosopher and religious teacher who claimed he had awakened himself from the everyday.

THE EIGHT-POINT PATH

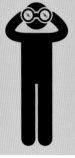
RIGHT VIEW

RIGHT INTENTION

RIGHT SPEECH

RIGHT ACTION

LEADING BY EXAMPLE

A key part of his appeal, then and now, is that—according to tradition—he did not try to force anyone to listen or to follow him. In effect Buddha approached leadership by saying: "This is what I have found—try it for yourself." Everything he taught was the product of his own experience. Moreover he lived his teaching in his way of being and in his interactions with others. In this he was like Mohandas Gandhi who, asked for a summary of his message, replied: "My life is my message" (see page 130). A leader acquires a special type of authority when she or he speaks from experience and embodies teachings in this way.

DISTURBED BY SUFFERING

The details of the Buddha's life are known from texts written down by his followers many centuries after his death. Their historical accuracy is open to question, but historians accept that the Buddha was a historical figure who became a teacher and founded a monastic order in the fifth century BC.

According to the traditional account of the Buddha's life he had many advantages and a comfortable existence. He was born as Siddhārtha Gautama, a prince in what is now southern Nepal—in an area that, in the fifth century BC, was at the northern edge of a society of warring city-states ruled by kings in the Ganges River Basin.

He had a sheltered upbringing due to his overprotective father. But as an adult, going out among his subjects with his charioteer, he had four encounters which would lead him to reconsider how he lived his life. First he saw an old man, then a sick person, a corpse, and an ascetic monk.

In this traditional narrative Gautama was deeply troubled by the knowledge that life was brief and full of suffering, Unlike the majority of people who witness human suffering, Buddha's experience motivated him to understand the causes of human unhappiness and how to prevent it. He determined he would not rest until he had done this. His key motivation, which carried him to greatness, was his desire first to understand and then to share what he learned.

RIGHT LIVELIHOOD   RIGHT EFFORT   RIGHT MINDFULNESS   RIGHT CONCENTRATION   FREE FROM SUFFERING

TIME LINE

Note traditional dates have the Buddha as being born in 563 BC but latest dates set his life as c.490–410 BC

c.490 BC
Siddhārtha Gautama is born.

c.474 BC
Gautama marries at the age of 16.

c.461 BC
Aged 29 he leaves the palace for the first time and witnesses human suffering and death.

c.455 BC
Aged 35 he achieves Enlightenment under the bodhi tree.

c.410 BC
Gautama Buddha dies; First Buddhist council is held.

c.250 BC
Indian Emperor Ashoka the Great issues edicts in support of Buddhism.

c.100 BC
Collections of the Buddha's teachings are written down on birch bark in the kingdom of Gandhara (northern Pakistan/northeastern Afghanistan). These are the oldest surviving Buddhist writings.

c.AD 150
Indian poet Aśvaghoṣa writes the first full biography of the Buddha.

Gautama abandoned his comfortable palace existence and set out as a wandering monk. He tried various methods of living, including an extremely harsh regime under which he almost starved to death, and diligently studied meditation and yoga under leading teachers.

According to the traditional accounts—which may have been devised for inspirational effect more than factual accuracy—he then sat himself down under a bodhi tree (a type of fig tree) and declared he would not move until he had reached understanding. He sat there for 49 days, until he achieved understanding. He became enlightened.

MIDDLE WAY TO HAPPINESS
It is said that Buddha's new enlightened way of seeing tempered his driving desire to know with an understanding—acquired through experience—of what really works in finding answers. People should not go to extremes, he said—as he had done when he almost starved to death through self-denial: Neither too much, nor too little; his followers should seek the Middle Way.

Buddha's teachings explain that we suffer because things are always changing and we cling to things that cannot last; the way to happiness and a good life is to be detached from this urgent desire to hold on to people or possessions. As a teacher the Buddha did not produce grand theories, elegant language, or wide-ranging philosophical schemes. He boiled things down to the simplest truth and then shared that with people.

Buddha began with just four followers. They were monks—fellow seekers. After his Enlightenment, he began to teach and founded a monastic community, and, within two months, according to the traditional accounts, he had 60 followers.

It is said that Buddha traveled tirelessly all year round, sharing his teachings, except in the rainy season where he and his monks settled in a forest or park and then seekers came to them. Sometimes people might come to challenge or attempt to upset the Buddha or to raise abstruse religious or philosophical questions. According to tradition, he remained calm and would not be drawn into long discussions; he emphasized the simple and the practical and encouraged people to try his teachings out.

UNDERSTANDING FOR ALL

Buddhism today is a global religion with 376 million followers. A person can be Buddhist without believing in a god or any gods and some people hold that Buddhism is an ethical system or a form of philosophy rather than a religion. There are various schools of Buddhism with their own unique traditions: Theravada Buddhism, which some argue is the closest to the original teachings of the Buddha, and Mahayana Buddhism. Tibetan and Zen Buddhism are both schools of Mahayana.

Key to Buddhism are the four essential truths. In these truths Buddha taught that life was suffering caused by attachment and craving. In order to free themselves from this suffering followers had to detach themselves from this craving by following the eight-point path set out by Buddha.

NATURAL AUTHORITY

According to all accounts the Buddha was anti-authoritarian. Because he did not struggle for pre-eminence, and merely presented what he had learned to people who were interested, he had natural authority. He stressed the availability of his method to all. Before his death at the age of around 80 it is said he told his followers not to follow a leader. He did not have any revelation from a god or divine spirit. Buddha is remembered as a scientist of the mind who investigated consciousness, not through the physical activities in the brain but through personal experience and observing others' behavior.

LEADERSHIP ANALYSIS

LEADER TYPE: *Leader by example*
KEY QUALITIES: *Determined, honest, gifted communicator*
LIKEMINDED LEADERS: *Jesus of Nazareth, Mohandas Gandhi, Nelson Mandela*
FACT: *The Buddha was the first person in history known to have condemned slavery.*

4 ALEXANDER THE GREAT

DRIVEN LEADER WHO CREATED ONE OF THE ANCIENT WORLD'S MOST POWERFUL EMPIRES

NATIONALITY: *Macedonian*
ACHIEVEMENT: *Created one of the ancient world's greatest empires*
WHEN: c.*325 BC*

Macedonian king Alexander the Great was a brilliant general who won an enduring reputation in creating one of the foremost empires of the classical world before he was 30. Full of energy, forceful, and imaginative—but also self-controlled and a great strategist—he inspired his army to astonishing achievements.

At the climax of the Battle of Gaugamela on October 1 331 BC King Alexander of Macedon exhibited all the bravery and strategic intelligence for which he was famous when he led his elite cavalry in a charge at the center of the Persian battle line. The Persian Royal Guard was thrown into disarray: King Darius III fled and the day belonged to Alexander.

Victory in the Battle of Gaugamela, fought near modern Mosul in present-day Iraq, led to the collapse of the great Achaemenid Empire. At the age of only 25, Alexander—already leader of the Greeks, ruler of Asia Minor, and pharaoh of Egypt—became Shahanshah ("King of Kings") in Persia. He did not rest. In the ensuing eight years he inspired his troops to follow him on a campaign that covered another 11,000 miles (17,000 km) and created an empire that ran from Greece in the west to the Indian Punjab in the east, stretching southward to Egypt and northward as far as the River Danube.

LEADER BY EXAMPLE

Alexander inspired fierce loyalty. He shared hardships with his troops. According to Greek historian Plutarch: When his army was reduced to a state of exhaustion during the invasion of Persia, Alexander refused the drink offered to him by passing travelers even though, after 11 days in pursuit of the fleeing Darius, he was desperately thirsty. Looking around and seeing his men gazing longingly at the water he handed the helmet back without drinking, thanking the passers-by and saying that if he alone drank the rest of his army would be disheartened. This show of camaraderie reinvigorated the soldiers who had previously been willing to give up. They called on Alexander to lead them on. With such a leader, they said, they could defy thirst and exhaustion.

Alexander's leadership, Plutarch noted, made his men feel unstoppable, immortal. In the 13 years of hard campaigning that filled his reign, Alexander's troops followed him loyally and passionately through grueling conditions—that they only once refused to

follow his lead, when they prevailed upon him to turn homeward rather than pressing on in India, is truly remarkable.

INVINCIBLE COMMANDER

Alexander never lost a battle, despite the fact that he was often outnumbered. He used his cavalry and the superb Macedonian infantry phalanx with consummate skill and tactical intelligence. He utilized troops to interrupt communications within the enemy army by striking at its center of command. At Gaugamela he planned the battle so he could make a decisive attack at the center of the enemy line, where he knew Darius was fighting: He deployed his army with the wings angled back from the infantry in the center and then rode with his elite cavalry, the Companions, to the extreme

IMAGE CONTROL

Alexander understood the importance of reputation and image. Having had a likeness made that pleased him, by the Greek sculptor Lysippos, he forbade any other artist to represent him. He encouraged the spread of colorful narratives about his exploits, such as the claim that he was a son of the Greek god Zeus. When his official historian Callisthenes passed from praising to criticizing his lord, Alexander acted with typical ruthlessness and eliminated his former ally. Though suppressing criticism in this way is not something to aspire to— paying attention to your image and public perception is key in modern leadership.

In the image above, artist Placido Costanzi depicts Alexander founding the city of Alexandria, which still thrives today.

TIME LINE

356 BC
Born in Pella, Macedonia.

343–340 BC
Studied with Aristotle.

336 BC
Unites Greek states.

334 BC
Invades Persian Empire.

334 BC
Defeats Persian army at Battle of the Granicus River.

333 BC
Defeats Darius in Battle of Issus.

332 BC
Besieges Tyre.

332 BC
Crowned pharaoh in Egypt.

331 BC
Founds city of Alexandria, Egypt.

331 BC
Defeats Darius a second time in Battle of Gaugamela.

329 BC
Defeats Scythians in the Battle of Jaxartes.

327 BC
Executes court historian Callisthenes, who had criticized Alexander's adoption of proskynesis.

326 BC
Defeats Indian King Porus in Battle of the Hydaspes.

326 BC
Alexander leaves India after his army mutiny.

323 BC
Dies, Babylon.

right of the field—both moves designed to lure Persian cavalry to come forward to attack—and then wheeled back to strike decisively in the center.

He also set out to limit the enemy's strength through careful tactical planning. At the Battle of Jaxartes in October 329 BC he came face to face with the widely feared Scythian horsemen, known for their speed and unpredictable movement in battle; no one to date had been able to defeat a nomad army of this type. Alexander planned the battle to limit the Scythians' ability to maneuver: He sent forward his mounted spearmen to engage the Scythians, happy to accept casualties in the knowledge that they would fix the enemy's position; once the Scythians surrounded the spearmen, Alexander was able to pin them in place with his infantry and archers. It was a triumph—1,200 Scythians were killed and 1,800 horses captured. Alexander here presents an inspirational example for leaders of how to make the most of limited resources by concentrating attacks on a rival's key strength.

GENERAL INSPIRATION

Because he achieved so much so boldly and so young, and because of his innovative and intelligent tactics, Alexander became an inspiration for later military leaders, his tactics regularly taught in military academies. In the Roman period, leaders including Pompey the Great and Julius Caesar sought to emulate him. Alexander's canny strategy and the means by which he settled such vast territories—by adopting local customs and using existing forms of government—also provided a lesson. This aspect of Alexander's achievement inspired French general Napoleon

Bonaparte. He declared that what he admired most in Alexander was not his military campaigns but his "political sense." Napoleon wrote that Alexander "knew the art of gaining the people's affection."

DESTINED FOR GREATNESS?

Alexander apparently believed himself bound for glory from his youth. His mother Olympias told him of her vision that her son would one day rule the world. She filled his head with stories of the legendary Greek warrior Achilles, whom she claimed as an ancestor. Moreover, his tutor as a young man was none other than Aristotle, the great Greek philosopher. Aristotle's influence was extremely important: He taught the young prince the benefits of detachment, of gaining control over your emotions, of understanding the consequences of what you do—of sometimes giving way in order to follow a long-term goal. In Alexander were combined the self-belief of a prince, the clear thinking of a philosopher, and the cunning of a strategist.

Alexander's vast empire did not last long after his death, but his chief legacy lay in the enduring influence of the Greek culture and traditions that he carried to the far-flung areas he conquered. He also founded no fewer than 20 cities in his name, most famously Alexandria in northern Egypt. Even in his lifetime he was the subject of colorful stories, and after his death his reputation grew through legends and romance narratives popular throughout the Middle Ages. They emphasized his boldness, energy, and often-stirring leadership alongside his astonishing achievements and his combination of intellectual strength and physical courage.

▲ *Detail of the late fourth century BC Alexander Sarcophagus that was discovered near Sidon, Lebanon. Here Alexander fights at the Battle of Issus.*

LEADERSHIP ANALYSIS

LEADER TYPE: *Strategist*
KEY QUALITIES: *Boldness, intelligence, energy*
LIKEMINDED LEADERS: *Pompey the Great, Julius Caesar, Napoleon Bonaparte*
FACT: *Great Roman leaders viewed Alexander with awe. Julius Caesar made a pilgrimage to Alexander's grave.*

5 JULIUS CAESAR

AMBITIOUS GENERAL WHO DICTATED THE FUTURE OF THE ROMAN EMPIRE

NATIONALITY: *Roman*
ACHIEVEMENT: *Won civil war and became the first dictator in Rome*
WHEN: *49-45 BC*

Imperious Roman statesman Julius Caesar defeated the Gauls, boldly triumphed over republican forces in a bitter civil war, and established himself as dictator—paving the way for the emperors who succeeded him.

In January 49 BC Caesar crossed the Rubicon—a river in northeastern Italy viewed as the Roman Republic's frontier—with his troops. This was an open challenge to his former ally Pompey, who had commanded Caesar to return from his governorship of Gaul. Caesar's audacious move began a civil war that he won to establish himself as dictator of Rome.

His audacious decision to challenge Pompey's authority came in the wake of his daughter Julia's death in 54 BC. Julia and Pompey's marriage had helped cement the relationship between the leaders, but with her death the uneasy alliance between the two men had disintegrated and they were now at loggerheads for control of power. Caesar knew he had to act or be eliminated. Roman generals were forbidden to enter the Roman Republic with their troops. Caesar knew that once he had done so he must either defeat his rivals or he would be executed. On crossing the river he declared, "the die is cast."

Pompey and his troops turned tail, but Caesar acted decisively and bravely. Accompanied only by the Thirteenth Legion he marched at speed to defeat Pompey's fleeing allies in Spain. Then in June 48 BC he came head to head with Pompey himself. Caesar overcame a defeat at Dyrrachium (near Durrës in what is now Albania) to win a spirited and decisive victory at the Battle of Pharsalus (near modern Fársala, Greece). In this triumph he out-thought and out-maneuvered his opponent, showing the brilliant strategic skill for which he was celebrated—and which was one of the key aspects of his eminence as a leader.

STRATEGIST SUPREME
Caesar's army of around 22,000 was outnumbered more than two to one by Pompey's 45,000-strong force. The two cavalry forces faced up on Pompey's left wing: Caesar saw that his outnumbered cavalry would be defeated and stationed 2,000 of his finest legionaries behind the cavalry. He also held back a third division. When Pompey's cavalry overpowered their counterparts in Caesar's army they were

BRITAIN

BELGICA

GAUL

Atlantic Ocean

AQUITANIA

EXPANDING THE EMPIRE

ILLYRIA

DACIA

Black Sea

ROME

MACEDONIA THRACE

GALATIA

ARMENIA

MESOPOTAMIA

NUMIDIA

Mediterranean Sea

SYRIA

MAURITANIA

JUDEA

EGYPT PALESTINE

Greatest extent of
Empire at death of
Julius Caesar 44 BC

Expansion of
territories to death of
Augustus AD 14

Further expansion of
territories to death of
Trajan AD 117

Battle of Pharsalus,
48 BC

Battle of Munda,
45 BC

surprised and terrified to come face to face with the fighting machine
of Caesar's legionaries, who were making a steady, deadly advance
using their *pila* (spears) for stabbing rather than throwing them like
javelins. Pompey's troops broke: One section fled, another—numbering
24,000, a larger contingent than Caesar's entire army—surrendered.
Pompey himself escaped to Egypt, with his tail between his legs.

In Rome Caesar was named dictator. It took Caesar three more
years to deliver a final defeat to his opponents in the Battle of Munda
in southern Hispania (Spain) in 45 BC.

BOLD AND INTELLIGENT

As well as strategic and tactical skill on campaign, Caesar was celebrated for his
boldness of character. Like Alexander the Great, George Washington, or Napoleon
Bonaparte, he commanded the loyalty of his men because he showed himself
willing to fight alongside them—and led them to great victories. He had immense
energy. He subdued the entire Roman province of Gaul in 58–50 BC and found time
to make two exploratory raids across the Channel into England, while also writing a
seven-volume history of these wars. A highly intelligent and a gifted writer, he also
authored a three-volume history of the civil war; both this and his history of the
Gallic Wars survive. Clearly and precisely written, they are celebrated by classical
historians as great works of art as well as valuable accounts of the events.

TIME LINE

July 13 100 BC
Born, Rome.

69 BC
Elected quaestor.

62 BC
Elected praetor.

61–60 BC
Governor of Further Spain.

59 BC
Elected consul.

58–50 BC
Governor of Gaul, conquers local tribes.

55–54 BC
Makes two expeditions to Britain.

52 BC
Defeats Gallic revolt led by Vercingetorix.

49 BC
Crosses the Rubicon river—an action that leads to civil war.

48 BC
Defeats Pompey in Battle of Pharsalus. Pompey is then killed in Egypt.

47 BC
Wins Egyptian power for Cleopatra in the Battle of the Nile.

January 1 45 BC
Julian calendar introduced.

45 BC
Battle of Munda is final defeat of civil war opponents; named Dictator for life.

March 15 44 BC
Assassinated, Rome.

42 BC
He becomes the first historical Roman to be deified—as "Divus Julius" ("The divine Julius").

CLEOPATRA

After his stunning victory at the Battle of Pharsalus, Caesar pursued Pompey to Egypt. Here he discovered that his opponent had been slain by an officer working for the pharaoh, Ptolemy. Whilst in Egypt Caesar made a romantic and political alliance with Ptolemy's wife, sister, and co-regent, the beautiful Cleopatra, and supported her in a civil war against her brother. He defeated Ptolemy's forces at the Battle of the Nile and established Cleopatra in power.

ENERGETIC, MAGNANIMOUS

He demonstrated great physical strength and vitality. In 49 BC, after crossing the Rubicon in January, he marched all the way to Brundisium (modern Brindisi, southeastern Italy) and from there to the Roman province of Hispania (Spain) to defeat troops supporting Pompey. Among Caesar's other qualities was his grace in victory—he could be brutal in his treatment of non-Roman barbarian opponents, as he was in the Gallic wars in putting down local tribes; but he was celebrated for being magnanimous to fellow-Romans in victory. Yet his greatest strength was undoubtedly his boldness.

REFORMER

His boldness on the battlefield was matched by his decisive governance— instituting sweeping reforms as dictator of Rome. He enlarged the senate, introduced a law to restructure debts, and arranged for land to be granted to veterans of his army. In Rome he built

Pellegrini's The Head of Pompey Presented to Caesar. *Caesar showed boldness in political maneuvering as well as on the battlefield.*

the Julian forum. He also reformed the calendar: This was previously aligned to the Moon, but he tied it to the Sun after the Egyptian model. He established a year's length of 365 and a quarter days by introducing an extra day at the end of February every fourth year. The calendar started on January 1 45 BC after three months were added to 46 BC. This calendar—named Julian after Julius Caesar—is still in use in some Eastern Orthodox countries; minor corrections by Pope Gregory XIII in 1582 established the Gregorian Calendar now used in Western countries.

POWER HUNGRY

At first Caesar established himself as dictator on a temporary basis, but in 44 BC he took the dictatorship for life. The movement of his rule toward absolute authority sparked a revolt and on March 15 44 BC he was assassinated. Among the conspirators were Marcus Junius Brutus and Gaius Cassius Longinus, former enemies he could have eliminated but whom he had pardoned: Here, perhaps, one aspect of his greatness a leader, his magnanimity, undermined him. But this generosity of spirit was a great part of what made him, and fed into the immortal reputation that has made his name ring down the ages. Indeed the source of the words kaiser in German and tsar in Slavonic languages—describing a paramount or supreme leader—is Caesar. He decisively changed Western history by reinvigorating the Roman state and paving the way for the emperors who would rule in Rome and afterward in Constantinople for several centuries.

LEADERSHIP ANALYSIS

LEADER TYPE: *Strategist*
KEY QUALITIES: *Boldness, energy, decisiveness*
LIKEMINDED LEADERS: *Alexander the Great, George Washington*
FACT: *Caesar's clan name Julius survives in that of the month of July.*

6 JESUS OF NAZARETH

THE CHARISMATIC LEADER WHO EMERGES FROM THE BIBLE

NATIONALITY: *Jewish, from Judea in Roman Empire*
ACHIEVEMENT: *Founded Christianity*
WHEN: *c.6 BC–AD 27*

Jewish teacher Jesus of Nazareth combined an intense charisma with powerful communication skills, an inquiring intellect with a profound compassion. He inspired great loyalty in his followers and was notable as a champion of the weak, the poor, and the outcast.

Jesus was at the start of his career as an itinerant teacher when he inspired his first followers to abandon their families and livelihoods and follow him. According to the account in the Gospels of Matthew and Mark in the Bible, Jesus was walking by the Sea of Galilee (now in northeast Israel) when he encountered two fishermen, Simon and Andrew, working at their nets. "Come, follow me," he said, "and I will make you fishers of men." They simply laid down their nets, the tools of their trade, and followed him.

Jesus's charisma is often evident in the accounts of his life. According to these narratives, he could connect powerfully and intimately with people—not just the likeminded souls, but also those who were opposed to his ideas; not only one to one or in small groups, but also when addressing large crowds.

The Bible stories show Jesus as a man who knew how to address people's concerns directly. As a leader of his disciples and other followers he could be forceful and challenging—daring people to take risks, to see things afresh and rethink conventional views, to live openly in an unguarded way, to believe in change; but he was also often mild, supportive, compassionate, and gentle. Over centuries these qualities have been a powerful example to Christians, and to leaders and teachers—religious figureheads such as Francis of Assisi or Mother Teresa endeavored to embody his vast energy and compassion; others like Martin Luther King, Jr, were inspired by his reforming zeal (see pages 62, 176, and 206).

Jesus inspired powerful loyalty. His disciples were energized by his transformational teachings and exemplary behavior to found the new religious faith of Christianity. Men such as Saint Peter, the first leader of the Christian church, traveled far and wide teaching and were willing to go to their deaths in support of Jesus (see page 34).

HISTORICAL JESUS?

There is no surviving archaeological or physical evidence of Jesus, but historians generally accept that he lived around c.6 BC–AD 27, was baptized by the man known

Jesus holds a book of the Gospels and makes a gesture that means "teacher" in this Byzantine mosaic from Cefalù Cathedral in Sicily, Italy.

to history as John the Baptist and was crucified at Jerusalem at the time when Pontius Pilate was Roman Prefect of Judaea in AD 26–36. Aside from references in the Qur'an and possibly also the Talmud, there are just three non-Christian documentary references to Jesus—two in the work of Jewish historian Josephus and one in that of Roman historian Tacitus. In a reference to early Christians, Tacitus gives the names of "Christus" who he writes, "suffered the extreme penalty during the reign of [Roman Emperor] Tiberius at the hands of one of our procurators, Pontius Pilatus."

GIFTED COMMUNICATOR

In the biblical accounts, Jesus delivered spiritual lessons by the medium of direct, accessible stories based on everyday situations: The parables. He was an immensely powerful teacher who grasped the power of stories to convey deeper lessons. Some of these lessons were difficult and seemingly counter-intuitive, such as those suggested by the Parable of the Prodigal Son or that of the Lost Sheep, which seem to reward negligence and selfishness over loyalty. In these stories Jesus emphasizes his central theme of compassion: God rejoices at the return of those who have strayed. Central to Jesus's teaching is the image of God as a forgiving father.

Jesus was a great champion of the weak and the poor. His celebrated Beatitudes (so called because they consists of a series of phrases beginning "blessed are...") suggest that the poor, the meek, those who mourn, and people who are persecuted are blessed. He was criticized by those in religious authority for associating with people deemed to be "sinners" such as publicans and prostitutes. When he was attacked for doing this, Jesus responded—according to the account in the Gospel

TIME LINE

c.6 BC
Jesus is born in Bethlehem, Judea.

c. AD 24
Jesus is baptized by John the Baptist and begins his ministry.

c. AD 25
Near Capernaum Jesus gives his celebrated Sermon on the Mount, which contains the Beatitudes.

c. AD 26
Jesus reputedly feeds a crowd of 5,000 at Bethsaida with five loaves and two fishes.

c. AD 27
In Jerusalem he is betrayed to the authorities by one of his disciples, Judas Iscariot, and crucified.

c. AD 30–69
Jerusalem is the center of Christianity.

c. AD 35–55
Saul of Tarsus (later known as Saint Paul) founds early outposts of the church in Europe and Asia Minor.

AD 64
Roman Emperor Nero persecutes Christians in Rome.

c. AD 70
The first of the biblical Gospels, according to Mark, is written.

c. AD 80
Second Gospel, according to Matthew, is written.

c. AD 90
The Gospels according to Luke and John are written, together with the Acts of the Apostles, which describes the history of the early church.

of Mark— "They that are whole have no need of the physician, but they that are sick." His main purpose, he stated, was not to preach to those who already had faith, but to reach out to and teach the outcast, "the sinners."

An important aspect of this outlook was holding back from judgment. According to the Gospel of Matthew, he told his followers, "Judge not, lest ye be not judged." Here again he used his gift for illustrating profound spiritual doctrine in homely language: Imagine a man with a piece of wood stuck in his eye, he

JESUS IN RELIGIOUS TRADITIONS

The narratives of Jesus's life given in the Gospels are theological documents. They belong to the Christian faith, which holds that Jesus was both a human being and the Son of God. In Islam Jesus is revered—like Moses—as a prophet and a Messenger of God. Known as Isa ibn Maryam (Jesus son of Mary), he is seen as the last prophet sent to the "Children of Israel," and as a precursor to the Prophet Muhammad. Jesus is also identified in the Qur'an, as al-Masih (the Messiah—in Jewish tradition, a leader anointed by God to unite the tribes of Israel and bring about an era of peace). In Judaism Jesus is seen as a teacher, sometimes identified as one following in the tradition of the Old Testament prophets Elijah or Isaiah. There are some possible references to him in the Talmud; a few refer to him as a sorcerer or magician because of the stories of healing and other miracles associated with him.

suggested. He goes up to his friend, who has a tiny speck of dust in his eye, and suggests he help him clear his vision.

COMPASSIONATE LEADER

Again and again in his teaching Jesus emphasized fellowship and understanding. According to the Gospel of Mark, Jesus taught that two rules for a good life stood out above all others. The first was, "thou shalt love the Lord thy God with all thy heart, and with all thy soul, and with all thy mind, and with all thy strength." The second was, "Thou shalt love thy neighbor as thyself."

Jesus's promotion of selfless love inspired generations of Christians, not least Saul of Tarsus, a Roman who converted to Christianity and founded many early Christian churches. Remembered as the Apostle Paul, he held that Jesus was an exemplar of how to live your life. Central to Paul's understanding of Jesus was his belief that at the end of his earthly life Jesus was betrayed to the authorities in Jerusalem and crucified, but then appeared to his disciples after three days, risen from the dead.

For any person viewing Jesus's achievements, his most extraordinary and inspirational quality was ultimately his steadfastness, his willingness to live out what he seemingly understood to be his destiny—to give up his home and worldly possessions to teach, and then to give up his earthly life and go bravely to his bodily death. His extraordinary achievements in inspiring his followers to build a new faith in the teeth of persecution by the Roman Empire, combined with the widespread and enduring effects of his teachings, make him both an immensely significant figure in human history and a notable exemplar as leader.

WORLD POPULATION OF CHRISTIANS TODAY

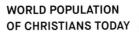

Christian 33.4%

Non-Christian 66.6%

CHRISTIAN POPULATION BY DENOMINATION

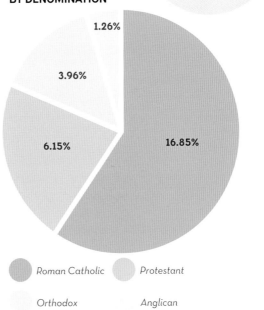

1.26%

3.96%

6.15%

16.85%

Roman Catholic   Protestant

Orthodox   Anglican

LEADERSHIP ANALYSIS

LEADER TYPE: *Leader by example*
KEY QUALITIES: *Steadfast, charismatic, challenging, compassionate*
LIKEMINDED LEADERS: *Saint Francis of Assisi, Mother Teresa, Martin Luther King, Jr*
FACT: *Scholars believe that Jesus spoke Hebrew and the Syrian language of Aramaic.*

7

SAINT PETER

LOYAL DISCIPLE WHO LED THE FIRST CHRISTIAN CHURCH

NATIONALITY: *Citizen of Judea in the Roman Empire*
ACHIEVEMENT: *First leader of the Christian Church*
WHEN: *c. AD 30-64*

Foremost among Jesus of Nazereth's disciples, Peter was handpicked by Jesus to take charge of the early Christians. He proved himself resolute and authoritative—the perfect shepherd to lead the church flock through its first years.

Peter's authority among the first Christians derived from a moment of profound insight. In the Gospel According to Matthew in the Bible, Jesus asked his disciples who they thought he was: Peter replied, "Thou art the Christ, the Son of the living God." Jesus responded to this bold display of absolute faith by declaring Peter to be the rock on which the church—the community of Christians—would be built.

Peter gained a new identity in this encounter. Among the first of Jesus's 12 disciples to follow him, Peter's original name was Simon, son of John. When he made his bold statement of Jesus's identity, Jesus renamed him Peter, from Greek *petros* for "rock." Peter's declaration revealed not only an openness to possibilities, but also self-confidence and bravery. In calling Jesus "the Christ," Simon Peter meant that Jesus had been sent to fulfil God's plan: "Christ" is the Greek translation of the word "Messiah," meaning "God's Anointed One."

RESOLUTE, NATURAL AUTHORITY

Jesus made his way as an itinerant teacher. As he traveled around with his disciples, he recognized Simon Peter's pre-eminent position in the group. Peter would be the one to question Jesus about the meaning of a parable (teaching story), demonstrating hunger for knowledge and confidence to speak out. A story in Matthew's Gospel further illustrates Peter's standing in the group: When tax collectors came up to ask whether Jesus paid the temple tax, they addressed Peter, who they assumed to be leader of the disciples, and he answered on behalf of the group.

In addition to this natural authority, Peter was also persevering, vigorous, and insightful as a leader, a man who overcame failure and used setbacks to strengthen his resolve. The biblical account of Christ's crucifixion includes the story of Peter's denial of Jesus. But, despite this setback, Peter resumed his position at the head of the disciples and, according to the Bible, later reaffirmed his love for Jesus three times—a counterpart to his triple denial. So the story goes, each time Peter answered his Lord "thou knowest that I love thee," Jesus responded: "Feed my lambs ... feed my sheep." Peter's authority to care for the early Christians was affirmed again.

Jesus had predicted Peter's triple denial, but he knew all along that Peter would recover and regain his status: He warned Peter of what would happen and instructed him, when he had recovered, to "strengthen thy brethren"— that is, support Jesus's other followers. In Jesus's eyes, the denial and subsequent recovery gave Peter more—not less—authority among the early Christians. Any leader may suffer setbacks, even personal failures of the kind Peter went through— but these do not necessarily undermine authority: As in Peter's case, a person who can demonstrate their recovery from difficulties may in fact gain in stature.

▲ Peter honors Jesus in his death—choosing to be crucified upside-down—in a painting by Caravaggio in the Church of Santa Maria del Popolo, Rome.

INDEPENDENT, SELF-RELIANT

Peter's openness and independence of mind were also shown on the day when, according to the biblical narrative, Jesus rose from the dead. On the third day after Jesus was crucified, three women—Mary Magdalene, Joanna, and Mary, the mother of James—visited his tomb to bring spices and perfumes for his body, but when they arrived they found it empty: Jesus's body was missing. They hurried back and told the disciples, but they would not believe them—except Peter, who ran to the tomb and saw for himself. The Bible also identifies him as the first among the disciples to encounter Jesus after his resurrection.

In the biblical narrative, following Jesus's ascension Peter became the leader of the community of Christians in Jerusalem: Playing a key role in the election of a new disciple, Matthias, to replace Judas Iscariot, who had betrayed Jesus;

TIME LINE

c.1 BC
Born in Bethsaida as Simon, Son of John.

c. AD 24
Gives up his business as a fisherman on the Sea of Galilee to follow Jesus of Nazareth.

c.25–26
Peter identifies Jesus as "the Christ;" Jesus renames him.

c.27
Jesus predicts Peter will deny him three times; Peter does so. Jesus is crucified.

c.28–44
Peter is leader of the disciples in Jerusalem.

c.44
Imprisoned by Herod Agrippa I, but freed from jail.

c.44
Peter quits Jerusalem, leaving the church in the hands of Jesus's brother James.

c.64
Dies in Rome.

c.80
One of Peter's successors as pope in Rome, Anacletus, builds a tomb over Peter's grave.

319
Emperor Constantine starts building of first Saint Peter's Basilica, Rome, on the site of Peter's tomb.

1506–1626
Second Saint Peter's Basilica is built on the same site.

1939
Bones of a man believed to be Peter found beneath Saint Peter's basilica.

June 26 1968
Pope Paul VI declares the bones to be those of Saint Peter.

1968
Archaeologists uncover house thought to have belonged to Peter in Capernaum beside the Sea of Galilee.

preaching inspiring sermons; and acting as the disciples' advocate before Jerusalem's religious authorities. His natural authority, which had been confirmed by Jesus, enabled him to take up the mantle of leadership and provide strong guidance for the disciples at a time when they faced persecution and hardships.

LEADER IN ROME—FIRST POPE

Peter remained based in Jerusalem until c. AD 44. In these years he traveled widely, preaching in the name of Jesus. He also converted the first Gentiles (non-Jews) to Christianity. After that he seems to have left Jerusalem and settled first in Antioch (near modern Antakya, Turkey) and then as the head of the Christian community in Rome. He was reputedly crucified there in the reign of Emperor Nero (AD 54–69), who severely persecuted the early Christians.

Tradition has it that Peter had one final encounter with Jesus before his death. Leaving Rome to escape the persecution of the Christians by Nero, Peter had a vision of Jesus going the other way,

QUICK DECISION

The most important moment in Peter's life was the one in which he decided to follow Jesus of Nazareth. There are three versions of this encounter in the biblical accounts, but in all Peter makes a swift decision and then sticks by it. He was clearly a decisive and loyal man, and it is this strength of conviction that has inspired the many admirers of his unflinching leadership.

THE 12 DISCIPLES OF JESUS AND THEIR SYMBOLS

ANDREW

Patron saint of Scotland and Russia.

BARTHOLOMEW

Worked as a missionary in Armenia and India.

JAMES THE ELDER

A former fisherman and brother of John the Apostle.

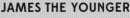
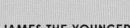

JAMES THE YOUNGER

Died a martyr after being sawn into pieces.

JOHN

Known as "beloved disciple" in Christian tradition.

JUDAS ISCARIOT

Betrayed Jesus to authorities.

JUDE

Brother of James the Younger.

MATTHEW

A former tax collector also called Levi.

PETER

Leader of the apostles and celebrated as the first Pope.

PHILIP

Probably a former fisherman like Peter and Andrew.

SIMON THE ZEALOT

Another fisherman before he became a disciple.

THOMAS

Known as doubting Thomas in Christian tradition.

---

carrying the cross on which he had been crucified. Peter asked, "Where are you going, Lord?" Jesus replied, "Into Rome, to be crucified again."

Understanding this to mean that he should return to Rome, Peter turned right around. On his return to the city he was crucified. Reportedly Peter asked to be crucified upside down, since he felt he was not worthy to be executed in the same way as Jesus. In such a way, according to this tradition, Jesus's most senior and loyal follower capped decades of devoted leadership of the early church. To this day Peter is celebrated as the inspirational figurehead of the Church of Rome, the first in the line of 266 popes that run to Pope Francis in 2015.

LEADERSHIP ANALYSIS

LEADER TYPE: *Paternalistic*
KEY QUALITIES: *Resolute, loyal, forthright*
LIKEMINDED LEADERS: *Jesus of Nazareth, Gregory the Great, Nelson Mandela*
FACT: *Peter is mentioned 195 times in the New Testament. The next most commonly mentioned disciple, John, gets 29 mentions.*

8

QUEEN BOUDICA

BRITISH TRIBAL QUEEN WHO DEFINED A NATION SPIRIT

NATIONALITY: *British Celtic*
ACHIEVEMENT: *Inspired British tribes to defy the Roman military machine*
WHEN: *AD 60*

Boudica—Queen of the Iceni in East Anglia, England—combined charisma, compelling rhetoric, and theatrical gesture in inspiring local tribes to revolt against the Roman Empire. She was bold and decisive—she seized exactly the right moment for military action and personally led her army to defeat the Ninth Legion and sack the surrounding Roman settlements.

Queen Boudica had been wronged by the Romans and wanted revenge. She used every resource at her disposal—her status as queen, her imposing physical appearance, her knowledge of the religious traditions that inspired local tribes, her quick wits, and ability to deliver dramatic and engaging speeches—to rouse the Iceni and their allies to bloody rebellion.

The event that sparked her rage was the death of her husband Prasutagus, King of the Iceni, and the dishonoring of his memory by their Roman overlords. After the Roman Empire had conquered southern England in AD 43, Prasutagus remained in power— effectively as a client ruler of his Celtic tribe. But when he died in AD 60, the Romans seized the lands of the Iceni and the possessions of the leading tribesmen, then stripped and whipped Boudica. Her daughters were raped.

The Romans had demonstrated contempt for the peoples of Britain, but Boudica set out to restore their pride. She possessed natural authority: Historians believe she may have been a princess of the neighboring Trinovantes tribe or the daughter of a local aristocrat before she became queen of the Iceni through marriage. As a leader she epitomized dramatic methods of leadership, using all her powers of charisma to inspire people, powers for which leaders like African-American activist Malcolm X or Nazi leader Adolf Hitler would later become famous.

SYMBOLIC THEATER

Boudica understood that anger, when controlled and directed against an enemy or a target, can be the most powerful of forces. Moreover, she knew when to wait—and when to act. She grabbed the opportunity to mount her rebellion when the governor of the Roman province of Britain, Gaius Suetonius Paulinus, was called away in AD 60.

Gathering the local tribes, Boudica gave an impassioned speech, calling them to arms. Understanding that physical performance is as powerful or sometimes more

VICTORIOUS

For centuries Boudica was forgotten, but after she was rediscovered in the Renaissance she became an iconic figure in the history of British defiance. She was particularly celebrated in the reign of Queen Victoria (1837–1901). Victoria's consort, Prince Albert, commissioned the celebrated statue of Boudica and her daughters that stands on the Embankment beside the River Thames in central London. Boudica was established for posterity as a symbol of Britons' bravery in defending their island.

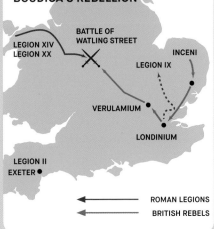

BOUDICA'S REBELLION

LEGION XIV
LEGION XX

BATTLE OF
WATLING STREET

INCENI

LEGION IX

VERULAMIUM

LONDINIUM

LEGION II
EXETER

← ROMAN LEGIONS
← BRITISH REBELS

TIME LINE

AD 43
Romans under Aulus Plautius and Emperor Claudius invade southeast England. Prasutagus, king of the Iceni, is allowed to remain in power as a nominally independent client ruler.

AD 47
The Iceni revolt when governor Publius Ostorius Scapula threatens to seize their weapons. They are defeated.

AD 60
Prasutagus dies; the Romans seize his lands.

AD 60
Boudica inspires a revolt of the Iceni and allies and leads them to victories at Camulodunum, Londinium and Verulamium, but is defeated in the Battle of Watling Street. She dies of poisoning or shock.

1534
Italian humanist Polydorus Vergilius learns about Boudica, who was forgotten in the Middle Ages, in the rediscovered works of Roman historian Tacitus.

1837–1901
In the reign of Queen Victoria, Boudica's popularity soars.

1902
A bronze statue of Boudica and her daughters in their chariot, by Thomas Thorneycroft, is unveiled in London.

2014
A buried stash of Roman jewelry is found in Colchester. Archaeologists suggest a Roman woman panicked by the approach of Boudica and her army in AD 60 buried it.

BRITISH FREEDOM FIGHTER

We know from accounts by Roman historians Tacitus and Cassius Dio that Boudica was an imposing figure. She was tall, with long, red hair that fell to below her waist. She had a powerful voice and a fierce gaze, and wore a golden necklace and a thick cloak clipped in place by a brooch. She made sure she looked every inch a war leader.

impressive than words alone, Boudica performed a rite of divination in which she released a hare from her cloak. When it raced off, her listeners saw that it had gone in an auspicious direction and followed, roaring their approval. She had perfectly judged the power of symbolic action to inspire people.

Following her rousing call to arms, Boudica led the Iceni alongside the Trinovantes and other local tribes into the revolt. Her army sacked and burned Camulodunum (modern Colchester), the capital of Roman Britain. There they tore down the temple to the Emperor Claudius: Boudica knew the importance of a symbolic target. She rewarded her followers with this chance to act out their anger and enjoy their victory.

LEADING BY EXAMPLE

The queen then galvanized her army anew to inflict a devastating defeat on the forbidding Ninth Legion under the command of Quintus Petillius Cerialis. Following her war-chariot into battle, her army understood that she was willing to put her life on the line in their common cause. In the ensuing battle, only a section of the Roman cavalry and Quintus Petillius himself escaped, while the infantry were killed almost to a man.

Boudica next headed for Londinium (modern London, at this stage not a city but an important trading center). Having heard of the destruction being wrought upon his strongholds, Roman governor Suetonius marched back to quash the rebellion, but—

judging his army severely outnumbered—he withdrew. The inhabitants of Londinium fled. The rebels burned it to the ground, then marched on Verulamium (modern St Albans) and ravaged that settlement, too.

Around 70,000 Romans and their allies among the British were killed in these attacks. The rebels showed no interest in taking prisoners, putting all they encountered to death. In gruesome scenes described by Cassius Dio, high-ranking women were impaled on sharp spikes; the victorious Britons celebrated raucously, feasting on the spoils of war and making sacrifices to Andraste, the local goddess of victory.

Finally Suetonius gathered sufficient troops to mount a response. He deployed his army—around 10,000 strong—on a narrow battlefield in the English West Midlands near the Roman road of Watling Street.

PASSIONATE AND PERSUASIVE

Preparing for the battle to come, Boudica once more demonstrated the force of her rhetoric—giving an impressively argued speech described in detail by Tacitus. Boudica appealed to her people as a woman who had been stripped and shamed by the brutish Romans, the mother of dishonored daughters; she declared that she was willing to go to her death rather than live as a slave of these invaders. The only Roman legion that had dared face them, she said, had been swiftly dispatched. The Britons' cause was just. The gods were on their side; not that of the Romans.

The passion of Boudica's rebels was now pitted against the might of the greatest armed force in the world. Her army poured forward in attack but the disciplined Romans stood firm, killing most of the first wave of warriors with well-aimed javelins. The Romans then marched steadily forward, driving the Britons back into the rebel encampment. It was an overwhelming victory for the Romans: Tacitus claims 80,000 Britons died while only 400 Romans were killed.

Boudica's revolt had been so effective that it had made the Emperor Nero, far away in Rome, consider abandoning the island of Britain to its inhabitants. But now the rebellion that had promised so much was finished. According to one account, Boudica took poison rather than accept defeat. In another version, she died from the shock of this setback.

Her people were taken into slavery or crept back to their own lands, and the Romans went on to occupy Britain until 410. Yet although it ended in failure, Boudica's extraordinary achievement in bringing the Roman military machine to the brink of defeat was celebrated in later centuries as a heroic narrative of a patriotic freedom-fighter defying the heavy hand of imperial rule.

LEADERSHIP ANALYSIS

LEADER TYPE: *Inspiring*
KEY QUALITIES: *Decisive, charismatic, fearless*
LIKEMINDED LEADERS: *Napoleon Bonaparte, Mohandas Gandhi, Nelson Mandela*
FACT: *According to legend, Boudica lies buried beneath platform nine at King's Cross Station, London.*

GREGORY THE GREAT

DEVOUT MONK WHO LAID THE FOUNDATIONS FOR THE MEDIEVAL CHURCH

NATIONALITY: *Roman/Italian*
ACHIEVEMENT: *Reformer and celebrated saint*
WHEN: *590-604*

The first monk to become pope, Gregory I led the way toward the spirituality of the medieval era and became known as the Father of Christian Worship for his revision of forms of religious service. He is renowned for his widely distributed handbook for the clergy as well as his superb leadership of the church in difficult times.

In 590, as Rome was in the grip of a plague that had killed scores of people, including Pope Pelagius II, his successor Gregory I led a penitential march through the streets. Many in the march reported seeing the Archangel Michael sheathe his sword, suggesting God would spare the city. It seemed that this unassuming monk had saved Rome with his piety and devotion, and promised the revitalization to come under his leadership.

Gregory was an extremely reluctant pope. In this period the appointment of each pope had to be approved by the emperor of the Eastern Roman Empire in Constantinople, and after he was chosen Gregory wrote to Emperor Maurice, asking to be spared the task. But Germanus, Prefect of Rome, confident of Gregory's abilities, did not send the letter and Gregory was duly confirmed as pope.

In spite of his initial misgivings, once in office this humble, diligent, and pious man rose magnificently to the task. Like leaders such as Saint Francis of Assisi, Mohandas Gandhi, or Mother Teresa, Gregory was profoundly humble in his person: He demanded respect for his position as pope, but he was famous for declaring that in carrying out his responsibilities, he was the "Servant of the Servants of God." His task was to lead the bishops and clergy of the church by serving them—by providing teaching and guidance in works such as his handbook *Pastoral Care* or the talks collected in his *Commentary on Job*, which extend over 35 books.

Gregory argued that the pope had moral primacy over other church leaders as the spiritual descendant of the first pope, Saint Peter, but that otherwise "all are equal by the law of humility." Gregory did not emphasize status or rank for its own sake; leaders of this sort who can engage warmly and directly with their followers are often able to inspire hard work and great loyalty.

PRACTICAL GUIDANCE
In pursuit of his aim to provide spiritual guidance, Gregory was highly prolific—his

THE SURVIVING WORKS OF GREGORY THE GREAT

41 BOOKS

854 LETTERS

11 HYMNS

60+ SERMONS
Including 22 on the Book of Ezekiel and 40 on the gospels, as well as two on the Song of Songs

voluminous writings in Latin were influential throughout the Middle Ages. They included his *Pastoral Rule* (591), a handbook for bishops and clergy, which was translated into Greek in his own lifetime on the request of Byzantine emperor Maurice and sent to every bishop in the empire. In the ninth century this book was translated into Old English by King Alfred the Great, who likewise despatched it to every bishop in his kingdom (see page 54). Gregory's *Dialogues*, a collection of saints' lives, was also widely popular—in the Eastern Church, he is celebrated to this day as "Gregory the Dialogist" on the basis of this book.

Gregory was also a great preacher and his sermons attracted large crowds. Many of these sermons survive. They show how Gregory used anecdotes to make his points in a way that anticipated the preachers of the Middle Ages.

CHURCH REFORMER

Before becoming pope, Gregory received a good education that probably incorporated training in the law. In 574 he retired from the world to become a monk, and founded Saint Andrew's monastery on the Caelian Hill in Rome. The sixth-century historian Gregory of Tours noted that Gregory had no equal in rhetoric, grammar, and argument. He also was learned in history, mathematics, and music. As pope, Gregory implemented all his learning in instigating wide-ranging reforms. He revised the liturgy (the forms of church worship), making a number of changes to the order of prayers in the service of Mass.

His learning and record as a reformer gave rise to the tradition that he standardized Western plainchant, the unaccompanied sacred singing in church services that later became known as "Gregorian chant." However, this chant was not standardized until the eighth or ninth century. Some historians suggest that the music became known

TIME LINE

SPEAKING WITH AUTHORITY

Gregory had a gift for engaging his audience. This was represented in a legend recorded by one of his biographers, Peter the Deacon. In this story, when Gregory was preparing his sermons on Ezekiel, an onlooker, peeking through the curtain behind which the pope sat, saw a dove (traditionally the symbol of the Holy Spirit) with its beak in Gregory's mouth. When the dove withdrew its beak, Gregory dictated his sermon. Representations of Gregory show him with a dove (see right). Like other spiritual leaders such as the Prophet Muhammad he was seen to be transmitting divine wisdom.

as "Gregorian" from Gregory's eighth-century namesake Gregory II (715–731).

CARE FOR THE POOR

After his election Gregory continued to live a simple monastic life and appointed many monks to key positions in his administration. Another side to Gregory's role as "servant" was his care for the poor and hungry of Rome. In this he led by example: He himself made generous donations as he reformed the system under which alms were distributed to the poor. He also sent out monks into the streets of Rome looking for those who had nothing to eat and reputedly would not eat himself until he had been told the poor had been fed. He regularly invited the poor and hungry to share his meals.

Gregory also improved the administration of church estates and sent out agents to manage them and prevent oppression of peasants by landowners. In a further attempt to provide peasants with protection he established a system under which the poor in each parish could apply to a deacon for help.

He believed that the church was steward of its property, which rightfully belonged to the needy: Under his rule the papacy became the ally of the people, so that on his death on March 12 604 he was popularly acclaimed as a saint. In a reign

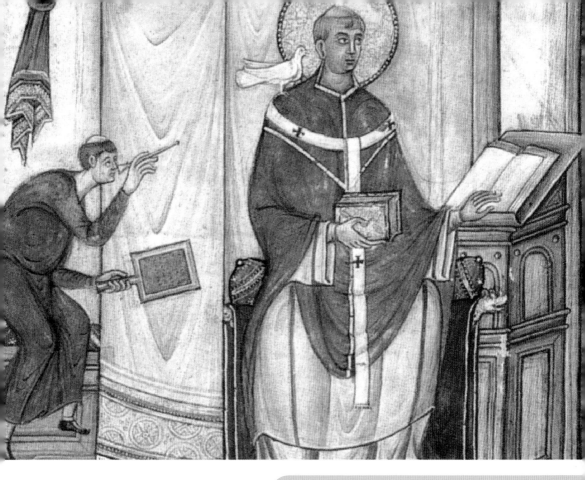

of 13-odd years, and despite his initial reluctance, he had produced a proud and enduring legacy in his reforms and his written work, which provided instruction for the bishops, clergy, and faithful for centuries. He was celebrated as a saint in both the Roman Catholic and the Eastern Orthodox churches and at the Reformation was appreciated even by Protestants: The outspoken Swiss Protestant John Calvin declared that Gregory I was the last good pope.

LEADERSHIP ANALYSIS

LEADER TYPE: *Reformer*
KEY QUALITIES: *Diligent, learned, humble*
LIKEMINDED LEADERS: *Saint Francis of Assisi, Mother Teresa*
FACT: *Gregory's mother Silvia is also celebrated as a saint.*

10

MUHAMMAD IBN 'ABD ALLĀH

INSPIRED PROPHET WHO FOUNDED THE WORLD FAITH OF ISLAM

NATIONALITY: *Arab*
ACHIEVEMENT: *Founded world religion of Islam*
WHEN: *610-632*

Muhammad's mystical encounter with the archangel Jibreel produced the revelations collected in the Qur'an as the words of Allah—whom he recognized as the one God. A deeply spiritual leader driven by the need to share these divine teachings, he gathered devoted followers and founded the religious and social community of Islam.

According to traditional accounts, in a mountain cave near Mecca, Saudi Arabia, Muhammad was disturbed while meditating by a man he later saw was the archangel Jibreel—or Gabriel. Jibreel embraced Muhammad and ordered him to recite. So Muhammad started to recite—and so began the revelations that would inspire the birth of Islam.

Having received Allah's teachings Muhammad became a great leader because of his ability to share them effectively with others. Open to spiritual guidance, he was God's messenger. Tradition holds that Muhammad had visions from early in his life. As a boy he was sent by his mother to live with the Bedouin in the desert, where he experienced an encounter in which two men dressed in white purified his heart with snow. Later, as a young man, he had visions that he described as breaking on him like the light of dawn.

SPIRITUAL AUTHORITY

Even before his transformative encounter, Muhammad was known for his wisdom and was often asked to arbitrate in disputes. He was devout, committed to prayer. It was for this reason that, in AD 610, he retreated to a cave for the month of Ramadan. Traditional accounts of Muhammad's encounter with Jibreel tells us that when he first witnessed the archangel, Muhammad initially fled the cave thinking he had been disturbed by a demon. He was stopped when he heard a voice declaring "Thou art the Messenger of God and I am Jibreel!" Looking back he saw that Jibreel had revealed his true angelic form—he was now so vast that he filled the sky, which had become green. In Islam, Judaism, and Christianity, Jibreel or Gabriel is the archangel sent by God with his communications to mortals—in the Christian tradition, Gabriel was the archangel sent to the Virgin Mary to tell her she was to give birth to Jesus Christ.

Muslims believe the Ka'aba was rebuilt by Abraham in the place where the first man, Adam, had built a shrine and that it is the most sacred place on Earth.

Muhammad took his role as God's Messenger very seriously. He shared the teachings first with his family, then friends, then the general public. The message was that there is no God except Allah and that every life should be lived in submission to Him—the word "Islam" means "to surrender" and the name for a follower of the religion, Muslim, has the same root. He continued to receive revelations from God—either through the voice of the archangel or the movement of truth in his heart—for the rest of his life.

COMMUNITY OF BELIEVERS

Among Muhammad's first followers was family friend Abu Bakr, who after Muhammad's death would become leader of the Muslims, the first caliph (or deputy to the Prophet). Muhammad made converts in Mecca, but also enemies among the ruling Quraysh tribe. His teaching stressed that there was only one God, while

TIME LINE

570
Born, Mecca; Father 'Abd Allah dies.

576
Mother Aminah dies; in care of uncle Abu Talib.

595
Marries Khadīja bint al-Khuwaylid.

610
Receives first revelation.

613
First public preaching.

619
Khadīja and Abu Talib die; experiences Miraj night journey to heaven.

622
Hijrah migration to Medina.

623
Draws up Constitution of Medina.

624
Muslims win first battle against Quraysh, at Badr.

629
Muslims make first conquest, of Khaybar; also capture Mecca.

631
Unites Arabia under Islam.

June 8 632
Dies, Medina.

c.652
Caliph Uthman ibn Affan compiles Qur'an in final form.

at this time the Arab tribes in Mecca worshipped many deities.

In 619 Muhammad had to come to terms with the death of his wife Khadīja and his uncle Abu Talib, who had been his protector since he had been left an orphan at six years old. Tradition holds that in the same year he had another profound religious experience in which he received further revelations directly from Allah.

The revelations that came to Muhammad in this episode provided guidance not only on a person's relationship with Allah, but also on the social arrangements among believers in the religious community. It was these social norms and conventions that Muhammad established for the Muslim community—a community further united by their common persecution at this time. Muhammad gained such a

CREATING COMMUNITY

Muhammad's authority was essentially spiritual, deriving from the fact that he was the bearer of Allah's teachings. He was also a highly effective teacher and leader of people: He built the community of Muslims patiently and with care over many years, creating a very strong bond among his followers, a brotherhood of believers. He appealed both to people's inward self, their relationship with Allah, and to their social self, their relationship within the community. In the modern day many Muslims believe that wherever they live they are part of an international community of believers, the Ummah Islamiyyah (the Islamic Community).

reputation as a powerful leader and a man of justice that in 621 people from Yathrib, a city north of Mecca, asked him to come to their city as their leader.

LAWMAKER

The Muslims and Muhammad traveled to Yathrib—an event later celebrated as the Hijrah ("migration"). On leaving Mecca he narrowly escaped assassination by leading Quraysh. His arrival at Yathrib on September 25 622 is remembered as the date on which Islam was established as a religious and social community of believers. The year of the Hijrah marks the start of the Islamic calendar, which was created by the second Caliph Umar I (ruled 634–644); the city became known as Medina ("the city of the Prophet"). The first Islamic mosque was built at the outskirts of Medina, at the place where Muhammad arrived. Muhammad drew up a constitution widely seen as the blueprint for an ideal Islamic society.

After many clashes with the Quraysh, Muhammad returned in 629 to conquer Mecca and by 631 he had brought the whole of Arabia under Islam. In 632 he made the first Islamic pilgrimage to Mecca—an event celebrated as Al-Hajj and repeated by millions of Muslims every year. On this occasion he reputedly received the final revelation of the Qur'an. Later that year, however, he fell ill and died on June 8 632. In just 23 years since the start of his revelations, he had founded a new religion, united the disparate tribes of Arabia under its umbrella, and established a powerfully bound community of believers who would carry Islam through al-jihad ("exertion as a believer" or "holy war") far and wide across the world.

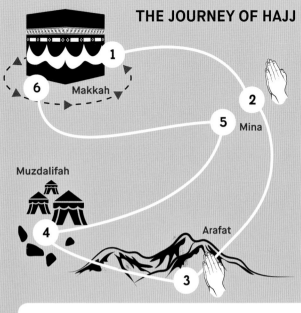

THE JOURNEY OF HAJJ

1 *Pilgrims circle the Ka'aba seven times*
2 *At Mina they stop to pray*
3 *Prayer at Arafat from noon to dusk*
4 *49 stones are collected at Muzdalifah*
5 *Returning to Mina, pilgrims throw the stones at three pillars that represent the devil*
6 *On return to Makkah pilgrims circle the Ka'aba another seven times.*

LEADERSHIP ANALYSIS

LEADER TYPE: *Leader by example*
KEY QUALITIES: *Mystical, great teacher, community builder*
LIKEMINDED LEADERS: *Moses, Jesus of Nazareth, Mohandas Gandhi*
FACT: *Muhammad never ate alone if he could avoid it. He preferred to eat with others.*

11 CHARLEMAGNE

DEVOUT EMPEROR WHO PROMOTED REFORM AND UNITED EUROPE

NATIONALITY: *Frankish*

ACHIEVEMENT: *Created Carolingian Empire*

WHEN: *771-814*

King of the Franks and founder of a great Christian empire, Charlemagne promoted learning and artistic activity in the Carolingian Renaissance. He had a major impact on life in medieval Europe and for centuries was revered as an ideal ruler.

On Christmas Day 800 Pope Leo III crowned Charlemagne Emperor of the Romans in St Peter's, Rome. The ambitious leader, who had already proved himself a powerful Christian warrior and effective protector for the pope, gained authority for his rule over the great empire he had built up since his accession as sole ruler of the Franks in 771.

This unprecedented imperial coronation at the hands of the pope revived the Roman Empire in the West, which had been in abeyance since the fifth century. It gave Charlemagne, hitherto King of the Franks and Lombards, equal standing with the rulers of the Roman Empire in the East, the Byzantine emperors based in Constantinople. The action also consolidated the authority of the papacy—the church was bestowing Charlemagne's authority.

The alliance between the Frankish kings and the papacy had been created by Charlemagne's father Pippin III the Short. Pippin, originally mayor of the palace (an important court position, who was effectively regent), had seized the Frankish throne from Childeric III in 751, then gained the pope's backing for his position. In 754 Pippin and the then pope, Stephen II, reached a mutually beneficial agreement: Military protection in exchange for the papacy's recognition of Pippin's dynasty as rightful Frankish rulers. In 756 Pippin, who had enjoyed considerable military success in Italy, made the famous Donation of Pippin in which he gave the pope a great swathe of territory in central Italy—the basis of the Papal States governed by the papacy.

AMBITIOUS, DIPLOMATIC

Charlemagne had all the ambition, military drive, and diplomatic skill of his father. On Pippin's death he inherited the kingdom alongside his brother Carloman, but Carloman's death in 711 opened the way for Charlemagne to build an empire in his own name. As was expected of a Frankish monarch, he embarked at once on energetic military campaigns to expand territory, over the course of many years defeating the Lombards, Saxons, and Avars and incorporating their territories into

his own. He was brave, strong-willed, and physically imposing—standing at 6 feet 3 inches (1.9 m) at a time when the average height was only 5 feet 7 inches (1.69 m).

Charlemagne was quick-witted and able to see the big picture. He improved administration of the territories in his empire and used diplomacy—backed by the force of his armies—to settle its borders: He maintained largely settled relationships with neighbors including Danes to the north, Slavic tribes to the east, Bretons and Gascons in what is now France, and the papacy in Italy. He also had good relations with the Anglo-Saxon rulers of Northumbria and Mercia in England and with the Muslim rulers of the Abbasid caliphate based in Baghdad—in the course of several diplomatic missions, Charlemagne received from Caliph Harun ar-Rashid an elephant, a chessboard, and a water-powered clock that greatly impressed Charlemagne's courtiers.

REFORMER

A devoutly religious man, Charlemagne was inspired by his Christianity to spread the faith: His conquests of the Avars and Saxons opened up vast territories for missionary work. He instituted a program of religious reform, calling several synods at his court and enforcing laws to make the church hierarchy stronger and more efficient, raise intellectual and moral standards among the clergy, and standardize forms of worship. He also took control of many matters that were previously governed by the church. In addition to these religious reforms, Charlemagne was also interested in promoting education throughout his empire. To this end he invited some of the best minds of Europe to his court, chief among them the Anglo-Saxon poet, cleric, and teacher Alcuin of York. Alcuin was head of the Palatine School that Charlemagne founded and

April 747
Born, Aachen.

751
His father Pippin III the Short seizes Merovingian throne.

753
Pippin makes alliance with Pope Stephen II.

756
"Donation of Pippin."

768
Pippin dies—Charlemagne and Carloman co-rulers.

771
Carloman dies—Charlemagne takes sole power.

772
Begins 32-year campaign against Saxons.

774
Defeats Lombards in northern Italy.

778
Failed invasion of Spain.

781
Creates kingdom of Aquitaine to protect border with Spain.

781
Invites Alcuin to Aachen.

789
Takes control of Bavaria.

796
Third of three successful campaigns against Avars.

December 25 800
Crowned "Emperor of the Romans" by Pope Leo III.

805
Palatine Chapel, Aachen, consecrated.

January 814
Dies, Aachen.

a leading light among the scholars who set out to improve education and standards in reading and writing Latin across the empire. They issued manuals for the teaching of Latin and the basics of the Christian faith and outlines for the correct performance of church liturgy. Monastic schools were established throughout the empire. At court the scholars founded a library and a scriptorium for writing illustrated manuscripts, developing a new system for writing later known as Carolingian miniscule.

The court scholars wrote history, theology, explications of the Bible, and poetry. Alcuin declared that a "new Athens" was being established at Charlemagne's favorite residence Aachen (now in Germany), where the emperor set magnificent building works in motion. The court-driven program of education produced a great flowering of culture in the Carolingian empire and inspired King Alfred the Great to attempt his own Anglo-Saxon cultural revolution in the ninth century (see page 54).

BORN LEADER

Charlemagne did not have much formal education, but he possessed a keen mind and great intellectual curiosity. In the modern world great emphasis is placed on education and qualifications, but Charlemagne is only one of many leaders—alongside people such as Charles de Gaulle or Giuseppe Garibaldi—who achieved great things while relying chiefly on their natural intelligence and leadership qualities.

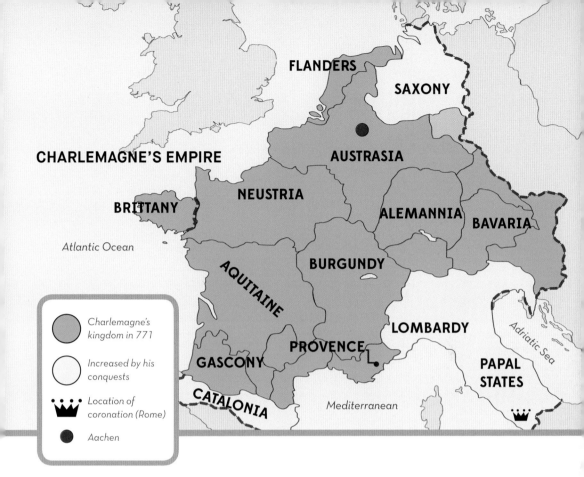

CHARLEMAGNE'S EMPIRE

FLANDERS
SAXONY
AUSTRASIA
NEUSTRIA
BRITTANY
ALEMANNIA
BAVARIA
Atlantic Ocean
AQUITAINE
BURGUNDY
PROVENCE
LOMBARDY
Adriatic Sea
GASCONY
PAPAL STATES
CATALONIA
Mediterranean

- Charlemagne's kingdom in 771
- Increased by his conquests
- Location of coronation (Rome)
- Aachen

ROLE MODEL FOR CHRISTIAN RULERS

Although Charlemagne's territorial empire did not long survive his death, he had a profound and lasting influence that was felt throughout the medieval period—and even beyond. He revived the Roman Empire in the West, establishing the possibility of a unified Europe that has lived on for centuries as an idea; the great cultural and educational renaissance of his reign had a major effect, and laid the foundations for later similar revivals. He himself became the model for subsequent rulers. Celebrated in his own lifetime as "Father of Europe," he became the subject of a great and widely popular body of legends that cast him as champion of Christendom, peerless warrior, and saintly leader.

LEADERSHIP ANALYSIS

LEADER TYPE: *Ambitious*
KEY QUALITIES: *Energetic, courageous*
LIKEMINDED LEADERS: *Alfred the Great, Süleyman the Magnificent*
FACT: *For all his commitment to education at court, Charlemagne never learned to read or write.*

KING ALFRED THE GREAT

ENERGETIC REFORMER WHO PROMOTED LEARNING AND RELIGIOUS DEVOTION

NATIONALITY: *English*
ACHIEVEMENT: *Promoted learning and law while defeating Danish raiders*
WHEN: *849-899*

The only English king to be celebrated as "the Great," King Alfred of Wessex not only achieved military success in holding off Danish raiders, but also promoted his people's education and welfare. He improved the legal system, encouraged literacy, and oversaw the beginning of English history-writing.

Alfred was characterized by a desire for wisdom. He believed there was an urgent need to raise standards of learning at his court and saw the brutal Viking raids that hit his kingdom as divine punishment. Ignorance led to the sins that angered God, Alfred argued, and only by acquiring wisdom through literacy and book learning could his people understand and follow God's will.

In 878–885, during a lull in Viking raids, Alfred invited to his court at Winchester, England, learned men from mainland Europe, Wales, and the kingdom of Mercia in central England. He decreed that all young English men of sufficient financial means must learn to read English and issued translations in English of what he called "those books most necessary for all men to know." To further his educational ambitions he established a school at court to teach the children of the nobility alongside his own offspring and poorer children who showed great promise. In providing this educational and cultural leadership for his people, Alfred aligned himself with the great Frankish ruler Charlemagne of the eighth and early ninth century, who in a similar way promoted learning at his court, and who, like Alfred, oversaw a flowering of arts and culture in his kingdom as a result (see page 50).

Alfred's recommended reading list included *Histories Against the Pagans* by Paulus Orosius and the *Ecclesiastical History of the English People* by the seventh/eighth-century English monk the Venerable Bede. Both books promoted understanding of God's will as evidenced in history. Alfred was also responsible for launching the writing of English history. The *Anglo-Saxon Chronicle* was a collection of annals (annual records) written in Old English, begun around 890 in Wessex. In one case these records were updated right up until 1154.

Alfred himself learned Latin and made translations of important books, including *Pastoral Rule*, a sixth-century book on the responsibilities of clergy by Pope Gregory the Great (see page 42), *Consolations of Philosophy* by the sixth-century Roman philosopher Boethius, and the *Soliloquies* of fourth/fifth-century bishop Saint Augustine.

In order for learning to thrive, Alfred had to protect his people from invaders—Walter Hutchinson shows the king's navy fighting off the Vikings.

The king's principal interest in learning was to educate and promote Christian teaching among his people. Alfred both led by example, taking an active part in his program of promoting religious learning, and also demonstrated genuine enthusiasm for the project. He was profoundly interested in books and culture for their own sake.

PROTECTOR AND DEFENDER

The king who wanted to elevate his people also wanted to protect them. As part of this endeavor he reworked his kingdom's law code, in particular taking measures to protect the weak against corruption and oppression. He imposed substantial penalties for the breaking of pledges and oaths.

Alfred was also his people's military defender—as far as he was able in the face of repeated and ruthless attacks by marauding Danes. His greatest hour as a soldier was in 878: He defeated the Danes when all had seemed lost. The invaders had launched a

TIME LINE

849
Born at Wantage.

853/55
Visits Rome.

867
Vikings seize York and establish own kingdom.

868
Campaigns with brother Aethelred I of Wessex and Kent against Danish army in East Anglia.

868
Marries Ealhswith, Mercian princess.

871
Aethelred dies, succeeds as king. Fights Danes in Wessex; makes peace.

876–77
Danes attack Wessex again.

878
Defeats Danes in Battle of Edington, near Chippenham, southern England.

885
Defeats Danish invasion of Kent.

886
Attacks and captures London.

887
Begins to translate books into Latin.

c.890
The compilation of the Anglo-Saxon Chronicle *begins.*

892/896
Further Danish attacks.

899
Dies and is buried in Winchester.

shock attack in January 878 and seized Chippenham, where Alfred had been spending Christmas. Most of the people there were killed, but Alfred escaped into the nearby marshes of the Somerset Levels, where he set up a base at Athelney and conducted a campaign of guerrilla warfare against the Danes.

GENERAL, STRATEGIST, DIPLOMAT

Gradually, combining local militias, he built up his forces until he was ready to take on the Danes in a pitched battle at Edington, probably near Westbury (in Wiltshire, England). He won the battle—fought sometime between May 6 and 12 878—and then besieged the Danes in

THE KING WHO BURNED THE CAKES?

Alfred's reputation has not faded across the centuries: He is remembered as one of England's greatest leaders—warrior, lawgiver, educator. One celebrated story—that of Alfred burning the cakes—emphasizes his devotion to his people. According to this legend, when Alfred was in hiding in the Somerset Levels he took refuge in the house of a goatherd and his wife: The woman asked the guest to keep an eye on her cakes while she attended to a task, but Alfred—focused so strongly on plotting a way to overcome the Danes in Chippenham and so save his kingdom—allowed the cakes to burn; when the woman returned, she roundly told the king off. This story, which does not appear in Asser's Life of Alfred, *is a legend that first appeared in twelfth-century stories of the king.*

Chippenham, taking care to remove all sources of food they might access in a sortie from the town. After two weeks the Danes were desperate and Alfred granted them peace, on condition that their leader Guthrum was baptized a Christian.

Alfred's success won him a period of peace that lasted until 885, but after that the Danes re-emerged as a threat. He proved himself an acute strategist and effective diplomat in seeking to limit the Danish onslaught. He built a network of 33 burhs (forts and fortified towns) to protect the kingdom, in some places strengthening existing settlements, in others building new fortifications. He reorganized the military, using naval defenses and introducing larger ships that he designed himself. He built a series of diplomatic alliances, notably with the princes of Wales.

A LIFE REMEMBERED

Alfred was unique also in being the only one of the Anglo-Saxon kings to have a contemporary full-length biography written. Alfred's life was recorded by his friend Asser, a monk from Saint David's Abbey in Pembrokeshire who taught Alfred Latin and whom the king later appointed Bishop of Devon and Cornwall. Written in 893 the biography does not cover the final years of Alfred's life, but captures him for posterity as a likeable man, one keenly aware of his responsibilities as king, merciful, compassionate, and devoted to learning. In later centuries Alfred was remembered as a truly great leader, not just for his success in holding off the worst of the Danish attacks, but even more so for the care he showed his people and the ways—through promoting education and the law—in which he improved the quality of life in his kingdom.

▲ Alfred may be most famous for the legend of the burnt cakes, here imagined by James William Edmund Doyle.

LEADERSHIP ANALYSIS

LEADER TYPE: *Reformer*
KEY QUALITIES: *Inquisitive, brave, cultured, resourceful*
LIKEMINDED LEADERS: *Charlemagne, Queen Elizabeth I*
FACT: *Alfred was only known as "the Great" from the sixteenth century onward.*

13 GENGHIS KHAN

FEARSOME MONGOL CHIEF WHO USED MILITARY MIGHT TO BUILD A VAST EMPIRE

Genghis Khan was a ruthless war leader who spread terror far and wide as he built one of history's largest empires, fusing together many of the nomadic tribes of northeast Asia.

NATIONALITY: *Mongolian*
ACHIEVEMENT: *Created Mongol Empire*
WHEN: *1206–27*

At a great assembly of the Mongol clans beside the River Onon in 1206, Temüjin was declared Genghis Khan—the overlord of all. Showing the determination, ambition, and ruthlessness for which he would become famous, Temüjin had been building up his power base for years. He had eliminated all his enemies and the Mongols were united. He was ready to embark on a campaign of world conquest.

Genghis Khan's initial target was China. He first attacked the border state of Xixia, then launched a full-scale onslaught in 1211. In 1214 he accepted a vast bribe to hold off, but attacked again the following year and captured Beijing. Then in 1219–23 he attacked the Muslim empire of Khwarezm in Central Asia and Persia (modern Iran), ruthlessly overrunning settlement after settlement, massacring populations and forcing survivors to serve in his army, and reducing agricultural fields and elegantly planned irrigation schemes to dust and rubble. On his death in 1227 he had aggressively expanded his borders and established the foundations of what would become the world's largest continuous empire.

In war Genghis Khan was utterly merciless. Most of what we know of him and his army's conquests—aside from what is described in the *Secret History of the Mongols,* a saga written down in c.1240—derives from accounts written by scribes in cultures ravaged by the raiders, detailing the horrors swiftly moving Mongol armies inflicted on more settled peoples. One such account relates the events of the attack on Khwarezm. Khan was provoked when Inalchuq, the governor of the city of Otrar (now a ruin in Kazakhstan), attacked a caravan of merchants he had sent to establish trading links with the shah of Khwarezm. When the shah failed to repair the damage, Genghis Khan unleashed the full force of his military machine, sending an army of 200,000 men. When he captured Otrar, he put Inalchuq to a grisly death by pouring molten silver into his eyes and ears. He then returned to unleash another overwhelming punishment in 1226, this time on the rulers of Xixia, who had refused to supply troops for the campaign against Khwarezm. Khan overran the capital and executed all the members of the imperial family.

▲ An anonymous chronicle image shows Genghis Khan and the Mongols fighting Chinese warriors in the Battle of the Badger Mouth, northern China, in 1211.

TWO KINDS OF LOYALTY

As vividly demonstrated by such episodes, Genghis Khan punished every slight against him. He never allowed an enemy or subordinate to feel that they had the upper hand. In this way Khan demanded loyalty by ruling with an iron fist.

The danger implicit in this often short-term approach to inspiring loyalty is that any slight relaxation of power will lead to revolts. However, Genghis Khan also built loyalty by other means. On occasion he was open to being merciful and promoting brave and skillful enemies so they could serve in his army. In 1201, he was shot in the neck with an arrow during a battle against the Taijut tribe. After he had won the victory and treated his wound, he confronted the Taijut prisoners and demanded to know who had fired the arrow. A warrior named Zurgadai, perhaps figuring that he had nothing left to lose, stepped forward and defiantly declared himself. Temüjin, admiring his spirit and his skill with a bow, spared his life and gave him a position in the Mongol army. He became one of the Mongols' foremost generals and one of Genghis Khan's most loyal subordinates.

The ruthlessness with which Genghis Khan dealt with defeated enemies meant that his reputation traveled before him. Enemies could be reduced to a state of abject terror before any fighting began and surrendered when they might have otherwise fled or fought. He was brutal, too, when building up his power base among the Mongol tribes before 1206. After he overwhelmed the Tatar tribe in battle, he slaughtered every survivor who was taller then the axle of a cart—anyone shorter would have been a child of impressionable age who would grow up in thrall to him.

TIME LINE

1162
Born, near Lake Baikal, Mongolia.

c.1171
Their tribe abandons him and his mother and brothers after his father's death.

c.1176
Kills half-brother Behter.

1178
Marries Börte of the Onggirat tribe.

1184
Rescues Börte after she was captured by the Merkit tribe.

c.1177
Enslaved by Tayichiud tribe, but escapes.

1190
Unites Mongol confederation of tribes.

1206
Sole ruler of Mongols after defeating all rivals.

1211
After making ruler of Xixia his vassal, turns against Jin dynasty in China.

1215
Captures Jin capital Zhongdu (Beijing).

1219–23
Overruns Muslim empire of Khwarezm.

1226
Campaigns against Xixia.

August 18 1227
Dies.

c.1240
The chronicle, A Secret History of the Mongols, details Genghis Khan's achievements.

OPEN-MINDED

For a man with such a fearsome reputation, Genghis Khan was remarkably tolerant when it came to religious faith. He was himself a follower of the Mongols' shamanistic religion that honored spirits of mountains, winds, and sky, and was known for his devotion to their supreme god "Eternal Blue Heaven" and to the mountain Burkhan Khaldun, but he allowed the peoples in his territories to follow their own faith freely—whether Christian, Buddhist, Muslim, or Taoist. He summoned Qiu Chuji, a Taoist from Shandong, east China, to attend on him and discuss means of prolonging life and the possibility of immortality. Genghis Khan put Qiu Chuji in charge of all the religious followers in his vast empire and gave him the name "Immortal Spirit."

LISTENING EAR

Genghis Khan's reputation is that of a man who was single-minded in pursuit of land and glory, swift to seek revenge and issue terrifying punishments. But he was also open to advice and willing to learn. As a nomad, he initially saw no use for the cultivated fields of northern China except as a place to graze his ponies. But he listened when a former adviser to one of the Jin emperors told him that these fields and the craftsmen living in the towns nearby produced foods and goods on which he could levy taxes. He also learned from captured enemies how to lay siege to towns and the uses of weapons such as catapults and mangonels that had been quite foreign to the Mongols.

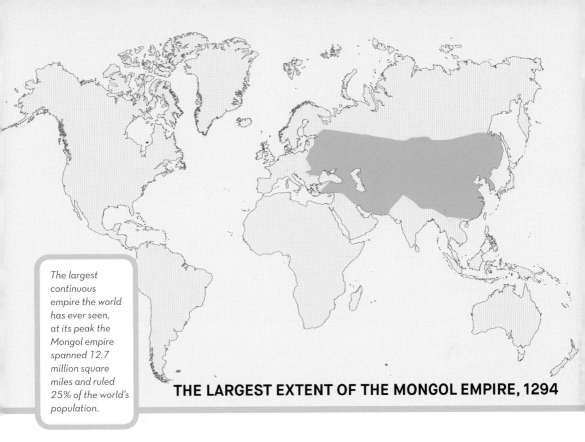

The largest continuous empire the world has ever seen, at its peak the Mongol empire spanned 12.7 million square miles and ruled 25% of the world's population.

THE LARGEST EXTENT OF THE MONGOL EMPIRE, 1294

By the end of his life his empire stretched right across Asia as far as the Adriatic Sea. An estimated 40 million had been slaughtered by his troops. In Mongolia he is celebrated as a national hero, founder of the country when he became ruler of all the steppe tribes in 1206. In his empire he opened a connection between Asia and Europe, between East and West. More widely, his conquests established a stable political environment across vast territories in Asia, boosting trade and cultural exchange along the 4,000-mile (6,500 km) Silk Route from Europe to China and India—as such he is credited with having expanded the horizons of East and West. Nonetheless, as a leader, Khan is generally considered the epitome of the cruel warlord, utterly ruthless in his pursuit and application of power.

LEADERSHIP ANALYSIS

LEADER TYPE: *Ruthless*
KEY QUALITIES: *Iron-willed, ruthless, disciplined*
LIKEMINDED LEADERS: *Attila the Hun, Napoleon Bonaparte*
FACT: *His original name Temüjin means "man of iron" or blacksmith.*

14 SAINT FRANCIS OF ASSISI

HUMBLE FRIAR WHO EMBRACED POVERTY

NATIONALITY: *Born in what is now Italy, in the Duchy of Spoleto*
ACHIEVEMENT: *Founded Franciscan monastic movement*
WHEN: *1181-1226*

Italian preacher and friar Francis of Assisi transformed the history of the medieval church through his commitment to a spartan lifestyle promoting charity and peace. With profound self-belief and integrity, he was a shining example to the members of the three Franciscan orders he founded.

In an extraordinary hearing before his local bishop in January 1206, Francis of Assisi was called before the authorities by his father, cloth merchant Pietro de Bernadone, after he sold a horse and a fine piece of cloth to raise money for the local church. During the course of the hearing Francis stripped entirely naked and handed his clothes to his outraged father. Having dramatically disrobed, he told his father, "Until today I have called you my father on Earth. But from now on I can truly say: 'Our Father who art in Heaven.'" Provided with a cloak by the bishop, Francis took himself off to live in the woods near his native Assisi and pursue a life of religious devotion.

Francis's driving force was his desire to follow the example of Jesus. As shown by the above story, Francis understood this to mean being willing to give up possessions, along with family ties, to humble his own self-will, and embrace poverty. A person who did this, he believed, could live as Jesus had done with passionate love for all.

INSPIRED BY FAITH

Francis was no dreamy idealist. He knew what he was rejecting when he denounced conventional attitudes and embraced poverty and peace. He had a comfortable life as the son of a well-to-do merchant, was a keen singer and musician, and was popular among his peers. The man who later preached peace to soldiers himself fought on the side of Assisi in a conflict with Perugia and endured a year as a prisoner of war. In 1205 he was on his way to fight for the papal forces against Holy Roman Emperor Frederick II when a religious vision inspired him to return to Assisi. This event marked the beginning of his journey to faith and eventual adoption of a pious life of poverty.

According to tradition, this was one of several divine visions that marked Francis's career and gave powerful impetus to his mission. One of the most important was that which led him to sell his father's horse and a length of cloth, resulting in the transformative encounter with the Bishop of Assisi.

POWER OF PERSONAL EXAMPLE

The founder and figurehead of the Franciscan orders of the Friars minor, the women's Order of Saint Clare, and the lay Third Order, Francis is also renowned as leader of the wider evangelical poverty movement in the thirteenth-century church. This movement encouraged the turning away from worldly riches in service of the way of life taught by Jesus in the biblical Gospels. In both, his key leadership quality was integrity, the force of his example.

He was inspired by Jesus's injunction to his disciples, given in Matthew, chapter 10: "And as you go, preach the message, 'The kingdom is at hand!' ... Take no gold, nor silver, nor money in your belts, no bag for your journey, nor two tunics, nor sandals, nor a staff; for the laborer deserves his food." Upon hearing this passage in a sermon at the Chapel of Saint Mary of the Angels in Assisi, 1208, Francis, already living a life of pious devotion and poverty, became convinced of his duty to teach his message. In an echo of his earlier symbolic disrobing, he took off his shoes, put on a rough tunic, and began to preach.

FEARLESS AND DETERMINED

Francis was profoundly determined, unfazed by authority, and self-reliant. In 1209 he traveled with his first 12 disciples to Rome and boldly asked Pope Innocent III to approve his fledging monastic rule. It was a simple rule, taken from passages in the Bible, which established the basic tenets of their way of life. The approval of the rule by the pope marked the official founding of the Franciscan order. Later in life, Francis

THE GROWTH OF THE FRANCISCAN ORDER

1209   **12 FOLLOWERS**

1221   **5000 FOLLOWERS**

2015

500,000 FOLLOWERS

TIME LINE

1181
Born Francesco di Pietro di Bernardone in Assisi.

1202/3
Fights for Assisi against Perugia.

1205
Visits Rome as pilgrim.

February 24 1208
Inspired by a sermon, Francis begins preaching.

April 16 1208
First followers join Francis.

1209
Francis has 12 followers and writes first rule of conduct.

1209
Pope Innocent III gives approval of their way of life.

1212
Founding of female branch of order—Poor Ladies of San Damiano.

1219
Francis travels to Damietta, Egypt, has audience with Sultan Malik al-Kamil.

1221
Francis founds Franciscan lay order—for those who are neither monks nor nuns.

November 29 1223
Pope Honorius III approves Francis's second rule for order.

September 14 1224
Vision at La Vernata, receives stigmata.

October 3 1226
Dies at Chapel of Saint Mary of the Angels in Assisi.

July 16 1228
Pope Gregory IX celebrates canonization of Francis.

1979
Named patron saint of ecology.

traveled with some of his followers to Egypt, where the Fifth Crusade was being waged, and fearlessly preached peace both to the crusaders and to the Muslim Sultan al-Kamil.

His continual demonstration that he would live wholeheartedly by his beliefs has been an inspiration to countless people—not least Pope Francis, who on being elected in 2013 announced that he had chosen his papal name in honor of Saint Francis of Assisi. Pope Francis declared: "He brought to Christianity an idea of poverty against the luxury, pride, vanity of the civil and ecclesiastical powers of the time. He changed history."

ESTABLISHING HIS LEGACY
In addition to gaining Pope Innocent III's backing for his monastic order in 1209, Francis won Pope Honorius III's approval on November 29 1223 of the rule of conduct he had written for his monks and nuns to follow. The rule called on

ECOLOGIST?

Francis saw the beauty of nature as a reflection of God's glory. He preached a sermon to the birds (a moment immortalized by the Italian artist Giotto di Bondone) and, according to one story, managed to convince a wolf to halt its attacks on the town of Gubbio on condition that the locals put out food for the creature. Francis has been a particular inspiration to modern environmentalists such as the American campaigner Robert F. Kennedy, Jr., and in 1979 Pope John Paul II declared Francis the patron saint of ecology.

According to tradition, Francis received the stigmata in 1224, depicted here by Caravaggio.

the monks "to follow the gospel of Jesus Christ, living in obedience and in chastity without any possessions of our own." He also appointed a vicar or subordinate to look after the order's practical affairs. The result was that the movement he founded not only survived but also grew and today has expanded beyond the Roman Catholic Church of its founder to embrace other Christians in the Church of England and Lutheran traditions.

Francis's life continues to cast an inspiring light in the modern world, not only through the Franciscan orders, but also in his inspiration of modern environmentalists and the appeal of the poems and prayers associated with his legacy. Most recently Francis's example of simple living has been embodied by Jose Mujica, the president of Uruguay who stood down on 1 March 2015.

LEADERSHIP ANALYSIS

LEADER TYPE: *Leader by example*
KEY QUALITY: *Integrity*
LIKEMINDED LEADERS: *Jesus of Nazareth, Mother Teresa, Pope Francis*
FACT: *In 1205 Francis's father chained him in a cellar for a month to prevent him becoming a religious hermit.*

15

SÜLEYMAN THE MAGNIFICENT

CELEBRATED LAWGIVER WHO PROMOTED REFORM AND THE ARTS

NATIONALITY: *Turkish*
ACHIEVEMENT: *Presided over the Golden Age of the Ottoman Empire*
WHEN: *1520-66*

After eight years' construction, the magnificent Süleymaniye Mosque in Istanbul was completed in 1558. Designed by the extravagantly gifted architect Mimar Sinan, it was built to glorify the name of Ottoman Sultan Süleyman I, a triumphant general but also a great patron of architecture and the arts.

Sinan based the design of the Süleymaniye Mosque on that of the venerable sixth-century church of Hagia Sophia in Istanbul. The new mosque symbolized the way in which emperor and architect were remaking the great city of Istanbul—formerly known as Constantinople and chief city of the Byzantine or Eastern Roman Empire—as a worthy capital for the expanding Ottoman Empire over which Süleyman I presided.

The Süleymaniye Mosque stood beneath a vast 185 foot (57 m)-high, 90 foot (27.5 m)-diameter dome—at the time the largest in the Ottoman Empire—at the center of a complex incorporating a hospital, four madrasas (Islamic schools), a refectory, medical school, baths, stables, and shops. The Süleymaniye remains today the largest mosque in Istanbul.

DEVELOPER OF TALENT

Mimar Sinan was Süleyman's generously supported chief architect, responsible for more than 300 buildings and other structures in Istanbul and across the empire—in addition to mosques, he built palaces, schools, bathhouses, hospitals, aqueducts, granaries, and caravanserais (travelers' inns); he is celebrated as the greatest architect in Ottoman history, a worthy counterpart to his Western contemporary Michelangelo, who in this period was drawing up his plans for the rebuilding of St Peter's Basilica in Rome.

At the Ottoman court Süleyman fostered talent in a range of artistic fields that produced a great flowering in the arts, for which his reign became celebrated: Under his rule, his Topkapi Palace in Istanbul was home to imperial artistic societies known as "communities of the talented." As early in Süleyman's reign as 1526 there were 40 such societies in existence, containing upward of 600 members. Like Catherine the Great at St Petersburg in eighteenth-century Russia (see page 86), he was determined to make the royal court an internationally renowned center for art and intellectual life.

The best artists and craftsmen were attracted to Istanbul from all corners of the empire—including conquered territories in Europe—by the offer of apprenticeships and then financial support in the form of a quarterly stipend. Artists, jewellers, goldsmiths, bookbinders, and furriers were among those working in Istanbul under Süleyman's protection. Fine calligraphy flourished. Under Süleyman's patronage, Ottoman arts and writing emerged from the shadow of Persian culture to assert their own character.

ARTIST AS PATRON

Süleyman was a practising goldsmith and poet who wrote under the pen name Muhibbi (The Lover). He composed in both Turkish and Persian, and wrote memorable poems to commemorate the death of his son Mehmed and to celebrate his love for Hürrem Sultan, the Christian concubine who became his wife.

▲ *Süleyman's fame spread to the West. This portrait, painted in c.1539, has been attributed to the celebrated Venetian painter Titian (Tiziano Vecelli).*

He was therefore a sympathetic patron of poets. Like Alfred the Great, he was a patron who himself engaged in artistic production (see page 54), and in this role was able to inspire and engage with those he sought to mentor. Major Ottoman poets who flourished at Süleyman's court included Muhammad bin Suleyman (who wrote under the name Fuzuli) and Mahmud Abdülbâkî, better known simply as Bâkî. Under Süleyman's patronage Bâkî achieved greatness as a court poet with works such as *Elegy for his Excellency Süleyman Khan* and *On Fall*. Such was his success that he became celebrated as "The Sultan of Poets."

LEGAL AND EDUCATIONAL REFORMER

Süleyman also gathered at his court experts on Islamic law including Kemalpashazade and Abū al-Suʿūd, and undertook a large-scale revision and codification of the law. The empire was governed under shar'iah (Islamic religious law), which the sultan could not revise; but he did collect and rework what he could—notably the kanuns, or canonical laws that governed areas such as taxation, land, and criminal laws. The code he drew up, known as the kanun-i Osmani (Ottoman laws) remained in force for more than 300 years. He also reformed tax laws to improve the plight of Christian subjects in the empire, and in criminal law he reduced the number of offences that attracted the death penalty, drawing up a scheme of fines and punishments.

Süleyman also promoted education, opening new primary schools in Istanbul and overseeing the establishment of a network of madrasas, where students studied astronomy, philosophy, grammar, and astrology as well as religion. Süleyman brought his discerning eye to bear in the appointment of administrators and statesmen, too. Gifted ministers Pargalı Ibrahim Pasha, Rüstem Pasha, and Sokollu Mehmed Pasha all served as grand vizier. The administration of the empire was in very good hands.

TIME LINE

November 1494
Born, Trabzon.

September 1520
Succeeds as sultan.

1521
Captures Belgrade.

1522
Takes Rhodes from the Knights of St John.

August 1526
Defeats King Louis II of Hungary at Battle of Mohács.

1529
Besieges Vienna.

1533
Agrees truce with Archduke Ferdinand.

1534
Fuzuli becomes court poet under Süleyman.

1534–35
First campaign against Safavid Persia.

1538
Sea victory off Greece by Süleyman's admiral Khayr ad-Din (Barbarossa) delivers Ottoman control of Mediterranean.

1543
Writes poem to mourn death of son Mehmed.

1548–49
Attacks Persia a second time.

1554–55
Third, largely unsuccessful campaign in Persia.

1558
Süleymaniye Mosque completed in Istanbul.

1565
Failed attempt to capture Malta.

September 1566
Dies.

ALWAYS VICTORIOUS

As a young man Süleyman had studied theology, literature, science, and military history. He admired Alexander the Great and drew inspiration from Alexander's creation of an empire that took in both West and East (see page 22). For, in addition to his wide-ranging patronage of artists and artisans, writers, and legal experts, Süleyman was an energetic and highly effective military leader—celebrated as "the one who is always victorious."

In the first years of his reign he captured Belgrade, took the island of Rhodes from the Knights of St John, and won a great victory in Hungary at the Battle of Mohács. By 1529 he was at the doors of Vienna but, partly on account of bad weather, he lifted the siege. He also captured large areas in the Middle East and North Africa and his navy under the

FAIR TO ALL

A key quality in leaders is justice—being seen to be fair to all. This is especially important for a legislator and administrator like Süleyman, ruler of a great empire containing varied populations. Here Süleyman led the way. His legal reforms eased the taxation burden on Christian subjects in the empire, and in fact made life better for poor Christians in Ottoman territory than it was outside the empire. This prompted the migration into the Ottoman lands of Christians looking to benefit from his reforms. In c.1554 he also issued a decree denouncing blood libels against the Jews (outlandish allegations that Jews kidnapped children to use their blood in ceremonies).

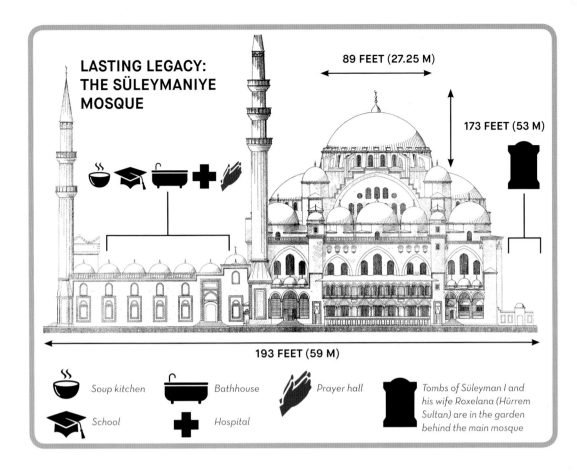

LASTING LEGACY: THE SÜLEYMANIYE MOSQUE

89 FEET (27.25 M)

173 FEET (53 M)

193 FEET (59 M)

Soup kitchen

School

Bathhouse

Hospital

Prayer hall

Tombs of Süleyman I and his wife Roxelana (Hürrem Sultan) are in the garden behind the main mosque

gifted admiral Khayr ad-Din—known in the West as "Barbarossa"—had control of the Mediterranean Sea after victory over a combined Venetian/Spanish fleet in the Battle of Preveza, off the coast of northwestern Greece, in 1538. Süleyman's great success as a military leader was in part due to the highly advanced Ottoman military and to the power of his navy.

Süleyman's reign was the high point of the Ottoman Empire—in terms of its size, artistic achievements, reform of law, and excellence of administration. His court patronage turned Istanbul into a great center of intellectual life. His dual legacy is reflected in the two names by which he is remembered; in the West as Süleyman the Magnificent and in Turkey and associated areas as Süleyman Kanuni (The Lawgiver).

LEADERSHIP ANALYSIS

LEADER TYPE: *Talent promoter*
KEY QUALITIES: *Brave, just*
LIKEMINDED LEADERS: *Charlemagne, Catherine the Great, Mustafa Kemal Atatürk*
FACT: *After Süleyman's death in Sziget, Hungary, his heart was buried where he died. It has not yet been found.*

16 QUEEN ELIZABETH I

PROUD TUDOR QUEEN WHO MADE HERSELF THE ICON OF A NATION

NATIONALITY: *English*
ACHIEVEMENT: *Defeated the Spanish Armada and was the heart of a nation*
WHEN: *1558-1603*

The 45-year reign of Elizabeth I, England's iconic Virgin Queen, saw the defeat of the Spanish Armada in 1588, the beginnings of the country's imperial power, and an extraordinary flowering of national theater, poetry, music, and art.

Elizabeth I told Parliament in November 1601 "Though God has raised me high, yet this I count the glory of my crown, that I have reigned with your loves." Over more than 40 years on the throne this shrewd, devoted leader had remained unmarried. In the carefully crafted national mythology of the "Virgin Queen," Elizabeth had chosen to be married not to a foreign prince but to her own country—to her people.

At the start of her reign, in 1558, Elizabeth's marital status had been a cause of concern for her subjects. Parliament twice urged the queen to wed, nervous that if anything happened to her while she had no heir the country would be plunged back into the dynastic feuding that had scarred England in the Wars of the Roses (1455–87). Elizabeth, however, remained firm and told her MPs that she had no intention of marrying at present:

> Nothing, no worldly thing under the sun, is so dear to me as the love and goodwill of my subjects ... in the end this shall be for me sufficient, that a marble stone shall declare that a queen, having reigned such a time, lived, and died a virgin.

In spite of numerous proposals of marriage, both before and after her accession to the throne, she declined them all. Elizabeth was the Virgin Queen.

THE TUDOR DYNASTY

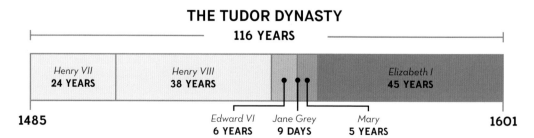

116 YEARS

| Henry VII | Henry VIII | | Elizabeth I |
| 24 YEARS | 38 YEARS | | 45 YEARS |

1485

Edward VI
6 YEARS

Jane Grey
9 DAYS

Mary
5 YEARS

1601

▲ The "Armada portrait" of c. 1588 shows the Virgin Queen at her most magnificent. In the background English ships see off the Spanish invasion fleet.

CONTROLLING TERMS OF ENGAGEMENT

By refusing to marry, Elizabeth was able to maintain her own and her country's independence. She could avoid any expectation that a wife—even a ruling queen—must be obedient to her husband. A marriage to a foreign ruler would likely involve England in another country's engagements; a marriage to an Englishman might spark conflict among noble factions. Elizabeth provides a powerful example of how a leader can benefit from controlling the terms on which she engages with her role and followers.

Meanwhile at the Elizabethan court, the customs and language of courtly love and chivalric engagement were embraced: In this world, she was a beloved mistress whose right was to grant or withdraw favors to her "knights." Deliberately ambiguous, Elizabeth expertly negotiated the potentially thorny issue of a woman in power.

She enjoyed a close relationship with a succession of favorites including Robert Dudley, whom she elevated to the earldom of Leicester, and Sir Walter Raleigh. But she kept the upper hand. According to courtier Sir Robert Naunton, she once furiously cut off Leicester's attempts to make her grant him a favor with the stinging rebuke, "I will have here but one mistress and no master."

NATIONAL ICON

Elizabeth was an icon, a figurehead, carrier of the dreams of her people: She oversaw a glorious era for England that included the defeat of the Spanish Armada—an attempted invasion by King Philip of Spain in 1588—and daring voyages of discovery and settlement

TIME LINE

September 7 1533
Born, Greenwich Palace.

November 17 1558
Accedes to the throne.

January 15 1559
Crowned, Westminster Abbey.

1572
Nicholas Hilliard appointed official limner (painter of miniature portraits) to the queen.

1575
Visits Earl of Leicester at Kenilworth Castle, Warwickshire, as part of "summer progress."

1575
Thomas Tallis and William Byrd publish Sacred Songs.

1577–80
Sir Francis Drake makes circumnavigation of world.

1584
Foundation of England's first overseas colony: "Virginia."

1585
Dispatches English army to back Protestant revolts in the Netherlands.

February 8 1587
Execution of Mary, Queen of Scots.

1588
Inspires defeat of Spanish Armada.

1589
Sir Edmund Spenser presents first three volumes of The Faerie Queene *to Elizabeth.*

1597
After enjoying the History of Henry IV, *asks Shakespeare for new play featuring Sir John Falstaff—the result is* The Merry Wives of Windsor.

February 25 1601
Former favorite the Earl of Essex is beheaded for treason.

March 24 1603
Dies, at Richmond Palace.

that resulted in the establishment in 1584–89 of England's first overseas colony, the land at Roanoke Island (now North Carolina) that Sir Walter Raleigh christened "Virginia" in Elizabeth's honor. Beginning in the 1570s, the date of Elizabeth's accession to the throne (November 17) was

THE ICON DESCENDS

Elizabeth's glittering elevation as the Virgin Queen made all the more stirring and inspirational her actions on August 9 1588 when she rode among her troops at Tilbury, Essex, to inspire them prior to the attack by the Spanish Armada. She was like a goddess descending or, in the words of an onlooker named James Aske, a "sacred general." Elizabeth's stirring words have gone down into English tradition alongside those of Winston Churchill, who in 1940 likewise rallied the country against a threatened invasion. The immortal lines:

> *I know I have the body of a weak and feeble woman, but I have the heart and stomach of a king, and of a king of England too, and think it foul scorn that Parma or Spain or any prince of Europe should dare invade the borders of my realm, to which, rather than any dishonour shall grow by me, I myself will take up arms, I myself will be your general, judge, and rewarder of every one of your virtues in the field.*

are forever associated with the image of Elizabeth as a fiercely loyal protector of her people.

celebrated as a holiday: There were bonfires, services of thanksgiving, and at Whitehall Palace in London tilts and pageants. This was a saint's day for a Protestant country. Her court was a place of lavish and magnificent display and she took it out with her when she made a summer progress around country houses in central England.

Moreover, Elizabeth was an enthusiastic patron of the arts, which enjoyed an remarkable flourishing in her reign—with William Shakespeare, Christopher Marlowe, and Ben Jonson active in the theater, the exquisite miniaturist Nicholas Hilliard at work as a portraitist, and Thomas Tallis and William Byrd proving their worth as composers of sacred music. In addition, Sir Edmund Spenser wrote his long, allegorical romance *The Fairie Queene* and dedicated it to Elizabeth as "Gloriana, queen of Fairieland" and mistress to brave knights in her Order of Maidenhead.

MATERNAL AUTHORITY

As she grew older, the stage-managed image of the Virgin Queen was shifted in a new direction that emphasized self-sacrifice and devotion: The queen had given up the chance to marry out of loyalty to her people. She was less a mistress in a courtly love-relationship and more a mother figure—with clear references to the devoted love of the Virgin Mary. The pearl and the crescent moon—symbols traditionally associated with the Virgin Mary—were linked to Elizabeth.

The image of the loving Virgin Queen was maintained right to the end. In December 1602, less than six months before her death, Sir Robert Cecil put on an entertainment that presented Elizabeth as Astraea, a saintly virgin from the Roman poet Virgil's *Eclogues*, who brought to Earth a golden age of peace and unending spring. In her November 1601 speech to Parliament—her final address to MPs, later known as the Golden Speech because a surviving manuscript was marked with the words "this speech should be set in letters of gold"—she declared "It is my desire to live nor reign no longer than my life and reign shall be for your good."

Elizabeth died in the early morning of March 24 1603, after an extraordinary 45-year reign in which she had managed to maintain the devotion of a people who arguably had loved her as no other English monarch has been loved before or since. The reign of Gloriana, the Virgin Queen, was indelibly inscribed as a golden age in the psyche of generations of English men and women, all too happy to believe and celebrate the declaration she made in her Golden Speech: "There will never Queen sit in my seat with more zeal to my country, care to my subjects and that will sooner with willingness venture her life for your good and safety than myself."

LEADERSHIP ANALYSIS

LEADER TYPE: *Proud*
KEY QUALITIES: *Iconic, engaging*
LIKEMINDED LEADERS: *Süleyman the Magnificent, Catherine the Great*
FACT: *Elizabeth was determined to limit the religious disputes that had caused such disruption in previous reigns.*

17

WILLIAM SHAKESPEARE

PROLIFIC PLAYWRIGHT WHO TOOK COMMAND OF LONDON THEATER AND REVITALIZED THE ENGLISH LANGUAGE

NATIONALITY: *English*
ACHIEVEMENT: *Greatest English dramatist in history*
WHEN: *1592–1611*

The son of a Stratford-upon-Avon glove maker and bailiff, William Shakespeare seized every opportunity to make himself a successful actor and theater manager and became the leading playwright in London. His works established him as the greatest English dramatist of all time.

Led by William Shakespeare and Richard Burbage, the theatrical troupe of the King's Men were licensed by King James I under a royal patent of May 19 1603. Lifted to greatness by extraordinary dramatic gifts, Shakespeare had established himself in little more than ten years as the pre-eminent playwright in London, a leading light of this troupe, and co-owner of the Globe Theatre.

The King's Men were at the height of their profession. Each member was supplied with four and half yards of red cloth so they could be suitably attired for King James's coronation procession, in which they duly took part on March 15 1604. They were often called to court—between November 1604 and February 1605 Shakespeare's plays *Othello*, *Measure for Measure*, *Love's Labour's Lost*, *Henry V*, and *The Merchant of Venice* were all performed at court.

Shakespeare rose from relatively humble beginnings to being courted and lauded by the king of England and Scotland. From his plays it is clear he had a rare ability as a writer, which he crucially combined with drive, ambition, and an eye for opportunity. Born in Stratford-upon-Avon, Shakespeare was married to Anne Hathaway and father of three children—a daughter Susannah and twins, Hamnet and Judith—before he journeyed to London, determined to make his name in the theater and as a poet.

UPSTART CROW, RUFFLED FEATHERS

Like all who seek to be leaders, Shakespeare demonstrated courage and determination in making the move—and he brought great self-belief with him. But success did not come without trial. In 1592 he was attacked by fellow-playwright, Robert Greene, as "an upstart crow."

This clash of words seems to have been a response to Shakespeare's success—by this date he had established himself as an actor and playwright. He had clearly upset a few established names in the theater world along the way to be lampooned by Greene in this way. He was also showing himself to be adept at self-publicity.

SHAKESPEARE IN NUMBERS

17 COMIC PLAYS

2 NARRATIVE POEMS

118,406 LINES

10 TRAGIC PLAYS

154 SONNETS

10 HISTORY PLAYS

884,647 WORDS IN THE COMPLETE WORKS

Shakespeare made the acquaintance of powerful patrons. His poems *Venus and Adonis* and *The Rape of Lucrece*, published in 1593 and 1594 respectively, were dedicated to Henry Wriothesley, third Earl of Southampton. Patronage was critical to a writer's success at this time. His other patrons included Robert Devereux, Earl of Essex, and Henry Herbert, Earl of Pembroke.

LEADER AMONG PLAYWRIGHTS

By 1594 Shakespeare was a key member of the Lord Chamberlain's Men, later granted a royal patent and renamed the King's Men. Shakespeare rose to become one of the leaders of the group on account of his talent, his wit, and his energy. He was the company's principal playwright, an occasional actor, and a partner in the enterprise. All profits were shared among the company members and the theater owners ("housekeepers"), who included Shakespeare, Burbage, and Burbage's father.

Shakespeare dedicated himself first and foremost to realizing his talent, but he also made sure he seized every chance that came his way and showed steely commitment to his art. In the early 1590s the Lord Chamberlain's Men mostly performed at The Theatre, in Shoreditch. After the lease on the site where this building stood expired, the company men demonstrated their commitment to the enterprise by dismantling the theater piece by piece and moving it to a riverside

TIME LINE

April 23 1564
Born, Stratford upon Avon.

1594
Became a member of the Lord Chamberlain's Men. The Rape of Lucrece *and* Titus Andronicus *published.*

1594
The Comedy of Errors *performed at Gray's Inn.*

1599
New Globe Theatre built in Southwark.

1601
Richard II *performed at The Globe.*

1602
Twelfth Night *performed at the Middle Temple.*

1603
Lord Chamberlain's Men renamed King's Men.

1608
King's Men perform at Blackfriars Theatre and The Globe.

1608
King Lear *published.*

1609
Shakespeare's Sonnets published.

1610
The Tempest *performed at court.*

1611
Retires to Stratford.

June 29 1613
Globe Theatre burns down during performance of Henry VIII.

April 23 1616
Dies, Stratford-upon-Avon.

1623
Mr William Shakespeares Comedies, Histories & Tragedies *published; this is the book referred as "the First Folio."*

warehouse; the following year they resembled the building as the Globe Theatre in a new location in Southwark.

DEDICATION AND HARD WORK
All worked hard—perhaps most of all Shakespeare, who from 1594 to 1611 wrote two plays a year as well as acting and managing the theater. Early plays included *A Midsummer Night's Dream*, *Titus Andronicus*, *The Merchant of Venice*, *Romeo and Juliet*, and *The Comedy of Errors*. Success came quickly. The Lord Chamberlain's Men were the most successful playing troupe in London: From 1595 they played at court before Queen Elizabeth I.

In 1596 Shakespeare's father John was granted a coat of arms, which his son must have financed, and in 1597 Shakespeare bought New Place, a substantial mansion in Chapel Street, Stratford-upon-Avon. He had made it. The following year English churchman and author Francis Meres declared that Shakespeare was the greatest writer of comedy and tragedy in England.

SUPREME TALENT
The gifts Shakespeare brought to bear were above all perception, wit, and poetic invention. He fashioned material from chronicles and various other sources into vibrant and powerfully immediate pieces of theater, driven by energetic and very often beautiful verse and inhabited by intensely memorable characters. His play *The Tempest*, performed at court in 1610, appears to present itself as a final work. The main character Prospero's renunciation of his magic at the play's end, has been interpreted as Shakespeare's announcement of his retirement as playwright. The passage may even

contain a reference to the Globe Theatre in the following lines: "Our revels now are ended. These our actors, As I foretold you, were all spirits and. Are melted into air ... the great globe itself ... shall dissolve." After 1611 Shakespeare lived more or less in retirement in Stratford-upon-Avon.

In an extraordinary career, Shakespeare proved himself a leader in two senses—both of the London theater scene of the 1590s onward in which he built his reputation, and of the timeless world in which his plays are performed, loved, and reinterpreted by generation after generation. As his contemporary poet and playwright Ben Jonson wrote of Shakespeare, "He was not of an age but for all time!"

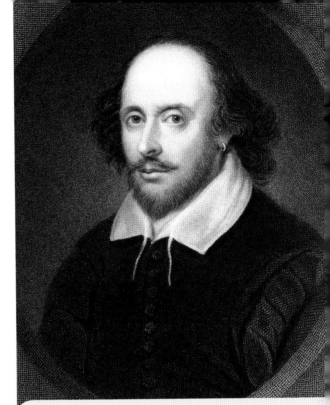

▲ Celebrated as one of the foremost writers of all time, Shakespeare had a lasting influence on the English language, introducing many words still in use today.

OPPORTUNITY

Shakespeare demonstrated his firm belief in the importance of making the most of every opportunity afforded to you in a passage in Julius Caesar. Brutus declares: "There is a tide in the affairs of men which, taken at the flood, leads on to fortune; omitted, all the voyage of their life in shallows and in miseries." Effectively: If you don't catch the tide, you may miss your chance.

Just as Shakespeare himself seized every chance as he moved from Stratford and made his way in the London theater world of the 1590s, quickly establishing himself as a leading player and the city's foremost playwright, so any leader needs to be alert to the moment of opportunity—be willing to take quick decisions and embrace risk.

LEADERSHIP ANALYSIS

LEADER TYPE: Innovator
KEY QUALITIES: Ambition, invention, drive
LIKEMINDED LEADERS: Pablo Picasso, Winston Churchill
FACT: Shakespeare's work has been translated into 80 languages—more than any other author.

PETER THE GREAT

AMBITIOUS REFORMER WHO LAUNCHED RUSSIA INTO THE MODERN WORLD

NATIONALITY: *Russian*
ACHIEVEMENT: *Modernized Russia*
WHEN: *1684-1725*

As tsar and then emperor, Peter I was an autocratic ruler whose modernizing cultural reforms transformed Russia. The nation's military victory over Sweden in the Great Northern War established his country as a major force in Europe.

Peter I ordered the introduction of a new Russian calendar on January 1 1700 as part of a program to modernize Russia and bring its social and cultural life closer to that of western Europe. With reforms to the military, nobility, government, education, and the church, and development of Russian industry, he replaced medieval traditions with more modern, forward-looking customs in harmony with the Age of Enlightenment.

The old calendar was notionally dated from the creation of the world: Peter changed the year 7207 to 1700, dated from the birth of Christ, to bring Russia in line with western European usage. He also moved the date of the New Year to align it with the Julian calendar. Another modernizing reform was his introduction in 1710 of a secularized alphabet to replace the Old Church Slavonic one previously in use.

In the same year the first Russian newspaper, *Vedomosti* ("Records") had been established. Under Peter's rule, the translation of Western works of literature was encouraged and the Russian Academy of Sciences was set up. Peter oversaw the creation of secular schools, which accepted children of priests and churchmen, soldiers, and government administrators as well as the offspring of the nobility.

AUTOCRAT TAKES ON BOYARS

Key among Peter's modernization program was his reform of the nobility. In 1722 Peter introduced the Table of Ranks, a new system of awarding positions in the nobility. Previously nobles had depended on their ancestry for access to roles in the service of the state and promotion within the hierarchy, but Peter's new system introduced a scale of 14 ranks that applied to all roles in the navy, military, and civilian life. A person rising up from the lowest 14th rank could attain membership of the nobility, regardless of birth, upon reaching the eighth rank: A new influx of nobles greatly diluted the power of the medieval elite of the boyars.

In central government Peter introduced autocratic rule to replace existing forms. In 1711 he swept away the boyar council and established the Senate as the supreme body of government, charged with implementing the edicts of the tsar. To carry out the administrative tasks of government he created a system of nine colleges in 1718 to replace the older, inefficient collection of around 80 offices.

HANDS-ON AND PRAGMATIC

While Peter maintained an autocratic rule, he did not stand on ceremony himself. He did not like fine clothes: He often appeared scruffily dressed in an old hat and shoes or in military uniform. In St Petersburg, the new capital he founded, he liked to sit and drink beer while passing the time with sailors and shipwrights that foreign ships had brought to port. A down-to-earth leader who enjoyed socializing with his subjects of all backgrounds, Peter was also highly intelligent, full of courage and had an immensely strong will. He was pragmatic in a changing situation but single-minded, acting always in the interests of his country. Like the similarly progressive leader Mustafa Kemal Atatürk Peter was happy to go face to face with the people he led—a powerful tool for a leader in motivating followers.

Peter also set out to reform the governance of the Russian Orthodox Church. The church was traditionally governed by the Patriarch of Moscow and All Rus', but when Patriarch Adam died in October 1700, Peter decided to leave the position vacant. In 1721 he abolished the role of Patriarch altogether and created the Holy Synod, a council of ten clergy, to govern the church; he made sure that this council was staffed by men loyal to his modernizing program and established the position of chief procurator, appointed by the tsar, to oversee its activities. Dissenters were punished severely and publications censored. Peter further limited church power by seizing monastic and ecclesiastical property and by decreeing that no serfs and no other men aged under 30 were permitted to become monks.

MILITARY REFORMER, CREATOR OF RUSSIAN NAVY

This last measure was in part a response to Peter's concern that too many men were becoming monks and so weakening the army. If Russia was to be a player on the international stage she needed a strong military force. Replacing the landholders' militia and royal bodyguards that existed before, Peter created a modern, regular army. The new army was uniformed, underwent regular drills, and was equipped with Russian-made muskets, mortars, and large guns—some designed by Peter himself. Beginning in 1696, he created a large navy containing 49 battleships.

PETER'S MODERN ARMY

49 SHIPS

800 GALLEYS (SMALL SHIPS)

- REGULAR DRILLS
- UNIFORMED SOLDIERS
- USED RUSSIAN-MADE MUSKETS

TIME LINE

June 9 1672
Born, Moscow.

1684
Co-tsar with half-brother Ivan V.

1696
On Ivan's death becomes tsar.

1697–98
Travels incognito abroad to the Netherlands, England, and Austria as part of the Grand Embassy.

1698
Back in Russia crushes revolt by Streltsy (royal bodyguard).

1700
Makes peace with Turkey: Peace of Constantinople.

1700
Start of Northern War: Russians defeated at Narva.

1703
Begins construction of St Petersburg.

1704
Russians capture Narva.

July 8 1709
Defeats Charles XII of Sweden in Battle of Poltava.

1712
St Petersburg new capital of Russia.

1714
First major naval victory at the Battle of Gangut.

September 10 1721
Treaty of Nystad ends Great Northern War.

November 2 1721
Proclaimed emperor.

1724
Russian Academy of Sciences established.

February 8 1725
Dies, St Petersburg.

To build these weapons and ships he needed to develop Russian industry. Peter was very hard-working and poured his energies into this project. His system of privileges allowed industrialists and businessmen to buy serfs to work in their workshops and factories: A new class came into being.

DOWN-TO-EARTH

To make this modernizing program effective, Peter decided he needed first-hand knowledge of industry and of modern customs in western Europe. In 1697–98 he traveled abroad incognito as part of a Grand Embassy—aiming to combine efforts to maintain and strengthen a coalition against the Turks with a fact-finding mission. Going by the name of Sergeant Pyotr Mikhailov, he worked for four months as a ship's carpenter in the Dutch East India Co. yard at Saardam in the Netherlands and then put in another stint at the Royal Navy Dockyard at Deptford, near London. He

VIEW FROM BELOW

Peter saw life in a shipyard from the worker's point of view when traveling incognito on the Grand Embassy Abroad. He began his service in the army on the lowest rank. When leaders truly understand what it is like to be one of the lowest ranks, they are more likely to make good decisions that are for the benefit of all their followers. In this Peter was like the great Napoleon Bonaparte, who rose to power from the position of a mere gunner and was at home among his troops, famously mingling with them amid their campfires (see page 96).

Peter—painted here by French artist Jean-Marc Nattier—loved military games and was interested in seafaring from a young age.

hired several experts to come to work in Russia and in addition visited museums, schools, arsenals, and factories, even going so far as to attend a session in the Houses of Parliament in London.

One of the defining aspects of Peter's leadership was the hands-on approach he took during the Grand Embassy. Throughout the Northern War against Sweden, the main military enterprise of his reign, he poured himself into all aspects—in the navy, in the shipyard, on the battlefield. Looking back on the Russian defeat at Narva, fairly early in the war, he declared, "Necessity swept away laziness and made me work day and night."

Peter drew up the battle plan for the great Russian victory over the army of Charles XII of Sweden at Poltava in 1709. In 1714 he fought in the Battle of Gangut in Riilahti Bay near modern Hanko in Finland, when the Russian navy he had done so much to build up won its first major victory in defeating the Swedes at sea. He also had personal oversight of all the treaties signed during the war, which ended with the treaty of Nystad on September 10 1721 that handed Russia control of the eastern shores of the Baltic.

The same hands-on approach led to his death. In 1724 he saw some sailors in difficulty aboad a ship that had run aground in the Gulf of Finland and dived bravely into the freezing waters to help them. He caught a chill from which he never truly recovered—he died on February 8 1725. His military achievements created a vast empire for Russia and his reforms transformed the country and its future. He made Russia a modern country with a key role in Europe.

LEADERSHIP ANALYSIS

LEADER TYPE: *Reformer*
KEY QUALITIES: *Down-to-earth, hard-working*
LIKEMINDED LEADERS: *Mustafa Kemal Atatürk*
FACT: *As part of his Westernization program, Peter banned the wearing of beards for all except peasants and clergy.*

19

FREDERICK THE GREAT

RULER WHO WIELDED ABSOLUTE POWER TO MODERNIZE AN EMPIRE

NATIONALITY: *Prussian*
ACHIEVEMENT: *Used rather than abused total power to make Prussia a great empire*
WHEN: *1740–86*

Frederick the Great led his well-drilled army to unprecedented success in the Seven Years' War—in the process transforming Prussia into the dominant force in Germany—while ruling as an enlightened autocrat.

The treaty of Hubertusburg, signed on February 15 1763, brought an end to the Seven Years' War in Germany, leaving Frederick II of Prussia in possession of Silesia, and confirming his country as a major European power. A gifted general and strict disciplinarian, Frederick established the Prussian army as a model to be emulated in other countries, while he himself was highly influential as an enlightened but absolute ruler.

The issues at contention in the Seven Years' War went right back to the start of Frederick's reign. Coming to the throne in 1740 he was highly ambitious for his country and, sensing weakness in Austria—where Holy Roman Emperor Charles VI had died and been succeeded by his daughter Maria Theresa—Frederick made a number of bold military moves that by 1745 had established Prussian possession of the wealthy and strategically important Austrian province of Silesia.

In summer 1756 Frederick became aware that an attack by Austria, Russia, and France was brewing and acted pre-emptively—invading Saxony and occupying its capital, Dresden. This was the beginning of the Seven Years' War, in which Prussia at various times faced France, Austria, Saxony, Russia, and Sweden with the support of only Britain and Hanover; the war was also fought further afield in North America and India between France and Britain.

Frederick conducted the war with great boldness: His (and Prussia's) fortunes waxed and waned. He won great victories in the battles of Rossbach and of Leuthen (both 1757) but suffered severe defeats in the battles of Hochkirch (1758) and Kunersdorf (1759). After 1759 Prussia's situation looked increasingly desperate and Frederick contemplated suicide. However, his enemies did not press home their advantage and he limped on. Then, in 1762, his fortunes changed when Russian Empress Elizabeth died and her nephew Peter III came to power. Peter was an admirer of Frederick and withdrew from the alliance against Prussia, leading to the signing of the Hubertusburg treaty. With determination and steadfast commitment, Frederick had succeeded in securing a crucial victory for Prussia.

BRAVE, GREAT STRATEGIST

Frederick regularly led his troops into battle himself. On campaign he shared the troubles and sufferings of his men, wearing his simple blue coat—the kind worn by an ordinary Prussian soldier. In the course of his military career he had six horses shot out from beneath him.

He is celebrated as one of the greatest generals in history. Napoleon Bonaparte admired him profoundly: He often studied Frederick's tactics and famously visited Frederick's tomb in Potsdam in 1807, where he declared to his officers, "Gentlemen, if this great man were alive still, then I would not be here."

Prussian military theorist Carl von Clausewitz, author of *On War* (1816–30), praised no other generals above Frederick and Napoleon. He particularly lauded Frederick's skillful and speedy movement of his troops.

A DISCIPLINED FORCE

Like Napoleon, Frederick was a fierce disciplinarian. He trained his soldiers to

Antoine Pesne's portrait shows Frederick as a young prince of 24, in 1736, shortly after his first military service and before his accession.

march faster and reload and fire their muskets more quickly than their rivals. He believed firm discipline was effective because it instilled the fear of failure—he declared that soldiers should be more afraid of their commanding officers than of the enemy.

The battle tactic of oblique order, with which his name is forever associated, depended on speed and discipline: A general would concentrate the main body of his force to attack one flank of the enemy, holding back a smaller group to keep the enemy in position. Using the flank attack, a smaller army could overwhelm a much larger foe. Frederick used this tactic at the Battle of Hohenfriedberg (1745) and the Battle of Leuthen (1757). In the second engagement, his army of around 36,000 defeated an 80,000-strong Austrian force.

Frederick said wars should be "short and fought quickly." He would often risk all to hit hard and decisively—he trusted his army. Leaders in any field learn that preparation and discipline are necessary so that when a move or strategy is implemented, it can be done speedily and effectively. When the moment comes, successful leaders act decisively and bravely—like Julius Caesar, Frederick, or Napoleon.

SURPRISE YOUR ENEMY

Frederick stressed the importance of flexibility and of taking the enemy by surprise, stating: "Everything that an enemy least expects will be the most successful." He

TIME LINE

January 24 1712
Born, Berlin.

1730
Attempts to escape Prussia but is caught and imprisoned.

1734
First military service.

May 31 1740
Accedes to throne on death of father, Frederick William I.

December 16 1740
Invades Silesia, sparking the War of the Austrian Succession.

June 4 1745
Defeats army of Austria and Saxony in Battle of Hohenfriedberg.

December 25 1745
Treaty of Dresden establishes Prussian possession of Silesia.

1756
Invades Saxony, provoking Seven Years' War.

November 5 1757
Defeats French-Austrian army in the Battle of Rossbach.

December 5 1757
Trounces much larger Austrian army in the Battle of Leuthen.

October 14 1758
Defeat by Austrian army in Battle of Hochkirch.

August 12 1759
Heavy defeat by Russo-Austrian army at Battle of Kunersdorf.

February 15 1763
Treaty of Hubertusburg ends Seven Years' War.

1772
Seizes territory in First Partition of Poland.

August 17 1786
Dies, Potsdam, near Berlin.

argued that if an enemy has deployed his army relying on the protection of a chain of mountains, you will wrongfoot him completely by bypassing the mountains and coming from a different direction; or if the enemy is deployed beside a river and defending a particular crossing, you will surprise him by finding a ford elsewhere and coming at him where he least expects it.

Leaders should cultivate the ability to act unexpectedly—and so unsettle opponents or rivals. Leaders need to be wily as well as strong—as Frederick himself put it, they should wear the skin of a fox as well as that of a lion in battle.

PATRON OF THE ARTS
Away from the battlefield Frederick modernized the Prussian civil and judicial

A LARGER DUTY

Like his father Frederick William I and like Queen Victoria in Britain, Frederick had a strong sense of duty as a monarch. He likened a ruling prince to the "soul of a state." He particularly focused on putting the needs of the state above his personal desires. This ability to prioritize the needs of the group, the faculty, or the company is a significant and impressive quality in a leader, which builds loyalty and encourages followers to work hard; it is a quality leaders can develop in themselves through discipline and the desire to improve their performance and that of the people they lead. A disciplined leader can expect and demand discipline in her followers.

services and was a great patron of the arts, responsible for major building work in his capital Berlin. The Berlin State Opera, the Berlin State Library, and St Hedwig's Cathedral were all built in his reign; at his summer residence, Potsdam, he built Sanssouci Palace in the Rococo style.

He was a keen musician, who played the flute and himself wrote four symphonies and 100 sonatas for his instrument. Among his court musicians was C.P.E. Bach, whose father J.S. Bach met Frederick at Potsdam in 1747 and wrote *The Musical Offering*, a collection of fugues and canons based on a theme composed by Frederick himself. Frederick was interested also in philosophy and maintained a correspondence with leading figures of the Enlightenment and, like Catherine the Great of Russia, was friends with Voltaire (see page 86).

Frederick's reign had a major influence on the development of Germany. He began the long and fierce contest between Prussia and Austria for dominance in Germany that was not settled until Prussian statesman Otto von Bismarck's Blitzkrieg (lightning war) humiliated Austria in 1866 (see page 114). As an absolute ruler who was nonetheless influenced by intellectual movements of the Age of the Enlightenment, he was a major influence on Catherine the Great and Holy Roman Emperor Joseph II, rulers celebrated as "enlightened despots." His architectural works remain an enduring legacy.

Frederick was an inspiration for German leaders for centuries right through to the Nazi era, when he was lauded and presented as a forerunner of Adolf Hitler. His emphasis on duty and discipline lived on for generations in Germany and across Europe.

▲ *The king as artist—Adolph von Menzel shows Frederick playing the flute with accompanying musicians during a concert at the Sanssouci Palace.*

LEADERSHIP ANALYSIS

LEADER TYPE: *Ambitious*
KEY QUALITIES: *Disciplined, bold*
LIKEMINDED LEADERS: *Julius Caesar, Catherine the Great, Napoleon Bonaparte*
FACT: *The Prussians viewed Frederick affectionately and nicknamed him Der Alte Fritz (Old Fritz).*

CATHERINE THE GREAT

ENLIGHTENED REFORMER WHO ENSURED THE RUSSIAN EMPIRE WOULD BE A WORLD LEADER

NATIONALITY: *Prussian*
ACHIEVEMENT: *Great patron of the arts, consolidated Russia as European power*
WHEN: *1762-96*

Empress Catherine the Great built on the achievements of Peter the Great, consolidating Russia as one of Europe's major powers. A great patron of the arts and of education, she regularly corresponded with many of the greatest thinkers of her era.

Empress Catherine the Great enthusiastically welcomed Louise Élisabeth Vigée Le Brun, one-time court painter to French queen Marie Antoinette, to St Petersburg in 1795. Catherine, a great patron of literature, education, and the arts, established a glittering aristocratic court in Russia. Her autocratic rule, which also saw the significant expansion of Russian territory and major administrative improvements in the country, is celebrated as a golden age of Russia.

Madame Vigée Le Brun painted several portraits of nobles and royalty, including one of Catherine's granddaughters Alexandra and Elena. Her memoirs, published in 1835–37, give a vivid picture of her encounters with the empress: "On the days when she made her appearances in public," she wrote of Catherine, "with her head held high, her stare like an eagle, and the expression of one accustomed to command, she had such an air of majesty that for me she might have been the queen of the whole world."

A self-professed lover of the arts, Catherine wrote memoirs, comedies, and fiction and even tried composing opera. Like Peter the Great in Prussia and Süleyman the Magnificent in Ottoman Turkey she was a patron and active participant in the arts. In the course of her reign she established literary reviews and encouraged the development of the sciences in Russia. French writer Voltaire, with whom she conducted a 15-year correspondence, praised her as "The Star of the North."

A SCANDALOUS START

Catherine came to power by an unorthodox route. She was not Russian, but the daughter of a Prussian prince. She married the heir to the Russian throne, Grand Duke Peter, becoming Empress Consort of All the Russias when her husband inherited the throne as Peter III in 1762. Within a year she had taken power in a coup and her husband, having been forced to abdicate, was murdered. She had the backing of the army and the Westward-looking enlightened elements of the aristocracy, for she had already established herself as one of the most cultured people in Russia. She declared herself Empress and Autocrat of all the Russias.

ENLIGHTENMENT CONTACTS

Catherine looked often to France and the thinkers of the Enlightenment for inspiration as she sought to remake Russia in the western European image. An essential part of her success as a leader was her ability to draw inspiration from, and build contacts with, key supporting figures. Her association with the French Enlightenment and the connection of her court to important Western artists, writers, and thinkers added considerable luster to her reign and her reputation as an enlightened ruler.

Catherine maintained a correspondence not only with Voltaire, but also with French Enlightenment figures Diderot and d'Alembert. She also attempted to offer practical help as a patron. At the very start of her reign, in 1762, she heard that the French government had threatened to suppress the *Encyclopedie* (Encyclopedia—or a dictionary of the sciences, arts, and crafts) that Diderot and d'Alembert had been issuing since 1751. She wrote to Diderot suggesting he emigrate to Russia and finish his work at her court.

An enduring display of Catherine's commitment to the promotion of art and culture is the collection of the Hermitage Museum in St Petersburg, the basis of which was Catherine's immense private holding of paintings.

DISPLAY

Leaders' displays of power and grandeur can be highly effective in the right circumstances. Of course they need to be backed up by real power to avoid the danger of looking foolish. In 1787 Catherine's former lover and now leading minister Grigory Potemkin arranged a grand voyage to Crimea, which Russia had annexed from Turkey in 1783. Catherine traveled part of the journey by river and her entourage became known as "Cleopatra's Fleet." Several diplomats and major figures including the Austrian emperor came to pay court to her.

Shown above is Catherine in 1780 as painted by Dmitry Grigoryevich Levitsky.

TIME LINE

May 2 1729
Born, Stettin, Prussia.

August 21 1745
Marries Grand Duke Peter, heir to Russian throne.

January 5 1762
Empress Elizabeth dies; Peter accedes to the throne.

July 9 1762
Peter abdicates and Catherine becomes sole ruler.

July 17 1762
Peter murdered.

1762
Secularizes clergy property.

1764
Smolny Institute opens.

1767
Grand Commission, Moscow.

1773
Rebellion of peasants and Cossacks is put down.

1774
Grigory Potemkin becomes Catherine's lover.

1774
Diderot visits Russia.

1783
Annexes the Crimea.

1785
Charter to the Nobility.

1786
Russian Statute of National Education.

1787
Voyage to Crimea.

November 17 1796
Dies, near St Petersburg.

CHARMING, ENERGETIC

Catherine had great charm, intelligence, and immense energy. Some of this found expression in the steady stream of lovers she took, including the nobleman Grigory Potemkin who had a brilliant career at her side.

She considered putting the ideas of the Enlightenment into practice in Russia. In 1767 she called a commission in Moscow with 652 members of all classes except the serfs to advise on a new legal settlement for the empire. She also wrote *Nakaz*, a draft code of law and constitution that was strongly influenced by French Enlightenment ideals, especially the political philosopher Montesquieu's *The Spirit of the Laws* whom she "pillaged," she wrote, "for the good of my empire." She sent a copy of *Nakaz* in French to Voltaire and one in German to Frederick the Great of Prussia (see page 82), and Diderot read and wrote a critique of the document when he visited Russia in 1774. However, although the commission met more than 200 times over the course of several months, none of its deliberations were put into practice.

A serious rebellion of Cossacks and peasants in 1773 led by former Cossack officer Yemelyan Ivanovich Pugachev gave Catherine pause. At one time she had considered freeing the serfs, but instead she strengthened the hand of the nobles. The Charter to the Nobility of 1785 cemented their power.

EDUCATIONAL REFORMER

In the field of education Catherine believed that new theories and systems of schooling inspired by western European models could create a new, more enlightened and forward-looking Russia. To this end she established an educational commission, which recommended the creation of a school system for all subjects—except the serfs—from the age of five to 18.

Though none of the commissions reforms were put into practise, Catherine strove to make reforms in other areas of education. She wrote a manual on the education of young children and opened a foundling home for destitute and unwanted children in Moscow and a school for the daughters of the nobility, the Smolny Institute, in 1764. In this stern institution, young women were instructed in French, music, and dancing. They lived in spartan conditions because warmth was considered harmful to the growing body; they were not permitted to run or play.

Some of the educational reforms mooted in the earlier educational commission were implemented in 1766 in a refashioning of the curricula and practices in military institutions—the Cadet Corps, Naval Cadet Corps, and Engineering and Artillery Schools. Then, in 1786, following the report of another educational commission, the Statute of National Education was issued, under which free primary and secondary schools were established in provincial capitals open to all free classes—that is, all except the serfs—with a detailed curriculum for all ages.

MILITARY EXPANSION

Catherine also carried through significant administrative reforms, reorganizing 29 provinces and establishing more than 100 new towns. She greatly expanded the borders of Russia southward and westward, incorporating lands including Belarus, Lithuania, and the Crimea. With Prussia and Austria, Russia took part in three partitions of Poland in 1772, 1793, and 1795: Poland was divided up and ceased to exist altogether until it was re-established in 1918.

Catherine died on November 16 1796 after suffering a stroke. Madame Le Brun's memoirs reveal that Catherine's body was laid out in state for six weeks, wearing a gold crown and a silver brocade dress on a ceremonial bed surrounded by coats of arms of all the towns in Russia. An enlightened despot, she had ruled with absolute power whilst seeking to bring about reforms in administration and education. Like Elizabeth I and Queen Victoria in England, she gave her name to a period of national history—the Catherinian Era of Russia. Her memory was celebrated in Russia—even in the Soviet era— with great national pride as a time of territorial expansion, a brilliant imperial court that attracted great minds from across Europe, and a golden age for the nobility.

LEADERSHIP ANALYSIS

LEADER TYPE: *Talent promoter*
KEY QUALITIES: *Energetic, ambitious*
LIKEMINDED LEADERS: *Frederick the Great, Süleyman the Magnificent*
FACT: *Catherine probably did not order the assassination of Peter III, but was implicated because of her association with the killers.*

21 GEORGE WASHINGTON

CHARISMATIC LEADER WHO UNIFIED THE STATES OF AMERICA AND LED THEM TO INDEPENDENCE

NATIONALITY: *American*
ACHIEVEMENT: *Led Continental Army to victory in American Revolutionary War; first US president*
WHEN: *1775-83; 1789-97*

Commander-in-Chief of the Continental Army in the American Revolutionary War and first US president, George Washington is celebrated as the Founding Father of the United States of America and as a role model for leaders in all ages.

When George Washington's Continental Army forced the surrender of British general Lord Cornwallis at Yorktown on October 19 1781, it was the decisive moment of the American Revolutionary War. This brave, moral, self-disciplined, and profoundly patriotic leader had held together an often ramshackle, ill-equipped American force and inspired it to victory over the might of the British army. Washington's standing was further enhanced when he served with utmost distinction as the first president of the United States in 1789–97.

In summer 1781 Washington was at Dobbs Ferry, New York, alongside an army from France—an ally since spring 1778—planning an assault on the British on Manhattan Island. Receiving news that the French fleet under François Joseph Paul de Grasse was available to support an attack on another British army under Lord Cornwallis, in Virginia, he marched swiftly southward and had his men transported in de Grasse's ships across Chesapeake Bay to land at Williamsburg.

The siege of Cornwallis's army in Yorktown, Virginia, began on September 28. Washington's 5,500 Continental Army troops were supported by 5,000 French and 3,500 Virginia militia. Cornwallis, expecting reinforcements, hung on for as long as he could but Washington's army picked off the defensive positions one by one and the British general was forced to surrender around 8,000 British troops and 240 guns into American hands. The Revolutionary War was all but won. Peace negotiations began in April 1782 and the Treaty of Paris was signed on September 3 1783.

Leader of a nation: Toward the end of his life Washington was happy to be celebrated as "father of the country." This is one of many copies of a portrait by Gilbert Stuart. ▶

TIME LINE

February 22 1732
Born, Westmoreland County, Virginia.

1753–55
Serves in army of colonial Virginia.

August 1755
Appointed commander of Virginia forces.

1758
Elected to Virginia House of Burgesses; resigns commission.

1774
Delegate to Continental Congress.

May 1775
Delegate to Second Continental Congress.

June 15 1775
Elected Commander-in-Chief, Continental Army.

1776
In March captures Boston. Defeat in the Battle of Long Island in August. The year ends with a victory in the Battle of Trenton, New Jersey, in December.

January 3 1777
Another victory, at the Battle of Princeton.

October 19 1781
Victory in the siege of Yorktown.

1783
Peace treaty ends war. Resigns military commission.

May 25–September 17 1787
President of the Constitutional Convention.

April 30 1789
Inaugurated as first US president.

March 4 1793
Second inauguration as US president.

December 14 1799
Dies, Mount Vernon, Virginia.

LEADER BY EXAMPLE

Washington was an exemplary military leader. Hardy and courageous, he inspired his men's loyalty by sharing all the dangers and difficulties of army life. Like Napoleon Bonaparte and Frederick the Great of Prussia his presence alone was an immense boost to his troops (see pages 82 and 96).

At the start of Washington's army life, fighting against the French at Fort Duquesne in 1755 in the colonial British Army of General Edward Braddock, he rode into battle despite being severely ill and had two horses shot from under him: Four bullets passed through his coat without hurting him. After Braddock was killed and his army defeated, Washington then led the troops to safety. In the 1777 Battle of Princeton during the Revolutionary War American troops and supporting militias were fleeing after an initial setback, but when Washington rode into the thick of the action he settled his men's nerves and they re-joined the attack. Again and again he proved himself self-reliant and cool under pressure.

Physically, he was an imposing and powerful man: He was 6 feet 2 inches (1.88m) tall, straight-backed, and broad-shouldered with a muscular build. In civilian life—at home, as a farmer on his estate of Mount Vernon, Virginia—he was known as a good horseman and keen hunter.

Washington had the utmost commitment to service in a cause in which he believed and a complete willingness to put the public good above his personal interests. He declined to accept payment when he became Commander-in-Chief of the Continental Army, on the understanding that the Continental Congress he served would

▲ *Washington leads a crossing of the icy Delaware river on Christmas day 1776 prior to defeating the enemy at Trenton. This image is by Emanuel Leutze.*

pay his expenses. (And at the end of war, when he resigned his military commission, Washington submitted a meticulous and exact statement of these expenses—totalling a modest $160,074.)

UNIFIER, DISCIPLINARIAN

Washington's early heroics gave him an enduring military reputation—one of the reasons that he was selected as Commander-in-Chief of the Continental Army in 1775. His experience in the British colonial forces also stood him in good stead when he took command in the Revolutionary War. In the war years his great strength was his ability to unify: He held together army and people through a five-year struggle when unthinkable defeat often looked likely.

He was a strict disciplinarian who insisted that his men should maintain a strong backbone, despite having poor pay, inadequate food, and inferior equipment. He clamped down hard on inefficiency and ill-discipline, especially infighting between regional units. He won the devotion of his troops by campaigning vigorously with Congress for their better treatment and for better food.

DEFIER OF THE ODDS

More than once Washington led the army to a great victory or sustained troop morale when all seemed lost. At perhaps the lowest point of the war, the turn of the year 1776–77, his inspirational victories at Trenton and Princeton reinvigorated the country and brought volunteers forward to the cause. After the British captured Philadelphia in September 1777 the future again looked very grim, but he maintained the unity of his half-starved, exhausted army in a freezing winter at Valley Forge.

Washington is the very archetype of the successful leader precisely because of this ability to combine inspiring his followers with maintaining strict discipline. The persona he projected was one in which virtue and bravery matched patriotic, selfless service.

SENSE OF DUTY

In 1783 the Treaty of Paris brought peace. After overseeing the entry of the American army into New York following the British evacuation, Washington bid his leading officers farewell, then resigned his military commission before the Continental Congress at Annapolis, Maryland. The following day, on Christmas Eve, he returned home to his large estate at Mount Vernon.

He hoped to return to being a farmer and landholder, but was called back to public life as president of the Constitutional Convention, which met in Philadelphia in May–September 1787 and issued the Constitution of the United States. During the search for a president of the country, he was seen as the only candidate capable of uniting the states and commanding respect for the new republic in Europe. He was unanimously chosen by the electors and, somewhat reluctantly, accepted.

Washington had a strong sense of duty and was never a man to shirk his responsibilities. In his first inaugural address as president he said: "There is no truth more thoroughly established than that there exists in the economy and course of nature an indissoluble union between virtue and happiness [and] between duty and advantage." He was a man of integrity, of great moral character. As president, he did his utmost to promote unity. He conducted a personal tour through first the northern and then the southern states.

SELF-CONFIDENCE: WORKING WITH THE BEST

In his first cabinet as president, Washington appointed men of great ability such as Thomas Jefferson and Alexander Hamilton—he did not fear them despite the fact that they were probably more able than he was. One reason why self-confidence is such a key leadership attribute is that it enables a leader to appoint and manage teams of the very best—as Clement Attlee did in the British Labour government and Steve Jobs did at Apple (see pages 164 and 215).

INDEPENDENT

As president, Washington was committed to keeping the United States independent of warring nations—when France and Britain went to war in 1793, he supported a move to put aside the US alliance with France. He wanted, he wrote, a United States that was "free from political connections with every other country … under the influence of none … I want an American character that the powers of Europe may be convinced that we act for ourselves, and not for others."

Washington was re-elected for a second four-year term in 1792, but refused public calls that he accept a third term in 1796. He retired in March 1797 settling once again to life at Mount

THE FOUNDING FATHERS

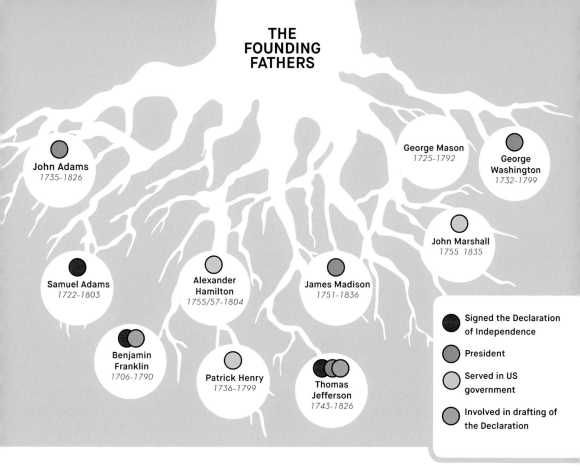

John Adams
1735-1826

George Mason
1725-1792

George Washington
1732-1799

John Marshall
1755 1835

Samuel Adams
1722-1803

Alexander Hamilton
1755/57-1804

James Madison
1751-1836

Benjamin Franklin
1706-1790

Patrick Henry
1736-1799

Thomas Jefferson
1743-1826

- ● Signed the Declaration of Independence
- ● President
- ○ Served in US government
- ● Involved in drafting of the Declaration

Vernon. He died on December 14 1799 two days after coming down with acute laryngitis, following a horse ride of several hours in freezing conditions. His death plunged the country into mourning. Celebrated in his lifetime as "the father of the country," he was revered after his death: Until the rise of Abraham Lincoln, president from 1861–65, Washington was held to be without equal among the great leaders of American history.

Fêted general, inspirational president, and well-loved leader, Washington was—in the words of the eulogy written by Henry Lee III, a cavalry officer in the Continental Army who in 1791–94 served as Governor of Virginia—"first in war, first in peace, and first in the hearts of his countrymen."

LEADERSHIP ANALYSIS

LEADER TYPE: *Unifier*
KEY QUALITIES: *Independent, confident, dutiful*
LIKEMINDED LEADERS: *Winston Churchill, Clement Attlee*
FACT: *Washington State, named in George Washington's memory, is the only state named after an American individual.*

22

NAPOLEON BONAPARTE

AMBITIOUS AND BRILLIANT GENERAL WHO ESTABLISHED FRENCH DOMINANCE IN EUROPE

Bold in battle and brilliant on campaign, Corsican general Napoleon Bonaparte rose to become French Emperor, winning the devotion of his troops and his people, and conquering much of Europe.

NATIONALITY: *French*
ACHIEVEMENT: *Built French Empire*
WHEN: *1804-15*

"One sharp blow and the war is over." With these words, Emperor Napoleon ordered an uphill attack on the Russian-Austrian troops occupying the Pratzen Plateau at the Battle of Austerlitz on December 2 1805. His battlefield genius and characteristic boldness delivered a crushing victory for France, one of the most celebrated triumphs of a glittering military career.

In summer 1805 Napoleon had abandoned plans to invade Britain and turned from the French coast to deal with the threat posed by Russia and Austria. After a brilliant campaign he outmaneuvered and captured Austrian general Karl Mack von Leiberich with 30,000 soldiers at Ulm in Bavaria on October 20; Vienna fell to the French in November. At Austerlitz Napoleon cunningly deployed his army with a weakened right wing, inviting the Russians and Austrians to attack there so that he could hit in force at their center.

The plan worked. His attack on the center of the enemy line captured the Pratzen Plateau. The Russian-Austrian army was divided in two and overwhelmed by the French—with 15,000 killed or wounded and 11,000 captured. The victory led to the dismemberment of the Third Coalition against France, the end of the historic Holy Roman Empire, and the establishment of the Confederation of the Rhine, a collection of German states under French control with Napoleon as Protector. Holy Roman Emperor Francis II abdicated as emperor, although he remained in power as Francis I of Austria.

Napoleon thought the Battle of Austerlitz, which took place on the first anniversary of his coronation in Paris as French emperor, to be the finest battle he fought as general and commissioned the 164 foot (50 m)-tall Arc de Triomphe in Paris to celebrate the victory.

BOLD, DECISIVE, COURAGEOUS

The boldness and willingness to take risks that he demonstrated at Austerlitz were Napoleon's greatest qualities as general and leader. When he saw that he had the advantage he acted decisively—unleashing the force of his army against an enemy's weak spot even when this meant leaving other parts of his deployment vulnerable. If the tactic succeeded, Napoleon's men could pour through the gap they had forced in the enemy line and attack the rest of the enemy army from the rear or on the flanks.

His masterful use of speed to concentrate strength and hit the enemy at the precise point where they were most vulnerable enabled him to win campaigns with a numerically inferior army. Key to this was the division of his army into independent groupings that were able to move quickly, interrupt enemy communications, and attack from different directions at once. He used these techniques superbly in the fall 1805 campaign that ended with the humiliation of Mack at Ulm. Leaders who move at speed and who empower subsidiary groups to take independent action often reap great benefits. They can achieve the upper hand or even outright victory while opponents are hesitating. Napoleon said: "In war there is only one favorable moment: The great skill is to seize it!"

▲ Jacques-Louis David represents Napoleon in a heroic pose as the general leads the French Army across the Alps through the Great St Bernard Pass in 1800.

However, he was certainly not reckless. Napoleon knew how to wait for the right moment—and then act boldly. One aspect of this, he said, was not to interrupt your enemy when they are making an error. Wait for them to do it, and enjoy the benefits. When your strength was inferior, Napoleon declared, the art of war lay in gaining time.

CLEAR-HEADED, AUTHORITATIVE

Napoleon was driven by ambition—both for himself and for France. Opponents made much of his short stature—standing 5 feet 6 inches (167 cm) tall—but this was in fact average height for the period. He had a very powerful presence, with an immensely strong will. With a strong memory for facts and maps, he had the strategic intelligence of a master chess player and is celebrated as a leading military strategist to this day.

He himself believed that the key quality of a leader at war was calmness and a clear head. It was essential, he explained, that good news did not overexcite a leader or bad news plunge him into despair. Information and sensations might be coming

TIME LINE

August 15 1769
Born, Corsica.

1798
Captures Cairo, with victory in the Battle of the Pyramids.

1799
Returns to France, stages coup, and becomes First Consul.

1800
Defeats Austria in Battle of Marengo.

1802
Peace of Amiens; Consul for life.

1804
Crowned Emperor of the French by the French Senate.

1805
Defeats Austria in battles of Ulm and Austerlitz.

1806
Battles of Jena and Auerstadt: Defeats Prussia.

1807
Defeats Russia in Battle of Friedland.

1808–14
Peninsular War.

1812
Invades Russia, victory at Borodino but disastrous retreat.

1813
Defeat by coalition of Russia, Austria, Prussia, and Sweden in Battle of Leipzig.

April 1814
Allies take Paris; abdicates and exiled to Elba.

1815
Escapes and returns to power for The Hundred Days. In August is defeated at the Battle of Waterloo; abdicates, and exiled to St Helena.

May 5 1821
Dies, St Helena.

hour after hour: A successful leader needed to file them away for later use.

Napoleon saw the success of a campaign depended on his being kept well informed: He sent out handpicked younger officers to gather information and make reconnaissance trips. He also gave them clear and detailed orders. He did not want to waste time or miss opportunities due to misunderstandings arising from poor briefing—an apt lesson for leaders in all fields.

INTUITIVE

In military strategy Napoleon learned from past masters, including Alexander the Great, Julius Caesar, and Frederick the Great (see pages 22, 26, and 82). But he also maintained that you could not learn what made a battle leader great from a book. Ultimately success in war came down to skill when making

TRIUMPHALISM

After victory at the Battle of Austerlitz Napoleon not only commissioned the Arc de Triomphe in Paris but also ordered the raising of a column in the city's Place Vendôme, made from cannon captured in the battle. There is a place for triumphalism in leadership, so long as the leader's power is secure. Napoleon cultivated his image through an active propaganda campaign— publishing battlefield bulletins and issuing medallions to celebrate his successes. In these triumphalist constructions he sought to project himself as all-powerful. And he was successful: His reputation struck fear into enemy armies.

decisions in the heat of battle—to intuition, to genius. On the battlefield Napoleon created an intense bond with his troops. Shortly after being made commander of the French Army in Italy in 1796 he led an assault on the Austrian-held Bridge of Lodi in Lombardy that entered army folklore: He rode forward to an exposed position and gave an impassioned speech that inspired his men to victory amid shouts of "*Vive la République!*" ("Long live the Republic!") Afterward the soldiers gave him the affectionate nickname of *Le Petit Caporal* (The Little Corporal).

In later times he would wander among the men as they huddled around their campfires: He himself had risen to greatness from being a mere gunner and he was able to connect naturally with them. They would do anything for him—he made them feel as if they were making history.

If Napoleon was bold, he expected boldness of his troops, too. He believed that courage and force could more than make up for lack of numbers. He said "The moral is to the physical as three to one." Napoleon knew he could rely on his army. His self-confidence and optimistic outlook—together with his success as a general—won and maintained the loyalty of his soldiers. He showed utmost confidence in his men and they rewarded him with dedicated service.

Napoleon certainly understood the importance of acting with confidence—a general can see the problems of his own situation, he said, but may not be able to see all those troubling his enemy. Those who betray uneasiness may embolden their enemies or rivals, but those who show confidence are likely to unsettle their opponents. Force of personality and reputation were weapons in themselves for Napoleon. British commander the Duke of Wellington declared that Napoleon's presence in battle was worth 40,000 soldiers since he inspired all ranks to greatness.

LEGACY

In his career as military commander and dictator, Napoleon transformed the face of Europe. Away from the battlefield he introduced major and enduring reforms in France—including the establishment of the Bank of France, the reintroduction of Roman Catholicism as the state religion, and the creation of a highly influential legal system—the Code Napoleon. He was undoubtedly a military genius—Wellington, when asked who was the greatest general of the age, declared: "In this age, in past ages, in any age: Napoleon." For the way in which he bound his army and country together and made them fight with such courage for him and for France he must go down as one of the greatest leaders in history.

LEADERSHIP ANALYSIS

LEADER TYPE: *Strategist*
KEY QUALITIES: *Bold, willing to take risks*
LIKEMINDED LEADERS: *Alexander the Great, Julius Caesar, Frederick the Great*
FACT: *A British nursery rhyme of the period threatened crying babies with the promise that "Bonaparte will pass this way."*

SIMÓN BOLÍVAR

DETERMINED REVOLUTIONARY WHO GRABBED FREEDOM FOR LATIN AMERICA

NATIONALITY: *Colombian*
ACHIEVEMENT: *Freed Venezuela, Colombia, Panama, Ecuador, Peru, and Bolivia from Spanish rule*
WHEN: *1808-30*

Simón Bolívar—the Liberator who led the struggle against Spanish rule of Latin America in the early nineteenth century—was a political visionary. Untiring and resourceful, he did not rest from efforts to realize his dream of freedom for Hispanic America.

In exile in Jamaica in 1815 after failing to seize control of his native Venezuela, Simón Bolívar could have sunk into despair. But determined to fight on he roused himself to write the "Letter from Jamaica," in which he declared "The ties that united us to Spain have been cut" and laid out his vision of constitutional republics throughout Spanish-speaking America.

Bolívar had experienced the failure of the first attempt by a Spanish-American colony to declare its independence—the establishment of the First Republic of Venezuela, which had ended in an armistice and the return of Spanish control in July 1812. Then, after a period of exile in Cartagena, New Kingdom of Granada (modern Colombia), he had launched a bold campaign for independence, winning no fewer than six battles in Venezuela before sweeping into Caracas on August 6 1813, where he was hailed as the Liberator and took power. But this—the Second Republic of Venezuela—was also short-lived and in 1814 Caracas fell to a Spanish royalist army under José Tomás Boves. Defeated, Bolívar fled to New Granada and then Jamaica.

VISION OF FREEDOM

The "Letter from Jamaica"—celebrated as the greatest document this visionary ever wrote—was an open address to Henry Cullen, an Englishman resident in Jamaica. Rebellion against Spanish rule was justified, Bolívar argued, because the Spanish had treated Latin Americans as little better than slaves. Shrugging off his recent disappointments, he predicted with utter confidence that the independence movement would succeed.

He married his enthusiasm to realism and took a realist's view of the kind of government that would then necessarily ensue. Having been treated as slaves, Bolívar reasoned, Latin Americans were not ready for liberal institutions, but needed paternalistic rule: Future independent states in the region should have a strong ruler granted a life term, alongside a constitution and a congress. "More than anyone," he declared in ringing tones, "I desire to see America built into the world's greatest nation,

SOUTH AMERICAN INDEPENDENCE DAYS

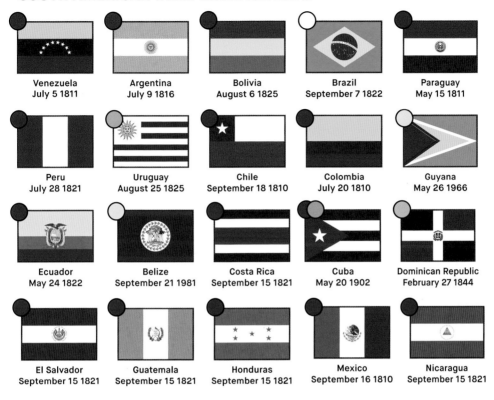

Venezuela
July 5 1811

Argentina
July 9 1816

Bolivia
August 6 1825

Brazil
September 7 1822

Paraguay
May 15 1811

Peru
July 28 1821

Uruguay
August 25 1825

Chile
September 18 1810

Colombia
July 20 1810

Guyana
May 26 1966

Ecuador
May 24 1822

Belize
September 21 1981

Costa Rica
September 15 1821

Cuba
May 20 1902

Dominican Republic
February 27 1844

El Salvador
September 15 1821

Guatemala
September 15 1821

Honduras
September 15 1821

Mexico
September 16 1810

Nicaragua
September 15 1821

FORMER IMPERIAL RULERS.

- ● Spain
- ● Brazil
- ○ Britain
- ○ Portugal
- ● Haiti
- ● US

greatest not so much in terms of her wealth and size as in freedom…" and to achieve this unity was necessary. Unity would be attained through sensible planning and once achieved, "Then will we march majestically toward that great prosperity for which South America is destined."

DARING CAMPAIGN

The vision Bolívar laid out in the letter carried him through the next stage of his freedom struggles. He demonstrated practicality and boldness, first gaining support in Haiti, recently liberated from French colonial rule, then setting himself up in the inaccessible Orinoco region, southeastern Venezuela, where the Spanish would struggle to reach him. He gathered a formidable force of foreign troops, principally Irish and British, and allied himself with other rebel groups. His next move was to lead an extremely daring

TIME LINE

July 24 1783
Born in Caracas.

1801
Marries Maria Teresa Rodriguez del Toro y Alayza.

1804
Maria Teresa dies of yellow fever; he travels to Europe.

1807
Returns to Venezuela, via the United States.

1810–12
First Republic of Venezuela is declared.

July 1812
After republic falls, goes to Cartagena in New Granada.

1813
Seizes power in Venezuela.

1814
Driven into exile.

August 7 1819
Defeats the Spanish at the Battle of Boyacá. Declared president and military dictator.

September 7 1821
Republic of Gran Colombia is established.

December 9 1824
Spanish surrender in Peru.

1825
Republic of Bolivia is established.

1826
Hispanic American Congress held in Panama.

April 27 1830
Resigns presidency.

December 17 1830
Dies in Santa Marta, Colombia.

and superbly executed attack across inhospitable territory to surprise and defeat the Spanish at the Battle of Boyacá on August 7 1819. Within three days he was in Bogotá and set about establishing the Republic of Gran Colombia with himself as president.

Final victory over the Spanish troops in Venezuela did not come until the Battle of Carabobo in June 1821. The state of Gran Colombia, incorporating most of Colombia, Panama, Venezuela, Ecuador, and northern Peru was formally established on September 7 1821. The following year the United States under President Monroe formerly recognized the republic.

INSPIRATION

Leaders of all types need access to inspiration, but this is particularly important for revolutionaries and visionaries who may have to sustain themselves through many setbacks. Bolívar was no exception. He drew his inspiration from the reading he undertook on a youthful trip to Europe: In 1804, suddenly bereaved by the death of his Spanish-born wife after only three years' marriage, he set out on a European tour during which he encountered a former tutor who introduced him to the work of European political and philosophical writers such as John Locke, Thomas Hobbes, Voltaire, Jean-Jacques Rousseau, and Montesquieu. Indeed in his "Letter from Jamaica" he quoted Montesquieu's statement that it is easier to enslave a free people than to free an enslaved one when discussing how Latin Americans would need the firm hand of paternalistic rule.

Bolívar next turned his attention to Peru, allying with Argentine revolutionary José de San Martin, who had already partly liberated the country from Spanish control. The Peruvian congress named Bolívar dictator and, with the help of his gifted general Antonio José de Sucre, Bolívar completely defeated the Spanish. In 1825 the region of Upper Peru was named the Republic of Bolivia in Bolívar's honor. He was at the height of his success.

In 1826 he took a further step toward realizing the dreams he had outlined earlier in his career, when he hosted a congress of Spanish-speaking American republics in Panama: Columbia, Peru, Central America, and Mexico attended and signed an alliance under which they planned common military defenses together with a twice-yearly assembly. In the end the plans did not come to fruition, although Colombia ratified the agreement.

The final years of Bolívar's rule in Gran Colombia were marred by increasing opposition. Ever the realist, he declared that Gran Colombia should be divided into three republics: Venezuela, Colombia, and Ecuador. Increasingly aware that his very presence was stoking unrest, he determined to stand down and resigned the presidency on April 27 1830. He set off for exile in Europe but died of tuberculosis en route at Santa Marta (now in Colombia). In his extraordinary life "the Liberator" had freed Venezuela, Colombia, Panama, Ecuador, Peru, and Bolivia from imperial Spanish rule, establishing his reputation as one of the founding fathers of democracy in Spanish-speaking America.

LEADERSHIP ANALYSIS

LEADER TYPE: *Revolutionary*
KEY QUALITIES: *Visionary, realist, brave*
LIKEMINDED LEADERS: *George Washington, Fidel Castro, William Morris*
FACT: *Asteroid 712 Boliviana, first observed in 2005, is named in Bolívar's honor.*

24

GIUSEPPE GARIBALDI

INSPIRATIONAL REVOLUTIONARY WHO CAMPAIGNED TIRELESSLY FOR A UNITED ITALY

NATIONALITY: *Italian*
ACHIEVEMENT: *Laid the foundations for a unified Italy*
WHEN: *1834-70*

Flamboyant general Giuseppe Garibaldi was a great propagandist in the cause of Italian unification. Acclaimed for his military successes at the head of his red-shirted guerrilla army, he played a vital role in the creation of the Kingdom of Italy and is remembered as a national hero.

On October 26 1860 at Teano, southern Italy, Guiseppe Garibaldi shook King Victor Emmanuel II of Piedmont-Sardinia by the hand and hailed him as king of Italy. A fervent patriot, Garibaldi gave up his dream of creating an Italian republic in the interest of establishing a united country.

At the head of a 1,000-strong volunteer army dubbed "*I Mille*" (The Thousand)—and celebrated as the Redshirts from the colored shirts they wore in lieu of a uniform—Garibaldi had seized control of the Kingdom of the Two Sicilies, the largest of the kingdoms that made up pre-unification Italy; it comprised the two kingdoms of Sicily and Naples, which together encompassed the entire southern half of the peninsula. In what is celebrated to this day as "The Handshake at Teano," he then handed control of this territory to Victor Emmanuel. The new Kingdom of Italy was declared on March 17 1861.

Garibaldi retired to his home on the island of Caprera off the Sardinian coast, refusing all honors or rewards. He was already an internationally celebrated patriot and military leader. Garibaldi was celebrated as the "Hero of Two Worlds" because of the freedom struggles he had led in Uruguay and Brazil during his exile in South America in 1836−48 as well as the renown he had won in Italy in 1848 and 1860−61.

REBEL FIGHTER

Garibaldi was a principled fighter, who inspired his followers in causes fought for passionately-held beliefs. A proven commander of guerrilla forces who repeatedly triumphed over professional armies, he had the appeal and standing of a lifelong rebel; throughout his life he wore the clothing of a South American gaucho (cowboy) and personified the struggle for freedom. Celebrated by leading authors such as George Sand and Victor Hugo, author of *Les Misérables*, he was a walking piece of revolutionary propaganda, rather as Ernesto "Che" Guevara, one of Fidel Castro's key allies in the Cuban Revolution, later became.

Garibaldi had been a soldier in the cause of Italian nationalism since 1834 when he met Giuseppe Mazzini, founder of the Young Italy society and a leading light of the campaign for a united Italy named Risorgimento (Resurgence). Garibaldi's role in an abortive uprising in Piedmont that year led to his fleeing into exile, first in France and then in South America, where he remained—at a safe remove from the death sentence that hung over his head in Italy—until 1848.

Whilst in South America he fought in freedom struggles for the republic of Rio Grande do Sul and for Uruguay and made his name as a general and liberationist, notably at the Battle of Sant'Antonio (1846) and the defense of Montevideo in 1847. His name was publicized by Alexandre Dumas, author of *The Count of Monte Cristo* and *The Three Musketeers*, and in 1846 a sword of honor in his name was paid for by subscription in Italy to pay tribute to his heroics with the Italian Legion in Uruguay.

HERO OF RISORGIMENTO

In 1848 Garibaldi returned to Italy with members of the Italian Legion to fight in the cause of the Risorgimento. In

▲ *Garibaldi in Naples, where he declared himself "Dictator of the Two Sicilies" in 1860. This referred to the lands of the King of Naples—Sicily and southern Italy.*

Rome, the Swiss Guard was disbanded and Pope Pius IX was effectively a prisoner. In November he fled Rome recognizing that he was no longer in control. After the pope left Rome, Garibaldi was elected a deputy in the city's assembly and proposed that Rome should be an independent republic. He led a heroic but ultimately doomed defense of the city against armies from France and the Kingdom of Naples sent to relieve it, and afterward led his volunteer troops to safety across Italy—these became celebrated events in the annals of the Risorgimento.

In 1861 the new Kingdom of Italy declared that its capital was Rome; but the government could not take possession of the city, which was in the hands of the papacy and was capital of the Papal States. Following the declaration Garibaldi twice led campaigns to capture Rome. In 1862 he successfully gathered an army but was injured and the campaign petered out after clashes with troops of the Kingdom of Italy. In 1867 he led another volunteer army against Rome but was defeated and again injured at the Battle of Mentana on November 3 that year. He was forced to withdraw.

TIME LINE

July 4 1807
Born, Nice.

1833–34
Serves in navy of Kingdom of Piedmont-Sardinia.

1834
Joins "Young Italy" movement; takes part in abortive plot to provoke republican revolution in Piedmont; sentenced to death, escapes to America.

1834–48
In exile in South America.

1848
Returns to Italy, leads troops in attack on Rome.

1849
Defends Rome, escapes with volunteers.

1855
Settles on island of Caprera.

1859
Fights in Piedmontese army.

September 7 1860
Takes Naples, declares himself Dictator of the Two Sicilies.

October 26 1860
Handshake at Teano—gives control of southern Italy to Victor Emmanuel II.

July 1861
President Lincoln offers Garibaldi command in Union Army in US Civil War.

1862
Fails in attack on Rome.

September 20 1870
Kingdom of Italy takes Rome, without Garibaldi.

June 2 1882
Dies, Caprera, Italy.

"HEADHUNTED"—GENERAL OF INTERNATIONAL RENOWN

In spite of his setbacks in trying to wrest Rome from the papacy, Garibaldi was internationally renowned. Indeed, in 1861 US President Abraham Lincoln offered him a command in the Union Army in the American Civil War. This came to nothing, however, as Garibaldi demanded supreme command and asked Lincoln to declare that the war's objective was the abolition of slavery, a more sweeping statement than Lincoln was willing to make at that point.

In 1863, however, after the Emancipation Proclamation of January 1 that year promulgated the freedom of slaves, Garibaldi wrote to the president, "Posterity will call you the great

SLOGANEER

Garibaldi's heroic campaigns are associated with the propagandistic rallying cries he devised to dramatize his cause or energize followers. In 1849 when he led the volunteer troops in a retreat from Rome they marched under the stirring slogan "Dovunque saremo, colà sarà Roma" ("Wherever we go, there will be Rome!") Then in 1862 he gathered an army for an assault on Rome under the slogan "Roma o morte" ("Rome or Death!") In Garibaldi's day, slogans like this might be shouted by rallying troops or declaimed in public speeches. They served to unite people in the cause. Garibaldi's effective use of propaganda is an important lesson for all leaders who wish to generate a sense of togetherness, united in a common cause.

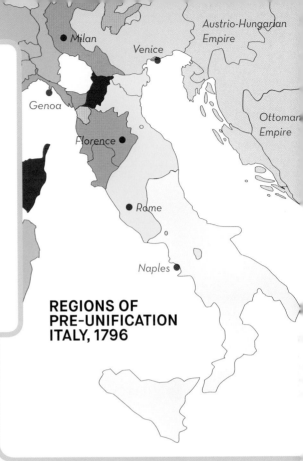

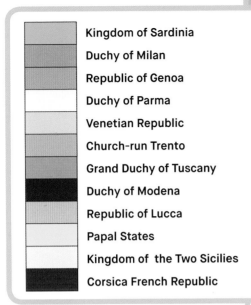

Kingdom of Sardinia

Duchy of Milan

Republic of Genoa

Duchy of Parma

Venetian Republic

Church-run Trento

Grand Duchy of Tuscany

Duchy of Modena

Republic of Lucca

Papal States

Kingdom of the Two Sicilies

Corsica French Republic

REGIONS OF PRE-UNIFICATION ITALY, 1796

emancipator, a more enviable title than any crown could be, and greater than any merely mundane treasure."

PRINCIPLED TO THE END

In his final years, Garibaldi was badly affected by rheumatism, arthritis, and the effects of his battle wounds and mostly remained at home in Cabrera. He campaigned for women's emancipation and the rights of working people and in 1879 founded the League of Democracy, which argued for the abolition of church property and universal suffrage— extending the vote to all. He defined himself as a socialist and revised his opinions on war, moving toward pacifism. His legacy was the Kingdom of Italy, for which he had laid the foundations. With Victor Emmanuel and Camillo Benso, Count of Cavour, the first prime minister of the new kingdom, he was celebrated as a national hero, father of the fatherland of Italy.

LEADERSHIP ANALYSIS

LEADER TYPE: *Revolutionary*
KEY QUALITIES: *Brave, passionate, principled*
LIKEMINDED LEADERS: *Simón Bolívar*
FACT: *Garibaldi used the red shirts worn by his men—according to one theory inspired by the red flannel shirts worn by New York City firemen he had seen while in exile—as a propaganda tool.*

ABRAHAM LINCOLN

GREAT WAR LEADER AND CHAMPION OF ABOLITIONISM AND CIVIL LIBERTY

NATIONALITY: *American*
ACHIEVEMENT: *Won Civil War and abolished slavery*
WHEN: *1861-65*

The enduringly inspirational president Abraham Lincoln abolished slavery in the United States and led the country through the great national crisis of the American Civil War.

On January 1 1863 President Lincoln issued the Emancipation Proclamation under which slaves in the Confederate states that had seceded from the Union were set free. This act—in tandem with the Thirteenth Amendment subsequently added to the US Constitution—brought about the end of slavery in the United States of America. A principled but pragmatic leader, Lincoln is celebrated as the Great Emancipator.

The proclamation was initially made as a war measure. The Civil War between the southern states of the Confederacy and the northern states of the Union had begun in April 1861. The outbreak followed the secession of southern states concerned that their way of life, which was based on slavery, was threatened by the election of Lincoln, who had campaigned in 1860 as an opponent of slavery, to the presidency.

Initially the principal war aim of the northern states was to undo this secession and so preserve the union. The Emancipation Proclamation was a largely symbolic act: It freed slaves only within Confederate-controlled areas. Nonetheless it greatly boosted morale on the Union side and attracted wide support for the Union cause in Europe. It made it clear that freeing the slaves was a Union war aim alongside preserving the unity of the country.

Subsequently Lincoln campaigned for re-election as president in 1864 on a platform that argued for the addition of a Thirteenth Amendment to the Constitution that would "terminate and forever prohibit" slavery, which it called "this gigantic evil." He viewed his victory in the election as a mandate to bring forward the amendment and he used all his well documented political and negotiating skills to get the necessary two-thirds support for the measure in Congress.

Lincoln famously grew a beard after being advised to do so in a letter from 11-year-old Grace Bedell in the 1860 election. ▶

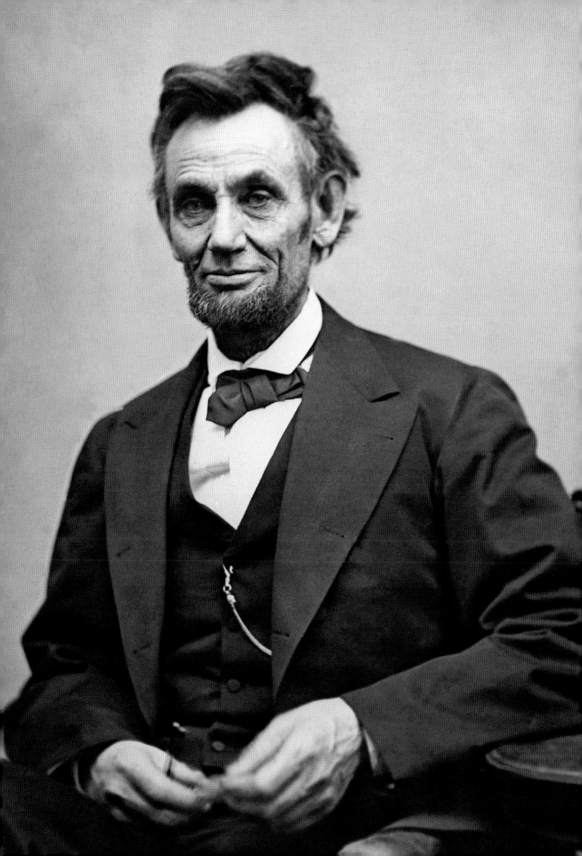

TIME LINE

February 12 1809
Born, near Hodgenville, Kentucky.

1836
Qualifies as lawyer—works in practice in Springfield, Illinois.

1834–42
State legislature.

1846
Elected to Congress.

1856
Joins Republican Party.

May 18 1860
Republican Party's presidential candidate.

November 6 1860
Elected president.

April 12 1861
Civil War breaks out: Northern states of the Union fight the southern states of the Confederacy.

January 1 1863
Issues Emancipation Proclamation.

July 1–3 1863
Battle of Gettysburg.

November 19 1863
Delivers Gettysburg Address.

April 9 1865
Confederate general Robert E. Lee surrenders, signaling the end of the war.

April 15 1865
Dies, after being shot in Ford's Theatre, Washington, D.C.

May 30 1922
Dedication of Lincoln Memorial, Washington, D.C.

SPEAKING FROM THE HEART

Lincoln's celebrated Gettysburg Address defined the Civil War as a battle to preserve the Union and bring forth a new freedom that promoted the equality of all. He gave the speech on November 19 1863 at the ceremony for Union soldiers killed in the Battle of Gettysburg on July 1–3, 1863 (the bloodiest of the Civil War clashes). In ringing tones, he recalled the foundation of the United States and looked forward to a brighter future:

> Four score and seven years ago our fathers brought forth on this continent a new nation, conceived in liberty, and dedicated to the proposition that all men are created equal. Now we are engaged in a great civil war, testing whether that nation, or any nation so conceived and so dedicated, can long endure … we here highly resolve that these dead shall not have died in vain— that this nation, under God, shall have a new birth of freedom—and that government of the people, by the people, for the people, shall not perish from the earth.

Lincoln was a superb communicator. His Gettysburg address has been likened by many historians to the funeral oration delivered by that chief of orators, the Athenian statesman Pericles (see page 14). One of Lincoln's most important characteristics was his ability to convince those who heard him. He was known as "Honest Abe" and had the ability to speak from the heart to listeners.

PRAGMATIST—WITH A MORAL CORE

As a politician and war leader Lincoln was a pragmatist. Like other great war leaders such as British Prime Minister

THE AMERICAN CIVIL WAR: THE BLOODIEST CONFLICT

AMERICAN CONFLICTS AND CASUALTY RATES

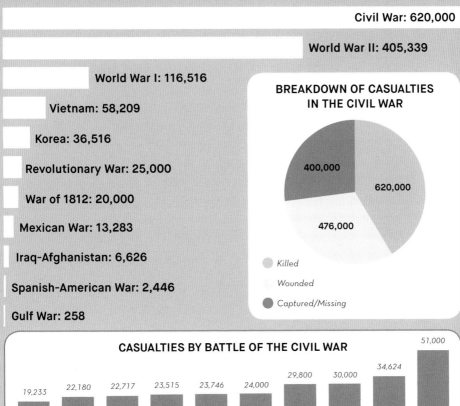

Civil War: 620,000

World War II: 405,339

World War I: 116,516

Vietnam: 58,209

Korea: 36,516

Revolutionary War: 25,000

War of 1812: 20,000

Mexican War: 13,283

Iraq-Afghanistan: 6,626

Spanish-American War: 2,446

Gulf War: 258

BREAKDOWN OF CASUALTIES IN THE CIVIL WAR

400,000

620,000

476,000

Killed

Wounded

Captured/Missing

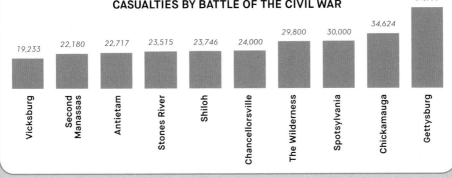

CASUALTIES BY BATTLE OF THE CIVIL WAR

Vicksburg	Second Manassas	Antietam	Stones River	Shiloh	Chancellorsville	The Wilderness	Spotsylvania	Chickamauga	Gettysburg
19,233	22,180	22,717	23,515	23,746	24,000	29,800	30,000	34,624	51,000

Winston Churchill and US President Franklin D. Roosevelt, he was immensely practical and flexible in responding to events (see pages 138 and 158). He was not tied to pre-determined plans. He wrote "My policy is to have no policy." However, this did not mean that he was easily swayed or incapable of sticking to a difficult line of action. Lincoln was a man of firm resolve.

He was closely involved in the day-to-day running of the war, repeatedly relieving generals of command until he found one, Ulysses S. Grant, who in his view was capable of delivering victory. The main planks of the war platform were maintaining a naval blockade of the southern states and seeking to mount a coordinated military attack on a large scale. Lincoln was known for his determination and—like former president George Washington—for his moral character (see page 90). He was calm and had a very good sense of judgment. During the Civil War the *Washington Chronicle* newspaper likened the two leaders, praising Lincoln's "great calmness of temper, great firmness of purpose, supreme moral principle, and intense patriotism."

Lincoln could in certain cases be hard-nosed and ruthless. He supported the suppression of certain newspapers and limits on civil liberties during the war, arguing that it was necessary to sacrifice parts of the constitution in order to win victory, preserve the Union and thus, ultimately, save the constitution.

MAN MANAGER

Lincoln was the type of leader who can work with opponents. Not only was he good at negotiating and reaching settlement, but he was also skilled in bringing former antagonists into his camp to work with him—men such as William H. Seward, his defeated rival for the Republican nomination for the presidency in 1860, whom he appointed Secretary of State in 1861 and who, after a number of initial disagreements, became the president's closest and most important adviser.

He was also skilled at managing dissenting individuals and groups within a coalition. He held the support of War Democrats (who backed the North against the South in the Civil War), and as far as he could he conciliated "Peace Democrats" or "Copperheads" who did not. Within his own party he did what he could to balance the demands of the Conservatives, the group to which he belonged, with the Radicals who, toward the end of the war, were calling for harsh treatment of the defeated southern states.

SENSE OF FUN

Abraham Lincoln was highly unusual among public men of his era in that he liked to tell jokes and humorous stories. He saw them as a release: When some members of his cabinet showed their disapproval, he said: "Gentlemen, why don't you laugh? With the fearful strain that is upon me night and day, if I did not laugh I should die, and you need this medicine as much as I do." Lincoln was also be able to laugh at himself. In 1858 during his debates with Stephen Douglas, Democratic candidate for the Illinois Senate, his opponent accused him of being two-faced and Lincoln reputedly replied: "Honestly, if I were two-faced, would I be showing you this one?"

MARTYR

In spite of Lincoln's conciliatory attempts, there remained committed secessionists who wanted the secession of the southern states to stand. Just six days after the surrender of Confederate commanding officer Robert E. Lee signaled the end of the war, one member of this group, actor John Wilkes Booth, shot Lincoln in Ford's Theatre, Washington, D.C. during a performance on Good Friday, April 14 1865. The president died of his wounds early the next morning.

▲ *Artillery reinforcements join the Union Army at Murfreesboro, Tennessee, in 1862.*

Lincoln's assassination set him up as a martyr in the cause of liberty: His reputation as a great war leader and champion of freedom was securely established. As Lincoln died, War Secretary Edwin M. Stanton reputedly declared "Now he belongs to the ages." His reputation was never higher than in the 1900–20s, culminating in the establishment of the Lincoln Memorial in 1922 in Washington, D.C. But throughout the twentieth century and into the twenty-first he has remained one of the most celebrated and revered figures of the American past, frequently cited—alongside George Washington and Franklin D. Roosevelt—as among the three greatest presidents in the history of the United States.

LEADERSHIP ANALYSIS

LEADER TYPE: *Persuasive*
KEY QUALITIES: *Humane, principled, moral*
LIKEMINDED LEADERS: *George Washington, Winston Churchill, Franklin D. Roosevelt*
FACT: *Lincoln was 6 feet 4 inches (1.93 m) tall—a huge size at a time when the average height was much less.*

26

OTTO VON BISMARCK

SHREWD MANIPULATOR AND SKILLFUL DIPLOMAT WHO CREATED THE GERMAN EMPIRE

NATIONALITY: *Prussian*
ACHIEVEMENT: *Established German Empire, maintained European peace*
WHEN: *1862-71*

Forceful Prussian statesman Otto von Bismarck unified the German states and established a great empire, then through moderation and astute diplomacy maintained peace in Europe for almost 20 years.

On January 18 1871 Otto von Bismarck proudly proclaimed the German Empire in a grand ceremony in the Hall of Mirrors in the Palace of Versailles, France. Just nine years after becoming prime minister of Prussia, Bismarck had transformed the face of Europe.

A great political tactician and diplomatic strategist, Bismarck had provoked France into war as a way of bringing the four southern German states into union with the existing North German Federation to form the German Empire. The war followed from the offer of the Spanish throne to Leopold, Prince of Hohenzollern-Sigmaringen, cousin of Wilhelm I of Prussia. French Emperor Napoleon III, already unsettled by the swift emergence of a Bismarck-directed Prussia as a major force in Europe, protested on the grounds that this would amount to an encircling of his country by the House of Hohenzollern. Bismarck encouraged Leopold to take the throne and further provoked France by making public a private communication between the French ambassador and Prussia which demanded the withdrawal of the offer to Leopold. His efforts succeeded: On July 19 1870 France declared war on Prussia.

The conflict quickly came to a head. The Prussians won a succession of battles, capturing Napoleon III at the Battle of Sedan on September 1 1870 and taking his whole army into captivity. This stunning defeat provoked a coup in Paris where Napoleon III was deposed and the Third Republic proclaimed. But this energetic response did not save the French: The Prussians took possession of Paris and imposed a humiliating peace treaty under which France lost Alsace and the German-speaking area of Lorraine and had to pay an indemnity of five billion francs, calculated to match precisely the sum that Napoleon Bonaparte had required Prussia to pay in 1807 after the War of the Fourth Coalition. Revenge was sweet for the Germans. In the same ceremony, Wilhelm I of Prussia was declared German Emperor. Bismarck served as chancellor.

BLOOD AND IRON

In 1862 Bismarck became Prussian prime minister having previously served as ambassador to St Petersburg and Paris. At the time Wilhelm I was in dispute with his parliament who were blocking his planned military spending. In an historic speech Bismarck declared the importance for Prussia of being militarily prepared: "Prussia's position in Germany will not be decided by its liberalism but by its power ... Prussia must concentrate its strength and hold it for the correct moment ... From the time of the treaties of Vienna, Prussia's frontiers have not been well designed for a healthy national life. The great questions of the day will not be decided through speeches and majority decisions ... but by blood and iron."

This phrase "blood and iron" became indissolubly linked to this forceful, powerfully determined statesman. Over the next nine years he drove Prussia forward to seize a pre-eminent position in the federation of German states that formed the empire. First came war with Denmark in 1864 over the duchies of Schleswig and Holstein that brought the first into Prussian control and the second under Austrian

▲ Otto Von Bismarck in 1881. Once a politician Bismarck rose rapidly and was a foreign ambassador by the late 1850s.

rule. Then he sought to provoke war with Austria and invaded Holstein in June 1866. After Austria declared war, Prussia struck with great speed—in a campaign described as Blitzkrieg (lightning war), just like the Nazi campaigns early in World War II—and inflicted a decisive defeat at the Battle of Königgrätz.

MODERATE IN VICTORY

Having bullied Prussia's way to power, Bismarck at this point displayed the moderation that was one of the defining characteristics of his leadership. Wilhelm and his generals wanted to press home their advantage and attack Vienna, but Bismarck insisted on restraint and a quick end to the war. In the subsequent peace Prussia took possession of Frankfurt, Hanover, Nassau, and Hesse-Kassel. Then, in 1867, Bismarck formed the North German Confederation, containing 21 states situated to the north of the River Main, to be governed by a Prussian president and chancellor.

Europe was transformed. Austria was a minor player beside a dominant Prussia. The next step was to provoke war with France and forge the German Empire.

DIPLOMAT

Moderation and skillful diplomacy were the hallmarks of Bismarck's rule as imperial chancellor from 1871 to 1890. He worked tirelessly to create alliances that would keep the peace. In 1873 he agreed the League of the Three Emperors with Russia and Austria-Hungary. In 1878, following the Russo-Turkish War, he hosted the Congress of Berlin to

April 1 1815
Born Schönhausen, Altmark, Prussia (now Germany).

1849
Elected to Prussian Chamber of Deputies.

1859
Becomes Prussian ambassador to Russia.

May 1862
Becomes Prussian ambassador to France.

1862
Becomes prime minister of Prussia.

1864
War against Denmark.

1866
War against Austria.

1867
North German Confederation established.

July 19 1870
France declares war on Prussia.

January 1871
Creation of the German Empire, becomes chancellor.

1873
Three Emperors' League with Russia and Austria-Hungary.

1878
Congress of Berlin.

1879
Dual Alliance with Austria-Hungary.

1882
Triple Alliance with Austria-Hungary and Italy.

1890
Resigns chancellorship.

July 30 1898
Dies, Friedrichsruh, near Hamburg.

balance the interests of Britain, Russia, and Austria-Hungary in the Balkans. Afterward, with the Three Emperors' League no longer in force, he agreed the Dual Alliance with Austria-Hungary of 1879 and the Triple Alliance of 1882 with Austria-Hungary and Italy as he sought to keep peace and consolidate the position of Germany.

For all these pacifying efforts he was widely respected through Europe. In his use of caution and moderation, he proved himself an immensely skilled political leader. Having established the empire, he deliberately reined in German expansionism, demonstrating great pragmatism through the 1870s and 1880s.

AUTHOR AND STATESMAN

In 1890 at the age of 75 he resigned as chancellor having fallen out with the new emperor, Willhelm II. He took a step

WRITING HISTORY

Like Winston Churchill, Bismarck was both one of the world's great statesmen and a highly skilled and lucid author. The reputation of both men greatly benefited from the fact that they were able to frame their achievements and their legacy through their own writings—as did Julius Caesar; the same can be said of leaders of a quite different type such as Mohandas Gandhi and Nelson Mandela, who both wrote autobiographies laying out their beliefs and actions. Leaders of all kinds benefit from maintaining control over how their actions and memory are viewed.

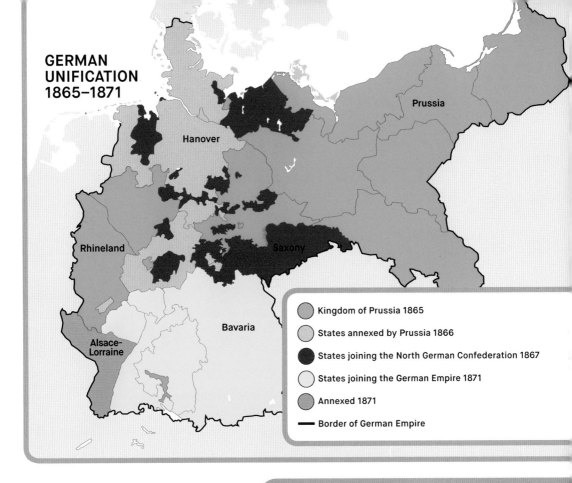

GERMAN UNIFICATION 1865–1871

Prussia

Hanover

Rhineland

Saxony

Bavaria

Alsace-Lorraine

- Kingdom of Prussia 1865
- States annexed by Prussia 1866
- States joining the North German Confederation 1867
- States joining the German Empire 1871
- Annexed 1871
- Border of German Empire

back from public life and wrote best-selling memoirs that launched the "cult of Bismarck" that would be prominent in Germany for decades.

Bismarck could be intimidating and harsh—a side effect, perhaps, of the great strength of will he needed to bring about his extraordinary achievements for himself and his country. But he was undeniably a great statesman. His enduring legacy was the unification of Germany and its establishment as one of Europe's most powerful nations. He established this through diplomacy and moderation after the creation of the German Empire. He reshaped the map of Europe and left his mark on an age.

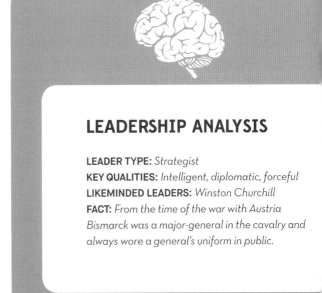

LEADERSHIP ANALYSIS

LEADER TYPE: *Strategist*
KEY QUALITIES: *Intelligent, diplomatic, forceful*
LIKEMINDED LEADERS: *Winston Churchill*
FACT: *From the time of the war with Austria Bismarck was a major-general in the cavalry and always wore a general's uniform in public.*

KARL MARX

SOCIAL REVOLUTIONARY WHO WORKED TIRELESSLY FOR A MORE EQUAL WORLD

NATIONALITY: *German*
ACHIEVEMENT: *Founder of Marxism and communism*
WHEN: *1848-83*

Historian and economist Karl Marx was the co-author of *The Communist Manifesto,* the book considered to be the founding document of communism, and author of *Das Kapital*, a hugely influential treatise on modern economics and the capitalist system. The innovative ideas he espoused in these two works shaped the twentieth-century world.

He was a leader in the fight for a better society. On May 30 1871 the German-born journalist and revolutionary delivered a stirring elegy for the recently crushed Paris Commune. He said "History has no comparable example of such greatness ... Its martyrs are enshrined forever in the great heart of the working class."

The Paris Commune was an insurrection in Paris against the French government following the defeat of Napoleon III in the Franco-Prussian war of 1870. Its revolutionaries—the Communards—had formed a commune but were crushed by government troops in a "bloody week" of fighting in late May. Marx's friend and collaborator Friedrich Engels declared the Commune the first example in history of the "dictatorship of the proletariat."

Radical theorists Marx and Engels had met in Paris in 1843. Five years later the two collaborated on the seminal work *The Communist Manifesto*. In the manifesto they argued that all of history was a succession of class struggles and that the current capitalist system was destined to be replaced by a society ruled by the proletariat— the workers in industrial society who sold their labor for a wage. In a stirring call to arms it declared: "The proletarians have nothing to lose but their chains. They have a world to win. Workers of all lands, unite."

FOR THE WORKING MAN

Having moved to London in 1849 Marx was one of the first members of the International Working Men's Association, founded in London on September 28 1864. He drew up its founding document, *Address and the Provisional Rules of the International Working Men's Association*, then served on its General Council and as corresponding secretary for Germany. He was a leading light in the organization as it grew in size and public profile: It supported a number of European trade unions in

▲ *A banner depicting Lenin, Friedrich Engels, and Karl Marx in Moscow's Red Square, to commemorate the Russian defeat of the German Nazis in WWII.*

struggles with employers and had around 800,000 members by 1869. The association has often been referred to as the "First International."

Marx's response to the crushing of the Paris Commune, contained in his 35-page pamphlet *The Civil War in France*, the official response of the First International, made him a public figure throughout Europe. He was seen as leader of the First International and representative of the revolutionary spirit that had fired the Communards.

Around this time, however, Marx's position within the First International came under attack—especially from firebrand Russian revolutionary Mikhail Alexandrovich Bakunin, a promoter of anarchism who accused Marx and the General Council of being authoritarian. A power struggle ensued: Marx succeeded in blocking the admission of Bakunin's organization, the International Alliance of Social Democracy, into the First International and overcame Bakunin's followers at the congress of the First International at The Hague in 1872. But soon after, the General Council was

TIME LINE

May 5 1818
Born, in Trier, Germany.

1835–1841
Studied at the universities of Bonn, Berlin, and Jena.

1842
Works as a journalist in Cologne.

October 1843
Moves to Paris, becomes a communist, meets Engels.

1845
Expelled from France, moves to Brussels. Publishes The Holy Family *with Engels.*

1846
Publishes The Poverty of Philosophy.

1848
Returns to Cologne and publishes The Communist Manifesto *with Engels.*

June 1849
First edition of newspaper, the Neue Rheinische Zeitung.

August 1849
Settles in London.

1859
Publishes A Contribution to the Critique of Political Economy.

1864
Foundation of International Working Men's Association.

1867–1873
Publication of First Volume of Das Kapital, *in German.*

14 March 1883
Dies, London.

1885
Second Volume of Das Kapital, *edited by Engels, published.*

1888
Marx's Theses on Feuerbach *first published and the* End of Classical German Philosophy *by Engels.*

transferred to the United States where it failed to thrive: It was disbanded in 1876 in Philadelphia.

UTTERLY COMMITTED

After the failure of the First International Marx remained in London, hard at work on his book *Das Kapital*. He had withdrawn from active politics but remained a leading figure to whom socialists and pioneers of working-class movements looked for guidance. In 1879 Jules Guesde, leader of the newly established French Socialist Workers' Federation, traveled to London to confer with Marx, who had significant input into that organization's program.

In his later years Marx's health declined, and with it his creativity. He

ENERGY OF THE COMMITTED

Marx was tireless in his work to effect change—to bring about the overthrow of capitalist society and the liberation of the proletariat. As a journalist and author of militant pamphlets, on the committees of organizations such as the First International, and in his own drive to understand and explain the workings of capitalism in Das Kapital, *he showed immense energy and commitment in the face of great economic hardship. This energy sustains such leaders through times when they might be expected to despair—it is a key requirement of leadership, all the more so in leaders like Marx whose chief gifts are as thinkers and communicators but who have to struggle in the face of indifference and opposition.*

suffered through years of poverty. For most of his London residency, both before and after his leading role with the First International, he and his family had endured severe financial difficulties. Marx was fully committed to the intellectual work on which he had embarked, but it did not pay. His only source of income was often what he earned as London correspondent of the *New York Tribune* and contributions from the financially better-off Engels. The family often had little more than bread and potatoes, lived in cramped conditions, and were hounded by creditors. Marx's wife Jenny had more than one breakdown and, partly due to these very difficult conditions, only three of the couple's seven children survived to adulthood.

Marx was devastated by the death of one of these adult children, Jenny Longuet, on January 11 1883, which followed hard on the heels of the death of his wife on December 2 1881. Marx himself died on March 14 1883.

GREAT THINKER—AND FIGHTER

In his funeral elegy for his friend, delivered on March 17 1883, Engels lamented that when Marx died "the greatest living thinker ceased to think." Marx was a leader in the world of ideas. Like many communicator-leaders Marx's legacy has spread out over years and decades. In *Das Kapital* he analyzed the functioning of the capitalist system and its tendency toward self-destruction. Engels praised Marx for having discovered "the law of development of human history." But Marx also emphasized the need for action derived from theory: He wrote in his "Eleventh Thesis on Feuerbach" (posthumously published, 1888) "The philosophers have only interpreted the world in various ways—the point however is to change it." This line was inscribed on his tombstone in Highgate Cemetery, London, beneath the imperative, taken from *The Communist Manifesto*: "Workers of all lands unite."

Marx was a tenacious fighter in the cause of social change and because his battles were chiefly conducted in the world of ideas and of culture he remains a powerful leader long after his death. His followers are still committed to social change: As Engels eulogized, "Marx was before all else a revolutionist. His name will endure through the ages, and so also will his work."

LEADERSHIP ANALYSIS

LEADER TYPE: *Revolutionary*
KEY QUALITIES: *Communicator, revolutionary*
LIKEMINDED LEADERS: *Saint Peter, Siddhãrtha Gautama*
FACT: *Marx often used an assumed name—in London "A. Williams" and in Paris "Monsieur Ramboz"—probably to avoid creditors.*

QUEEN VICTORIA

DUTIFUL YET POWERFUL QUEEN WHO CONSOLIDATED A MONARCHY AND ESTABLISHED AN EMPIRE

NATIONALITY: *British*
ACHIEVEMENT: *Safeguarded the future of the British Crown*
WHEN: *1837-1901*

The longest-reigning British monarch gave her name to the Victorian age, an era of significant British achievement and great change. Victoria stabilized the monarchy while overseeing the creation and consolidation of the vast British Empire—the largest the world has ever seen.

Cheering crowds greeted Queen Victoria as she made a triumphant 6-mile (10-km) procession through London on June 22 1897 to celebrate her Diamond Jubilee, the sixtieth anniversary of her accession to the throne. In her embodiment of stability and dignity, and through the creation of a vast British empire, this proud leader had restored the prestige of the British monarchy.

When Victoria came to the throne, the monarchy's reputation and status had been severely damaged by the failures and excesses of the first four kings of the House of Hanover, and only partly repaired by Victoria's uncle King William IV, whom she succeeded in 1837. The young queen was determined to put things right. Her strongly developed sense of duty was one of the central aspects of her character and a prime motivation behind her greatness as a leader.

DUTIFUL APPROACH—"I WILL BE GOOD"
Victoria inherited the crown as the only legitimate child of Edward Augustus, the Duke of Kent, the fourth son of King George III—and brother to both George IV and William IV. Her father died shortly after Victoria's birth and she spent a lonely childhood in the care of her mother Victoria, the Duchess of Kent, and a forbidding German governess, Louise (later Baroness) Lehzen.

The princess was initially kept uninformed of her status as heir to the throne. Her reaction upon discovering her true position exemplifies the steadfast determination and dutiful commitment that Victoria was to carry throughout her life: "I will be good" she declared.

Victoria was honest, full of vitality, and straightforward in her strong commitment to the institution of the monarchy. A central way in which she restored dignity to the crown was through her marriage to Prince Albert of Saxe-Coburg and Gotha and the family life they made together. The match was originally planned by Victoria's uncle, King Leopold of the Belgians, but met opposition from Victoria initially, who resisted

VICTORIA'S EMPIRE

MAP OF ALL AREAS OF THE WORLD THAT WERE EVER PART OF THE BRITISH EMPIRE

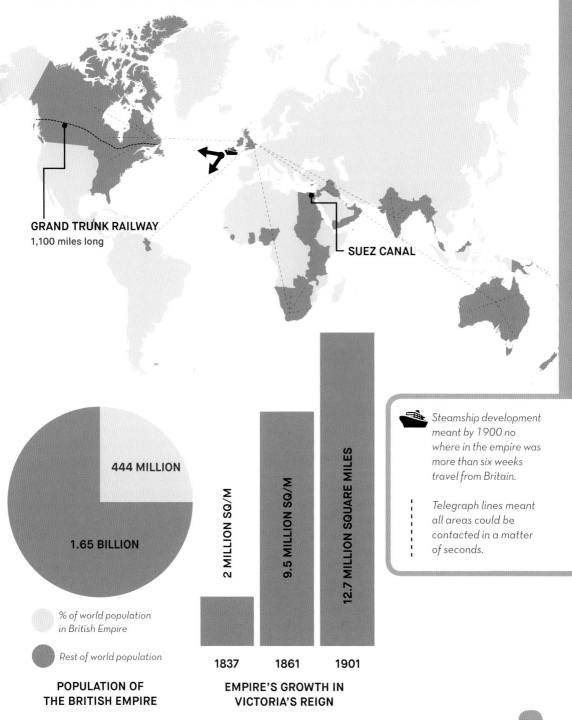

GRAND TRUNK RAILWAY
1,100 miles long

SUEZ CANAL

Steamship development meant by 1900 no where in the empire was more than six weeks travel from Britain.

Telegraph lines meant all areas could be contacted in a matter of seconds.

444 MILLION

1.65 BILLION

○ % of world population in British Empire

● Rest of world population

POPULATION OF THE BRITISH EMPIRE

2 MILLION SQ/M

9.5 MILLION SQ/M

12.7 MILLION SQUARE MILES

1837   1861   1901

EMPIRE'S GROWTH IN VICTORIA'S REIGN

TIME LINE

May 24 1819
Born, Kensington Palace, London.

June 20 1837
Accession to throne.

June 28 1838
Coronation.

1840
Marries Prince Albert of Saxe-Coburg and Gotha. Birth of firstborn child, Princess Victoria Adelaide.

November 9 1841
Birth of Prince Albert Edward, future King Edward VII.

1842
Twice escapes injury in shooting attacks.

May 1849
Fired at while driving in her carriage.

May 1 1851
With Prince Albert, opens the Great Exhibition.

1854–56
Crimean War. Victoria Cross instituted for bravery in battle.

December 14 1861
Prince Albert dies.

April 8 1871
Opens the Royal Albert Hall.

January 1 1877
Becomes Empress of India.

June 20–21 1887
Golden Jubilee.

June 22 1897
Diamond Jubilee.

1899–1902
Boer War.

January 22 1901
Dies at Osborne House, Isle of Wight, and is buried at Frogmore.

attempts to rush her into marriage. However, in the course of Albert's visit to Windsor in October 1839 she fell in love with him, writing in her diary "It was with some emotion that I beheld Albert, who is beautiful." On October 15 she proposed to him and they were married at St James's Palace in London on February 10 1840.

EMBODIMENT OF FAMILY VIRTUE
The couple had nine children, all of whom survived to become adults—unusual even among the well-to-do in this era. They included Prince Albert Edward, born on November 9 1841, who would eventually succeed his mother as King Edward VII. In their family life at Windsor, Balmoral in Scotland, and Osborne House on the Isle of Wight Victoria and Albert were widely seen as presenting a model of domestic happiness.

FIGURE OF PRIDE

Victoria's sense of duty meant that she applied herself assiduously to her new role when she acceded to the throne aged just 18 in 1837. Although she was only 4 feet 11 inches (1.5 m) tall she had a proud and noble bearing and a pleasant voice. First impressions can be highly important and leaders need, like Victoria, to make sure that no matter how they are feeling about new developments or particular challenges, they maintain an outwardly calm and steady demeanor. As her reign lengthened, her public image grew stronger and stronger as she became consolidated as figurehead of the British Empire.

Albert was behind that major symbol of the Victorian age—the Great Exhibition of 1851, an international trade show held in the vast Crystal Palace in Hyde Park. The exhibition put Britain's technological achievements and great wealth on show. Victoria commented, "I do feel proud at the thought of what my beloved Albert's great mind has conceived."

Victoria was plunged into mourning by Albert's sudden death from typhoid fever on December 14 1861. "He was my life" she later wrote, and she recalled that she had "leant on him for all and everything." She honored his memory with the Royal Albert Hall in Kensington, London, which was opened in 1871 and the 175 feet (53 m)-tall Albert Memorial, built at a cost of £120,000 to designs by celebrated architect George Gilbert Scott, and opened in 1872.

▲ *Victoria posed for this photograph in 1897, at the time of her reign's Diamond Jubilee.*

STRONG-WILLED, FORTHRIGHT

In her dealings with government ministers Victoria was independent-minded and forthright. She was no pushover. At the start of her reign she formed a close relationship with her prime minister, whom she called "dearest, kind Lord Melbourne," but when he was forced to resign in 1839 she was uncooperative, even obstructive with his proposed successor, the Conservative Sir Robert Peel. In the end Victoria won the day: Peel did not form a government and Melbourne returned.

After her marriage, Victoria was initially determined that Albert should not share the responsibilities of government, keen as she was to retain her independence. Over the course of their marriage, however, she came to rely on his advice and, notably during her pregnancies, Albert played a major role. Later, after Albert's death in 1861, she had a close and very important relationship with Benjamin Disraeli, twice prime minister in 1868 and 1874–80, who was highly supportive of her in her grief.

Victoria could be formidable and inspired awe in many. She was renowned for never forgetting—not just in her unwavering devotion to Albert's memory but also in recalling slights or failings of those who served her.

She was thick-skinned and physically courageous. This bravery was called upon in the early years of her reign when the Crown seemed under threat. At a time of republican unrest, Victoria was physically attacked—once in June 1840 and twice in summer 1842 dissidents got close enough to her in London to fire pistols at her. Attacks on the queen resurfaced in the wake of revolutionary outbursts in continental Europe in 1848, in the course of which her cousin King Louis Philippe of France was

The royal procession at the Great Exhibition, 1851. Victoria and Albert are joined by their two eldest children.

deposed. She saw herself as God's dutiful and ordained ruler: She wrote "Revolutions are always bad for the country ... Obedience to the laws and to the Sovereign, is obedience to a higher Power, divinely instituted for the good of the people, not the Sovereign, who has equally duties and obligations."

The central importance of the monarch's duty to her country would inspire Victoria's descendant Elizabeth II just as it had been a key aspect of the ruling propaganda espoused by her forerunner as queen, Elizabeth I.

VICTORIOUS

By 1897, Victoria was widely acclaimed wherever she went on her Diamond Jubilee procession. She wrote in her diary "A never to be forgotten day. No one ever, I believe, has met with such an ovation as was given me ... The cheering was quite deafening, and every face seemed to be filled with real joy." Taking part in the procession were representatives from all corners of the British Empire, including British Africa, Canada, India, and Australia. Eleven colonial prime minsters attended the celebrations.

In her lifetime Victoria was likened to Queen Boudica, the leader of British Celtic resistance against the Romans—not least because both queens' names are versions of a word meaning "victorious." She was certainly that—ruler of history's greatest empire, she became an icon of imperial might.

From 1877 she was Empress of India and was hailed as Victoria Regina et Imperatrix (Victoria, Queen and Empress). By 1900 the empire controlled 20 percent of the globe's territory and almost one-quarter (23 percent) of the world's population. Yet for all that there is little doubt that Victoria's most significant legacy was in securing the future of the British monarchy. While she oversaw a significant shift from political to ceremonial power—part of the movement toward the modern constitutional monarchy—she restored the dignity and standing of the British Crown, and in so doing safeguarded its future.

LEADERSHIP ANALYSI

LEADER TYPE: *Proud*
KEY QUALITIES: *Industrious, independent-minded, dutiful*
LIKEMINDED LEADERS: *Winston Church*
FACT: *The quote "We are not amused" often attributed to Victoria, but there no evidence she ever actually said it.*

WILLIAM MORRIS

CREATIVE REVOLUTIONARY WHO PROMOTED THE VITAL IMPORTANCE OF ART IN THE EVERYDAY

NATIONALITY: *British*
ACHIEVEMENT: *Leader of Arts and Crafts movement*
WHEN: *1875-96*

English designer and craftsman William Morris was the groundbreaking leader of the Arts and Crafts movement that brought new life to the decorative arts in Victorian Britain and has had a powerful influence right into the twenty-first century. Morris was also a practicing revolutionary socialist whose writings inspired generations to work for change.

William Morris believed in the power of beauty to change people's lives. In a lecture of 1880 he advised "Have nothing in your houses that you do not know to be useful or believe to be beautiful." Morris was a creative innovator who proved himself a leader in artistic and craft production, literature, and revolutionary thinking as well as a pioneer of social transformation.

Morris was dismayed by the effects of nineteenth-century industrialization. In response he founded a movement that took a fresh approach to the decorative arts and design. Drawing inspiration from the crafts of the medieval period, the Arts and Crafts movement emphasized the value of work for its own sake, the importance of taking notice of the beauty of natural materials, and the pleasures of craftsmanship.

GENIUS FOR DESIGN

As a leader of the movement Morris combined his artistic genius with tremendous energy: He committed himself to understanding and mastering the process involved in producing goods to the standard he desired, involving himself in every stage. Nothing was too much trouble.

He also exhibited great business acumen in building up his design, manufacturing, and interior-decorating business, "the Firm." Founded in 1861 as Morris, Marshall, Faulkner & Co., from 1877 it had a shop and showroom at no. 449 Oxford Street, in one of the smartest shopping areas of central London. Morris founded the company out of an urge to create things of beauty, in part inspired by his experience of decorating his own home when he had been dismayed by the low quality of furnishings and decorations available.

The company was quickly successful, winning two gold medals at the 1862 International Exhibition in South Kensington and in 1866 creating a decorative scheme for St James's Palace. The firm came under Morris's sole ownership in 1875, and he expanded production of wallpapers and woven fabrics made to his own design.

March 24 1834
Born in Walthamstow, London.

1856
Launches The Oxford and Cambridge Magazine.

1858
Publishes first book of poems, The Defence of Guenevere.

1859
Marries Jane Burden. Philip Webb designs Red House, Bexleyheath, for Morris.

1861
Founds Morris, Marshall, Faulkner, & Co.

1862
First Morris wallpapers designed.

1866
Designs and makes stained glass windows in Jesus College Chapel, Cambridge.

1875
Company reconstituted as Morris & Co.

1877
Founds Society for the Protection of Ancient Buildings. Opens Morris & Co. shop in Oxford Street.

1879
Lectures on "The Art of the People" in Birmingham.

1883
Joins Social Democratic Federation.

1884
Founds Socialist League.

1885–91
Edits Socialist League newspaper The Commonweal.

1891
Establishes Kelmscott Press.

October 3 1896
Dies in Hammersmith, London.

ARTS AND CRAFTS COMMUNITY

Morris's pre-eminence as leader of the Arts and Crafts movement rests in significant part on the fact that his company established an appreciative community who passed on the tastes he promoted. This community expanded through the social classes—from the aristocracy and through the middle classes—and had a lasting international legacy. It was a key influence in the North American Craftsman style and in continental Europe where it fed into Art Nouveau, de Stijl, and Bauhaus. In Japan its influence was seen in the Mingei (Arts of the People) movement in the 1920s and 1930s.

CRAVING FOR BEAUTY

As envisaged by Morris, a key element of the movement's program was the responsibility of the craftsmen and -women for the products they made—in stark contrast to the grinding repetitive processes of industrialized production in

ENERGETIC CREATIVITY

Morris was always open to new creative directions. He taught himself wood engraving and embroidery, and experimented with tapestry. In 1877 he founded the Society for the Protection of Ancient Buildings in the wake of proposals for a "restoration" of the medieval Tewkesbury Abbey in Gloucestershire. From 1891 he was also running the Kelmscott Press in Hammersmith. His effectiveness as a leader in so many fields derived from his extraordinary capability and drive, hands-on approach, and the force and range of his creativity.

factories. The craftsman's joy in making the pot or rug, cabinet or tapestry was an essential element of its quality.

In 1890 Morris published a utopian fantasy, *News from Nowhere*, in *The Commonweal*, the newspaper of the Socialist League to which he belonged. He envisaged a post-revolutionary future in which art is made by the people: "The art ... sprung up ... from a kind of instinct amongst people ... to do the best they could with the work in hand." People had freedom to do this because after the revolution they no longer felt driven to "painful and terrible overwork." People would be free to do what he believed came naturally—work, but not for another person's profit as under the capitalist system, or even to seek personal wealth, but work to create things of beauty.

▲ *On top of all his other achievements, Morris, shown here in 1887, was a founding father of fantasy literature.*

Morris's progressive ideas were integral to his understanding of artistic production. His engagement with revolutionary politics began in 1883 when he joined the Social Democratic Federation. He engaged enthusiastically, first on behalf of the SDF and then as founder of the breakaway group, the Socialist League. As a leader in this sphere, he was fearless and bold. He was arrested more than once, and in November 1887 walked alongside playwright George Bernard Shaw at the head of a banned demonstration in Trafalgar Square, London, at which police and troops drove protesters from the square in a violent encounter remembered as "Bloody Sunday."

CREATIVE REVOLUTIONARY

Morris was a pioneer and a leader of international standing in the field of creative expression. In building his own enterprise he led a revolt against the industrial production methods of the nineteenth century. The landscape in interior decoration and domestically focused fine arts of twenty-first century Britain is unimaginable without Morris's achievements. Artist and craftsman, businessman, shopkeeper, and poet, he was also a revolutionary thinker who in books such as *News from Nowhere* gave birth to provocative and enduring ideas.

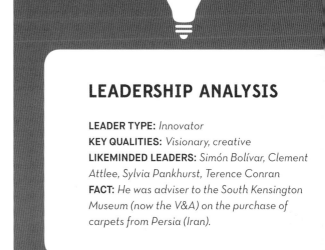

LEADERSHIP ANALYSIS

LEADER TYPE: *Innovator*
KEY QUALITIES: *Visionary, creative*
LIKEMINDED LEADERS: *Simón Bolívar, Clement Attlee, Sylvia Pankhurst, Terence Conran*
FACT: *He was adviser to the South Kensington Museum (now the V&A) on the purchase of carpets from Persia (Iran).*

MOHANDAS GANDHI

PIONEERING EXPONENT OF PEACEFUL PROTEST WHO SET INDIA FREE

NATIONALITY: *Indian*
ACHIEVEMENT: *Led India to independence; key proponent of nonviolent resistance*
WHEN: *1920-47*

Indian lawyer Mohandas Gandhi faced down the might of the British Empire and led his country to independence, gaining the honorary epithet Mahatma (Great Soul).

Mohandas Gandhi marked August 15 1947, the day on which India became independent, with fasting and prayer in Kolkata—demonstrating the simplicity and commitment to God that informed all he did. In the city Hindus and Muslims celebrated side by side. Those present joyfully called it "the miracle of Kolkata."

Gandhi, a long-term leader of the struggle to free India from British rule, had strongly opposed the division of the Indian subcontinent into a predominantly Hindu India and predominantly Muslim Pakistan. But when the split went ahead, he threw himself into efforts to heal divisions between the two religious communities. In the days before independence he was in Kolkata seeking to establish peace. When in September 1947 Hindu/Muslim rioting did break out, he declared he would fast until peace returned. He succeeded in restoring calm in Kolkata, and in Delhi in January 1948, Gandhi once again brought peace between the warring factions by fasting.

SELF-SACRIFICE

Gandhi was always willing to put himself on the line. He did not expect others to make sacrifices that he was not willing to make himself. He led by example—but was also keenly aware of the symbolic force of his actions. He declared in September 1947, "My fast isolates the forces of evil; the moment they are isolated they die, for evil by itself has no legs to stand upon." The function of his fast, he explained, was "to purify, to release our energies by overcoming our inertia and mental sluggishness." The forces of change could not, in his view, be generated or marshaled outside the individual; they must be brought into being through inner personal transformation.

Gandhi's understanding of the central importance of peace and of fasting as a way of self-purification went back to his childhood with his very religious mother in Gujarat. The Hinduism celebrated in his home contained a strong strain of Jainism—a major Indian religious tradition centered on *ahimsa* (the principle of nonviolence to all living beings). In character he was diffident and at school he was not particularly successful, but from early in life he had a fierce desire for self-improvement and a willingness to experiment with methods of achieving this.

Gandhi (right) confers with Jawaharlal Nehru (later first prime minister of independent India, 1947-64).

This drive to improve himself morally and spiritually was his great motivation and carried him to the heights he attained as a nationalist leader and religious exemplar. Throughout his life he always stressed how ordinary he was—in everything except his devotion and drive. The change he embodied was available to everyone. He wrote "I have not the shadow of a doubt that any man or woman can achieve what I have, if he or she would make the same effort and cultivate the same hope and faith."

Gandhi studied law in London and while there became a leading light of the London-based Vegetarian Society, where he met idealists and critics of modern society and first encountered, in an English translation, the Hindu scripture the *Bhagavad Gita* (*The Song of the Lord*), which had such a profound effect on his life. From the *Bhagavad Gita*, which he studied in great depth, he took the key concepts of *aparigraha* (nonpossessiveness), detachment from possessions and also the fruits of what you do, and *samabhava* (evenness or cheerfulness). He wrote "you must not worry whether the desired result follows from your action or not, so long as your motive is pure, your means correct."

TURNING POINT IN AFRICA

Returning to India from his studies, Gandhi struggled to find suitable work and in 1893 moved to South Africa to take a job with an Indian firm there. On his arrival he was shocked by the treatment of his fellow Indians. It was in response to this injustice that Gandhi developed his strategy of nonviolent resistance: *Satyagraha* (holding to the truth). In the face of injustice, he decided, civil disobedience was a citizen's duty. It

October 2 1869
Born in Porbandar, India.

1893
Having failed to find work in India, takes job in Natal, South Africa.

1894
Founds Natal Indian Congress.

1906
Leads Indians in South Africa in satyagraha protest.

1914
Returns to India.

1919
Launches satyagraha in India.

April 13 1919
Amritsar Massacre—British fire on Indian demonstrators, killing 379.

1922–1924
Arrested and jailed.

1928
At Kolkata Congress, demands dominion status for India within a year.

1930
Satyagraha against salt tax.

1931
Attends Round Table Conference in London.

1934
Resigns from Congress Party.

1942
Demands immediate British withdrawal from India.

1942–44
Imprisoned.

August 15 1947
Indian independence.

January 30 1948
Assassinated, Delhi.

should be, he wrote, "sincere, respectful, restrained, never defiant"; it must "have no ill will or hatred behind it." Its purpose was to win one's opponent over: "The satyagrahi's object is to convert, not to coerce, the wrongdoer." The strength of the satyagraha was in its endeavor to actively engage with opponents and win disputes through persuasion, to bring about change without creating an enemy.

Gandhi remained in South Africa for more than 20 years, returning to India in 1914. In 1919 he announced a new campaign of satyagraha to counter legislation that empowered the British to imprison people suspected of sedition without trial. He soon became an

CHANNELING ANGER

Anger can be a powerful tool for a leader so long as it is controlled and channeled for use. When asked what was the most creative incident in his life Gandhi recalled an insult in his early days in South Africa in 1893. While traveling by train across the state of Natal, South Africa, he was told he had to leave his seat in the first-class compartment because of the color of his skin. He refused to move since he had a valid ticket, and was thrown off by a policeman at Maritzburg, where he was left shivering overnight in the station—without overcoat and luggage, which were still on the train. He committed himself that night to the basic premises of his nonviolent resistance: Never to give in to force and never to use force to effect change. He did not repress the anger he felt at his treatment. He transformed it into the energy that drove his peaceful revolution.

important political figure in India, leading a boycott of British institutions and goods that saw thousands of satyagrahis go cheerfully to jail. He rebuilt the Indian National Congress party into a force for Indian nationalism. In 1922 he called off the satyagraha following an outbreak of violence when a nationalist crowd set fire to a police station. Gandhi was resolute in his decision to accept absolutely no use of violence in pursuit of his cause.

Ironically, it was this incident that led to Gandhi being charged with inciting violence and imprisoned. He was released in 1924. In 1930 he called a new and highly effective satyagraha against the British tax on salt. In the wake of this in 1931 he attended the first Round Table Conference in London as the only representative of the Indian National Congress. However, once back in India in 1934 he resigned from the Congress because he felt members were using nonviolent resistance as a political tool and not with the absolute belief he had in its tenets. He concentrated on a program of educating rural India, promoting cottage industries and campaigning against the tradition of the "untouchables" (those below the levels of the traditional caste system).

Independence finally came under the British Labour government of Clement Attlee after World War II. In its immediate aftermath Gandhi's devotion of himself to efforts to break down barriers between Muslims and Hindus in India led to his death. He was assassinated on January 30 1948 in Delhi by a fanatical Hindu nationalist, Nathuram Godse.

PRACTICAL INSPIRATION

The Mahatma was undoubtedly one of the greatest and most transformative figures of the twentieth century. While his political strategy might have seemed new, he stressed that it was not. He wrote "I have nothing new to teach the world. Truth and nonviolence are as old as the hills. All I have done is try experiments in both on as vast a scale as I could do." Yet, despite his protestations, he is remembered as a pioneer in the use of nonviolent protest for social reform. In particular, he was a profound influence on the African-American civil rights leader Martin Luther King, Jr.

Gandhi's nonviolent revolution in India opened the way to the dismantling of the British Empire in both Asia and Africa and inspired those working against colonialism, racism, and violence around the world. Gandhi himself would never have separated his political from his religious life: He wrote "What I have been striving and pining to achieve ... is to see God face to face." On Gandhi's death, Prime Minster Nehru called him "our beloved leader ... the father of the nation" and declared, "the light has gone out of our lives, and there is darkness everywhere."

LEADERSHIP ANALYSIS

LEADER TYPE: *Leader by example*
KEY QUALITIES: *Self-disciplined, peacable*
LIKEMINDED LEADERS: *Saint Francis of Assisi, Martin Luther King, Jr, the fourteenth Dalai Lama*
FACT: *Gandhi was nominated five times for the Nobel Peace Prize but did not win it.*

31

JOHN MCGRAW

HIGH-ACHIEVER WHO AIMED FOR SPORTING GLORY AND BECAME A GIANT SUCCESS

NATIONALITY: *American*
ACHIEVEMENT: *Led New York Giants to ten championships and three World Series*
WHEN: *1902-32*

John McGraw—who led the New York Giants to ten National League championships—was a winner, devoted to victory above all. He was a great motivator of players and, like any general, he proved himself willing occasionally to bend the rules of competition in pursuit of victory.

Playing third base for the Baltimore Orioles in the 1890s and as manager of the New York Giants from 1902–32, John McGraw waged war on his opponents. He was just 5 feet 7 inches (1.7 m) tall, and his stature and approach to the game won him the nickname "Little Napoleon."

"In playing or managing," he proclaimed, "the game of ball is only fun for me when I'm out in front and winning," then added, "I don't give a hill of beans for the rest of the game." He had a formidable personality combined with single-mindedness and an aggressive approach.

This determination inspired the New York Giants to go on an unprecedented winning streak. McGraw was Giants' manager for many years, which was crucial for the building of discipline. New players arrived to find an established team ethic and a disciplined way of doing things. McGraw was the kind of manager players come to love: Unafraid to take on people others have rejected as past their best, he helped them to recover their performance levels and carry on for a few more seasons. To succeed in this McGraw demonstrated unswerving self-confidence and immense courage. Highly self-disciplined, McGraw demanded similar standards from his team, allowing him to create a winning side from perhaps a less than obviously first-rate team.

EFFECTIVE TACTICS

When McGraw was a player at the Orioles in the 1890s the team was famous for tactics such as the Baltimore chop, in which a batter hit the ball hard at the ground, making it bounce over the fielder's head, so giving the batter time to reach base. To increase the bounce and make the hit work even better, the Baltimore groundsman packed the earth tightly around the home plate (where the batter stands) and mixed it with hard clay. The Baltimore chop was part of a tactical approach known as inside baseball that was developed by Ned Hanlon, McGraw's manager at the

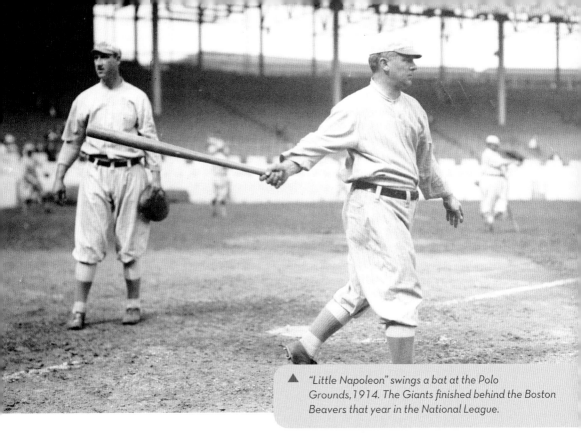

▲ *"Little Napoleon" swings a bat at the Polo Grounds, 1914. The Giants finished behind the Boston Beavers that year in the National League.*

Orioles in this period. Inside baseball—so called because it did not rely on big hits but on keeping the ball in the infield—was based on the bunt (hitting the ball softly to a part of the infield so runners on bases can advance) and other methods designed for moving the team little by little around the bases. McGraw wrote of the tactic, "Inside baseball ... is merely the working out of definite plans that the public does not observe."

As manager, McGraw built his teams on similar tactics—definite plans centered on good pitching, excellent defense, and aggressive running of bases. He was able to revitalize players' careers because he had a knack for seeing how a particular player would fit into this system. The general consensus at the time was that the Giants were not so talented as some of the other top teams but succeeded because of McGraw's tactics and superb leadership. Giants' pitcher Christy Mathewson recalled how in the team's 1904 pennant-winning season, every play was made by John McGraw from the sidelines. He had a system of signals, such as blowing his nose, which told the players what to do next. Mathewson wrote: "He won the pennant from the bench." Much later in McGraw's career, Johnny Evers, manager of the Chicago Cubs in 1921, declared that the Giants were a second-class team saved by a first-class manager.

Sometimes, both as player and manager, McGraw pushed at the very edge of what he could get away with. In 1901, as player-manager of the Baltimore Orioles in the newly formed American League, he bought African-American player Charlie

April 7 1873
Born Truxton, New Jersey.

August 26 1891
Makes Major League debut, for the Baltimore Orioles.

1899
Completes ninth season with Orioles.

1900
Plays a single season for the Saint Louis Cardinals.

1901
Player-manager for Baltimore Orioles in American League.

1902
Player-manager for the New York Giants.

1904
Wins National League pennant with New York Giants.

1905
Giants win National League. In the World Series they defeat Philadelphia Athletics 4–1.

1911, 1912, 1913
Giants win three consecutive National League pennants.

1917
Giants win sixth National League pennant.

1921, 1922, 1923, 1924
Giants win four consecutive National League pennants.

1921
Giants win World Series, defeating New York Yankees 5–3.

1922
Giants win World Series, defeating New York Yankees 4–0–(1).

June 3 1932
Ill health causes him to resign as Giants manager.

February 25 1934
Dies, New Rochelle, New York.

1937
Elected to the Baseball Hall of Fame

Grant, who had been playing in the separate Negro League for the Chicago Columbia Giants. At this time baseball was segregated and black players were not permitted in the American League: McGraw tried to claim that Grant—who was light-skinned and had straight hair—was a Cherokee Indian named Charlie Tokohama. This would have been permitted, but the deception was found out when the team traveled to Chicago and White Sox President Charles Comiskey recognized Grant.

CHARACTER ON AND OFF THE PITCH

Off the pitch McGraw was a larger-than-life character and became something of a celebrity. He went into business with gambler Arnold Rothstein, co-owning a pool hall, and even went on stage in a vaudeville act in 1912.

FEARLESS

Christy Mathewson—star pitcher in John McGraw's New York Giants—said of his boss "I have seen him go onto ballfields where he is as welcome as a man with the black smallpox and face the crowd alone ... I have seen him take all sorts of personal chances. He doesn't know what fear is." McGraw said that a person had to fight all the time to survive in baseball. He was unafraid to take on the fiercest umpires and frequently delivered savage reprimands to his players. Arlie Latham, coach of the New York Giants, said of him, "[he] eats gunpowder every morning for breakfast and washes it down with warm blood."

HALL OF FAME: JOHN MCGRAW

THREE BEST ON-BASE PERCENTAGES OF ALL TIME

Ted Williams .482

Babe Ruth .474

John McGraw .466

MANAGER VICTORIES

3,731	Connie Mack 53 years as manager
2,763	John McGraw 33 years as manager
2,728	Tony LaRussa 33 year as manager

WORLD SERIES VICTORIES AS MANAGER

1905 NY GIANTS

1921 NY GIANTS

1922 NY GIANTS

National Baseball
Hall of Fame
1937
★ ★ ★

His sporting record was extraordinary. In his playing career he scored 1,024 runs including 13 home runs and his on-base percentage (a record of how often a batsman reaches base) was .466—the third-best of all time after Babe Ruth and Ted Williams.

He was the first baseball manager to win four consecutive league pennants—with the New York Giants, winning the National League in 1921, 1922, 1923, and 1924. In the first two of these four seasons, the Giants also won the World Series, both times defeating the American League Champions, the New York Yankees.

As manager McGraw won 2,763 victories—second only to Connie Mack, who won 3,731 times as manager of the Philadelphia Athletics in 1901–51. But Mack had a much longer period as manager and himself declared McGraw to be the greatest, saying: "There has been only one manager—and his name is McGraw." He is celebrated as one of the all-time greats in baseball history, a record-breaking player and manager, and one of the sport's most colorful characters.

LEADERSHIP ANALYSIS

LEADER TYPE: *Ambitious*
KEY QUALITIES: *Tough, motivator*
LIKEMINDED LEADERS: *Winston Churchill, Indira Gandhi, Vince Lombardi*
FACT: *Umpires ejected McGraw from 118 games in his career—more than any other baseball manager.*

WINSTON CHURCHILL

ICONIC WARTIME LEADER WHO RALLIED BRITAIN AND THE WORLD AGAINST NAZI THREAT

NATIONALITY: *British*
ACHIEVEMENT: *Led Britain and inspired the British people and her allies to defeat Nazi Germany*
WHEN: *1940-45; 1951-55*

Winston Churchill was the indomitable premier who inspired the British people and the world at large in the darkest days of World War II, leading them from the brink of defeat to victory over Nazi Germany.

Winston Churchill defied the threatened Nazi invasion of Britain in a stirring speech delivered in the House of Commons on June 4 1940. "We shall fight on the beaches, we shall fight on the landing grounds ... We shall never surrender." With inspirational rhetoric, canny leadership, and his commitment to building an alliance with the United States he delivered victory by 1945.

Churchill had been prime minister less than a month when he delivered his address on June 4. It is one of three immortal speeches that together encapsulate the power of Churchill's inspirational vocal leadership in rallying the embattled people of Britain to fight back, and fight on—first in the face of the threat of a likely Nazi invasion and then under the bombardment of the Blitz (the Nazis' strategic bombing campaign of London and other British cities from September 1940 to May 1941).

Two weeks later, on June 18 1940, he announced to the House of Commons and the people of Britain in a radio broadcast that "the Battle of Britain is about to begin." Nazi

THE UPS AND DOWNS OF CHURCHILL'S CAREER

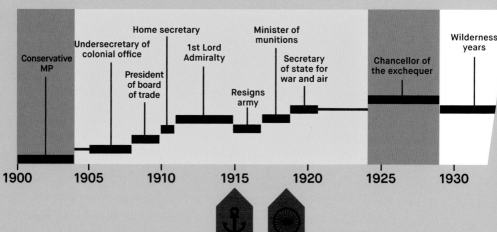

leader Adolf Hitler, Churchill stated, knew that he had to conquer Britain to win the war. If Britain could defy him then Europe could be saved. In a rousing conclusion he urged "Let us therefore brace ourselves to our duties, and so bear ourselves, that if the British Empire and its Commonwealth last for a thousand years, men will still say, 'This was their finest hour.'" His third piece of rhetorical genius was delivered on August 20 1940 when he paid stirring tribute to the actions of RAF fighter and bomber pilots who, he said, were turning the tide of the war by their prowess. "Never," he declared, "in the field of human conflict has so much been owed by so many to so few."

In 1940 Churchill was the right man in the right place: His qualities were exactly what the people of a beleaguered Britain needed. Fiercely patriotic and full of energy, he was a gifted communicator and experienced writer—an astute historian with no reticence at all about Britain's status and historic importance. Trained at Sandhurst academy, he was a World War I army veteran as well as an experienced politician, an unflappable man who seemed to thrive in a crisis.

PERSUASIVE

Central to any leader's success is his or her ability to convince others to follow. Churchill's energy, political experience, and forceful personality were key here, as was his innate imperturbability. In 1940 Churchill had to convince the Cabinet to fight on when some considered that an agreement could be brokered with Hitler to avoid a great deal of suffering. The situation looked hopeless. The Nazis had overrun northern France and Britain appeared ill prepared to defend herself. But Churchill projected confidence and convinced his colleagues in Cabinet and then MPs in Parliament that Britain should resist. The next job was to convince the people that resistance was not futile, even that victory was possible. He broadcast his great parliamentary speeches to the nation on BBC radio. They were powerfully effective. Labour MP Josiah Wedgwood commented

⬤	Conservative Party
◯	Liberal Party
◯	Wilderness years
⚓	Gallipoli Campaign
⚙	Against Indian self-rule
👑	Support of Edward VIII in abdication crisis
✕	Battle of Britain
📖	Wins Nobel Literature Prize
▲	Negative event
▲	Positive event

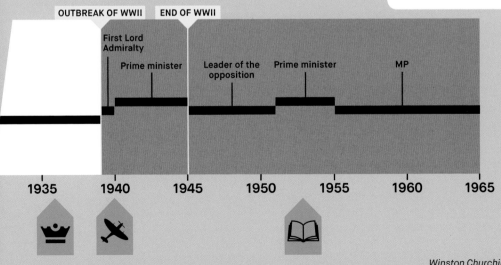

TIME LINE

November 30 1874
Born, Blenheim Palace, Oxfordshire.

December 1894
Graduates from Sandhurst Royal Military College.

1895
Commissioned in Fourth Queen's Own Hussars.

1899
Resigns army commission to enter politics.

1900
Elected Conservative MP for Oldham.

1904
Joins Liberal Party.

1910–11
Home secretary.

1911–15
First Lord of the Admiralty.

1924
Rejoins Conservative Party.

1924–29
Chancellor of the exchequer.

1939–40
First Lord of the Admiralty.

1940–45
Elected prime minister.

1945–51
Leader of the opposition.

1951–55
Elected prime minister for a second term.

1953
Wins Nobel Prize for Literature.

January 24 1965
Dies, London.

of the "We shall never surrender" speech, "That was worth 1,000 guns, and the speeches of 1,000 years."

Churchill conducted the war effort with immense energy and dedication. In 1940 he seemed to be everywhere—visiting bombsites, checking on coastal defenses and fighter headquarters, giving frank but defiant radio broadcasts. Press pictures showed him making his "V for victory" sign and smoking his cigar.

PRAGMATIC, PERSEVERING

For all his reputation as a great orator, a defender of values, Churchill was highly pragmatic as a leader. His principal aim was simply to persevere—in his own colorful words, "keep buggering on." This meant he and his war planning were highly adaptable to new developments.

Overall, however, he had a keen strategic sense. He understood the importance of alliance in warfare and saw that the key to victory was involving the United States on Britain's side. Upon becoming prime minister

TOTAL COMMITMENT

On becoming prime minister in May 1940 Churchill told the House of Commons, in another of his ringing phrases, "I would say to the House as I said to those who have joined this government: I have nothing to offer but blood, toil, tears, and sweat." Quite simply his goal was "Victory at all costs—victory in spite of all terror—victory, however long and hard the road may be." He promised full effort and utter commitment to achieving this aim.

Unfailingly energetic, Churchill pushed himself so hard that he had two serious bouts of pneumonia in 1943.

he began at once what became a long correspondence with US President Franklin D. Roosevelt, which was crucial to the British war effort (see page 158). When the Americans joined the war in December 1941 he was exultant. As he later recalled: "So we had won after all! ... How long the war would last ... no man could tell, nor did I at this moment care ... Our history would not come to an end."

The alliance was indeed crucial to victory. For the remainder of the war Churchill was tireless, traveling relentlessly, holding no fewer than 11 face-to-face meetings with Roosevelt and several with Soviet leader Joseph Stalin, including the Yalta Conference in February 1945 that drew up final plans for the defeat of the Nazis and the Potsdam Conference of July–August 1945 that began planning for the postwar world.

In 1945, having led the country to victory, Churchill was swept from power in the 1945 general election, a landslide victory for the Labour Party led by Clement Attlee (see page 164). During the campaign he had been cheered up and down the country, but the acclaim was for his role as war leader rather than as a potential prime minister in the postwar world.

Out of office, he set to work on his six-volume history of World War II while, on the international stage, he urged the need for the United States and Britain to combine in the face of the communist Soviet Union and promoted European union. He returned to power as prime minister in 1951–55 but he is remembered above all for his defiance of Hitler and leading Britain to victory in alliance with United States and the Soviets. For these achievements he is rightly celebrated as one of the greatest war leaders in history.

LEADERSHIP ANALYSIS

LEADER TYPE: *Defiant*
KEY QUALITIES: *Gifted orator and writer*
LIKEMINDED LEADERS: *Queen Boudica*
FACT: *During the war Churchill often traveled under the name "Colonel Warden" to disguise his whereabouts.*

VLADIMIR ILYICH LENIN

REVOLUTIONARY MASTERMIND WHO ORCHESTRATED THE RUSSIAN REVOLUTION IN 1917

NATIONALITY: *Russian*
ACHIEVEMENT: *Leader of October Revolution of 1917 and of the Soviet Union*
WHEN: *1917-24*

On November 7–8 1917 Vladimir Ilyich Lenin swept to power in Russia as his Bolsheviks ousted the existing Provisional Government. He had spent much of his life in exile from his homeland and had been in hiding until the last minute, but this resolute and ruthless revolutionary leader remained level-headed in power. Hailed as a great thinker, he was an inspirational figure for revolutionaries throughout the twentieth century.

Lenin had carefully plotted the events of the October Revolution and shown considerable courage in traveling from exile in Finland to Petrograd—the city founded by Peter the Great as St Petersburg and later renamed Leningrad—to force events to a head. (Lenin's Soviet coup is referred to as the October Revolution because the crucial events took place on October 25–26 in the old Julian calendar; the Gregorian calendar was not adopted in Russia until 1918, after these events.)

The Provisional Government had been in control only since March 1917, when Tsar Nicholas II was forced from power. In exile in Switzerland at the time of the tsar's abdication, Lenin rushed home to denounce the Provisional Government as being formed by bourgeois liberals and call for a government that truly represented the Soviets (workers' councils)—government by the peasants, industrial workers, and soldiers. For his outspokenness he was censured by the Provisional Government and forced into exile yet again—this time in Finland where he continued to agitate for an armed uprising.

Lenin was resolute, unbending in his determination to bring these events to a head—and decided to risk his life by returning to Russia to forward the revolution. On October 20 (Gregorian calendar) he crept disguised into Petrograd and succeeded in winning support for an armed takeover. In the immediate aftermath of the revolution, the All Russian Congress of Soviets voted to take power and elected Lenin as chairman of the Council of People's Commissars. This was the moment of triumph to which Lenin had built patiently and tirelessly over many years.

Lenin's revolutionary legacy was enduring. This Soviet propaganda poster by Victor Ivanov, inscribed with the legend "Lenin lived. Lenin is alive. Lenin will live," dates to 1967. ▶

ЛЕНИН –
ЖИЛ,
ЛЕНИН –
ЖИВ,
ЛЕНИН –
БУДЕТ ЖИТЬ!

ВЛ. МАЯКОВСКИЙ.

TIME LINE

April 22 1870
Born Vladimir Ilyich Ulyanov, Simbirsk.

1889
Reads Marx and declares himself a Marxist.

1895
Union for the Struggle for the Liberation of the Working Class.

December 1895
Arrested as one of leaders of the Union; exiled to Siberia.

1900
Goes into exile in Munich; founds Iskra (The Spark).

1901
Adopts name Lenin.

1903
Bolsheviks split from Mensheviks at Second Congress of the Russian Social-Democratic Workers' Party (RSDWP).

1905
Revolution.

1912
Lenin splits RSDWP, forming Bolshevik party.

March 1917
Tsar forced from power; replaced by Provisional Government.

October 1917
October Revolution; Soviets take power.

1918–20
Civil War: Red Army defeats Whites.

1921
Famine kills five million.

1922
Formation of Union of Soviet Socialist Republics.

March 10 1923
Suffers third stroke in under a year; loses power of speech.

January 21 1924
Dies, in Gorki, following another stroke.

STRONG-WILLED MAN OF DESTINY

Lenin saw himself as a man of destiny, working in the cause of a revolution in which he believed with all his being. He was charismatic, with a powerful mind allied to extraordinary strength of will, drive, and purpose.

He had been radicalized as a teenager, in part by the execution of his elder brother Aleksandr for allegedly plotting against Tsar Alexander III. After being expelled from university for taking part in an illegal gathering of students he enthusiastically read the works of Karl Marx, aligning himself with the Marxist ideology that would inspire him throughout his life. Working as a lawyer in St Petersburg in the 1890s, Lenin was arrested as one of the leaders of the Union for the Struggle for the Liberation of the Working Class, jailed for 15 months, and exiled for three years to Siberia.

After 1900 he spent many years in exile abroad, where he co-founded and edited *Iskra* (*The Spark*), a newspaper intended

PERSONALITY

After British philosopher Bertrand Russell met Lenin, he declared "I have never met a personage so destitute of self-importance." Lenin was modest. But in the revolution a cult of personality was built around him—just as it was around Fidel Castro in Cuba and in the modern age around Kim Jong-il in North Korea. Lenin did not like this but accepted it as necessary to achieve his goal. Sometimes leaders have to be willing to take their image or leadership style in directions that do not come naturally to achieve success.

to unite Marxists in Russia and across Europe. From 1903 he established himself as leader of the Bolsheviks, initially a faction in the Russian Social Democratic Workers' Party (RSDWP), opposed by the Mensheviks. In 1912 he split the Bolsheviks from the RSDWP. World War I found Lenin in Switzerland, agitating unsuccessfully for socialists to withdraw from a war in which, he argued, they were fighting against their comrades in the interests of capitalists and imperialists.

FULL COMMITMENT

After the October Revolution Lenin fought with every fiber of his being to prevent the collapse of the new regime. The country was soon engulfed by a brutal civil war, in which the Workers' and Peasants' Red Army fought the Whites, whose former tsarist generals were financed and supported by the Allied forces of World War I. Lenin showed iron will and leadership of the most forceful kind in balancing the needs of the industrial workers, the peasants, and national groups within Russia and dragging the Red Army to victory. In August 1918 he was almost a victim of the violence himself: Shot twice, his strength of will and strong constitution enabled him to recover, but he was never again quite himself.

In the aftermath of the war, in 1921, Lenin displayed his pragmatism when, faced with a mass revolt by the peasantry against the government's requisitioning of their grain supplies, he introduced the New Economic Policy that allowed peasants to sell their grain—a turning back from the revolution to a form of capitalism. From 1922 Lenin's health was in severe decline. By the end of the year he was no longer able to lead the country and dictated his Testament to his secretary, expressing concern about the party's future stability under Joseph Stalin, general secretary of the Central Committee. Stalin later suppressed this document.

GLOBAL TEACHER

Lenin died on January 21 1924. His corpse was carried by train to Moscow and more than a million mourners came to pay their respects at his lying in state. By the communists he was officially declared "the leader and teacher of the peoples of the whole world." His life and writings certainly had a transformative effect. His political theory (Leninism) was integrated with the theoretical outlay of Karl Marx (Marxism) to form Marxism–Leninism, the cultural–political structure embraced by the Soviet Union and communist countries existing in its ambit. This great revolutionary theorist—an inspiration for the revolutions of Fidel Castro in Cuba, Mao Zedong in China, and Ho Chi Minh in Vietnam—is widely accepted as the most significant revolutionary leader in history.

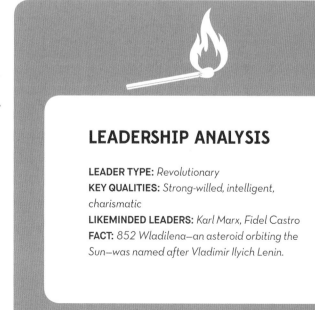

LEADERSHIP ANALYSIS

LEADER TYPE: *Revolutionary*
KEY QUALITIES: *Strong-willed, intelligent, charismatic*
LIKEMINDED LEADERS: *Karl Marx, Fidel Castro*
FACT: *852 Wladilena—an asteroid orbiting the Sun—was named after Vladimir Ilyich Lenin.*

34 SAM GOLDWYN

THE MOVIE MOGUL WITH A KEEN EYE FOR TALENT IN HOLLYWOOD'S GOLDEN AGE

NATIONALITY: *American*
ACHIEVEMENT: *Among most successful Hollywood producers of the Golden Age*
WHEN: *1923-59*

Sam Goldwyn—salesman, film producer, and talent-developer supreme—helped build the "Dream Factory" of Hollywood with his steely determination and created a democratic American art form that conquered the globe.

In 1947 *The Best Years of Our Lives* won Best Picture at the Oscars. In the same year its producer Samuel Goldwyn also won the Irving G. Thalberg Memorial Award, given to creative producers of consistently high-quality work. Goldwyn, whose company produced the first feature film made in Hollywood in 1913, was at the peak of his success and had proved himself to have a great eye for filmmaking talent.

Before 1947 Goldwyn had produced a string of films nominated for a Best Picture Academy Award made by leading directors and featuring major stars. They included *Arrowsmith* (1931), directed by John Ford and starring Ronald Coleman, as well as several films directed by William Wyler, including *Dead End* (1937; starring Humphrey Bogart), *Wuthering Heights* (1939; starring Merle Oberon and Laurence Olivier), and *The Little Foxes* (1941; staring Bette Davis). In 1947, in another accolade for Goldwyn's *The Best Years of Our Lives*, the same director, William Wyler, won Best Director.

Goldwyn was a brilliant salesman as well as a creative producer with a gift for hiring the most gifted directors, actors, writers, and cinematographers in Hollywood and putting together popular and critically acclaimed movies. He rose from poverty to a position at the top of arguably the world's highest-profile industry.

AMBITIOUS, ENERGETIC

Goldwyn needed energy, self-belief, and an optimistic outlook to make his way to the top. It wasn't an easy ride. He was born Szmuel Gelbfisz, the son of a Hasidic Jewish peddler in Poland, at the time part of the Russian Empire. After being orphaned he left his birthplace, Warsaw, on foot and without a penny to his name; he made his way first to Germany and then to London, before emigrating in 1898 to the United States by way of Liverpool and Nova Scotia, Canada. In the course of his journey he changed his name to Samuel Goldfish. He had drive and immense ambition: On arrival in the United States he found a job at the Elite Glove Company in Gloversville, upstate New York, and then—after becoming self-employed—proved himself a stupendously successful salesman.

His first steps in the movie business came through a family venture, undertaken with his brother-in-law and vaudeville producer Jesse L. Lasky—together with Cecil B. DeMille and Arthur Friend. The new company, the Jesse L. Lasky Feature Play Company, bought rights to Edwin Milton Royle's 1905 stage play *The Squaw Man* and began filming on December 29 1913—the first feature film made in Hollywood.

After a merger with the Famous Players Co., owned by Adolph Zukor, Goldfish was chairman of Famous Players-Lasky (later part of Paramount Pictures). After a number of run-ins with Zukor, however, he resigned and formed Goldwyn Pictures with brothers Edgar and Archibald Selwyn who were established producers of plays for Broadway. Starting this new venture he changed his name again—to Goldwyn.

PERFECTIONIST

Goldwyn was endlessly energetic, inventive, and determined. Once he set his mind on a goal, there was nothing that would stop him. This quality of utmost determination had carried him from Warsaw to London to Birmingham to Liverpool to Canada to New York City and thence to Hollywood. He had strong and inspiring dreams and set himself to realizing them.

▲ A Time *magazine article about soldiers returning to the United States after World War II inspired Goldwyn to develop this picture. It won five other Academy Awards on top of the directorial and best picture prizes.*

When in 1924 Goldwyn Pictures merged with Metro Pictures to form Metro-Goldwyn-Mayer, the new company immortalized Goldwyn's name but he had no formal role there and instead worked independently as a producer under the title Samuel Goldwyn Productions. This outfit became the most successful and critically lauded independent production house in the Golden Age of Hollywood. The firm concentrated on production and had no distribution arm, releasing most of its pictures through United Artists in the 1930s and from 1941 through RKO Radio Pictures. From its first film, *Potash and Perlmutter* (an ethnic Jewish-themed silent comedy) of 1923, the production house was active for 36 years until 1959.

After the success of *The Best Years of Our Lives*, Goldwyn took a new direction, moving from dramatic features to musicals—and scoring hits with *Hans Christian Andersen* (starring Danny Kaye) and *Guys and Dolls* (starring Frank Sinatra, Jean Simmons, Marlon Brando, and Vivian Blaine). His final film was a labor of love, a movie

July 1879
Born Warsaw, then part of Russian Empire.

1898
Emigrates from England to United States.

1899
Settles in New York; works as glove salesman.

1913
Co-founds the Jesse L. Lasky Feature Play Company and films The Squaw Man.

1916
Famous Players-Lasky; Goldwyn Pictures.

1923
Founds Samuel Goldwyn Productions.

1924
Metro-Goldwyn-Mayer.

1946
The Best Years of Our Lives; *Irving G. Thalberg Memorial Award.*

1950
Daily Variety *votes Goldwyn Best Movie Producer in America.*

1952
Hans Christian Andersen, *starring Danny Kaye.*

1955
Guys and Dolls, *starring Marlon Brando.*

1959
Porgy and Bess, *starring Sidney Poitier.*

March 27 1971
President Nixon visits Sam Goldwyn's house to present him with Presidential Medal of Freedom.

January 31 1974
Dies, Los Angeles.

version of the George Gershwin opera *Porgy and Bess*. The film, which starred Sidney Poitier and Sammy Davis Jr. alongside Dorothy Dandridge and Pearl Bailey, was a critical and financial flop. Its lack of success left Goldwyn heartbroken.

He lived on until 1974, honored by Hollywood—he has a Beverly Hills theater named after him and a star in the Hollywood Walk of Fame—and by the American nation: In 1971 he was presented with a Presidential Medal of Freedom. Late on in life he declared, "Hollywood owes me nothing. I owe Hollywood everything." He declared that he had been inspired to make movies by the idea of films as family entertainment. "People knew that when they saw the Goldwyn name on a picture, it was a family picture. I've proved that fine things, clean things, can be fun."

PUBLICITY IN A PHRASE

In a row with Jack Warner at the Motion Picture Producers and Distributors of America, Samuel Goldwyn reportedly declared "include me out"—instead of "count me out." He became well known for his colorful and amusing misuse of language—and the label "Goldwynism" was invented for this kind of skewed phrase. Eventually Goldwyn's publicity men had a team of writers creating new ones. Leaders benefit from being open to using any and all idiosyncrasies to promote their name and standing. Other Goldwynisms include "I'll answer you in two words: Im. Possible" and "Anyone who goes to a psychiatrist should have his head examined."

In the Famous Players-Lasky days. Goldwyn (center) with (left to right) Jesse L. Lasky, Adolph Zukor, Cecil B. DeMille, and Albert Kaufman.

Goldwyn took pride in the democratic art his company produced: He emphasized that Hollywood workers—producers, writers, directors, actors, artists, and technicians—were interested in the same areas of life as other Americans. "Hollywood has expressed America," he declared, "and in so doing it has created an art form which is a real embodiment of the American democratic spirit." Such was the tremendous achievement of this peddler's son from Warsaw who—along with other studio owners such as Darryl F. Zanuck (co-founder of Twentieth Century Pictures), David O. Selznick (of Selznick International Pictures), and Jack and Harry Warner of Warner Bros Studios—turned film into the world's most popular form of entertainment from the 1920s to the 1940s.

LEADERSHIP ANALYSIS

LEADER TYPE: *Talent-promoter*
KEY QUALITIES: *Perfectionist, energetic, ambitious*
LIKEMINDED LEADERS: *William Shakespeare, William Morris*
FACT: *Goldwyn declared "I make my pictures to please myself."*

35

MUSTAFA KEMAL ATATÜRK

CHAMPION OF MODERNIZATION WHO CREATED AN INDEPENDENT TURKEY

Mustafa Kemal Atatürk ("Father of the Turks") was a great modernizer who founded the Republic of Turkey in the years after World War I from the surviving parts of the defeated Ottoman Empire. He promoted European ways in building a secular state and restoring his people's pride.

NATIONALITY: *Turkish*
ACHIEVEMENT: *Established the modern, secular Republic of Turkey*
WHEN: *1923–38*

In 1928, the president of the Republic of Turkey went into country villages with a blackboard and chalk. An energetic leader devoted to remaking his country's future, he set out to teach his people face to face how to read and write the Latin alphabet used in western Europe.

In November 1928, Mustafa Kemal's government had abolished reading and writing of the Arabic script that has been used for centuries in the Ottoman Empire. The move was part of a large-scale program of modernization and secularization of a country that for centuries had been ruled by Ottoman sultans as an Islamic state.

The sultans had claimed to be caliphs (spiritual leaders) of all Muslims in the realm: Within six months of the establishment of the new Turkish republic on October 29 1923, the new government abolished the caliphate and in March 1924 closed the country's religious schools. The next month, religious courts were wound up. A new civil law code was gradually introduced, and in 1926 the Western calendar replaced the Islamic one. Mustafa Kemal was untiring in his efforts to bring Turkey into the modern world.

GIFTED GENERAL

Before becoming their modernizing president, Mustafa Kemal had played an essential part in Turkey's survival and rise from the shattered remains of the Ottoman Empire in the wake of World War I. He made his name as a general in 1915–16, when he thwarted the Allied invasion of the Dardanelles and was celebrated as "savior of Istanbul." Fate marked him out in this campaign, when a piece of shrapnel that would have killed or seriously injured him was stopped by a watch he carried in his breast pocket.

Mustafa Kemal and his Western-educated wife Latife Hanim embodied Turkey's move toward modern practices. ▶

TIME LINE

1881
Born in Salonika.

1915–16
In World War I thwarts Allies in Dardanelles. Promoted to general and fights on Russian front.

March 1917
Sent to Syria but resigns in disgust at state of army.

1918
Reinstated, sent to Syria. End of World War I.

1919
Establishes nationalist movement in Anatolia.

April 23 1920
Grand National Assembly in Ankara elects him as president.

November 1 1922
Grand National Assembly votes to abolish Ottoman Sultanate.

November 17 1922
Sultan Mehmed VI escapes into exile.

October 2 1923
Nationalists occupy Istanbul.

October 29 1923
Turkish republic proclaimed, with Mustafa as president.

March 3 1924
Ottoman caliphate abolished.

February 1925
Defeats revolts by Kurds in Anatolia.

June 5 1926
Signs peace treaty with Great Britain.

December 30 1930
Signs treaty of friendship with Greece.

1934
Takes surname of Atatürk.

November 10 1938
Dies, Istanbul.

In 1919 he took history by the scruff of the neck, establishing himself as leader of a Turkish nationalist revolt, based in Anatolia, against the peace terms the Allies were imposing on Ottoman Turkey. The next year he set up a provisional government in Ankara and, after the Ottoman sultanate was abolished and Sultan Mehmed VI fled into exile in 1922, he and the nationalists occupied Istanbul and declared the Turkish republic with Mustafa as president.

REVOLUTIONARY

The new regime immediately embarked on its modernization program, based on six main goals: Republicanism, nationalism, populism, the establishment of state-owned and operated industry, secularism, and revolution. The country was to be in a permanent revolution—a state of change and development. Mustafa Kemal's revolutionary aim was to make the Turks forward- and outward-looking,

FATHER FIGURE

Mustafa Kemal's central quality as a leader was that he was more interested in the long-term future of his country than in his own glory and achievements. As a leader, he was a builder—and his achievement was the establishment of a new Turkey, at peace with its neighbors, well connected to Europe, and confident in its own status. His standing as his country's educator and role model was recognized in the surname he was given by the national assembly in 1934: Atatürk, "Father of the Turks."

to equip them to take their place in the fast-developing world of the twentieth century. He saw that the introduction of the Latin alphabet was key to this program and to the development of education in Turkey because it encouraged students to open themselves to Western learning.

EMBODIED FREEDOM

Mustafa Kemal had a direct relationship with the people he led, inspiring their urge to freedom and always leading by example. In 1925 the government outlawed the customary wearing of the fez, a red felt-hat in the shape of short, cut-off cone traditionally associated with the Ottoman civil service and military. As he would repeat in 1928 to promote teaching of the Latin alphabet, Mustafa Kemal embarked on a tour of the country, this time sporting a European-style hat of the kind people were now being urged to wear.

A key part of the modernization program was the emancipation of women. In the new law code introduced in 1926, polygamy—a man's right to have several wives, traditional in Ottoman society—was abolished. Marriage and divorce were established as matters covered under civil rather than religious laws.

Mustafa Kemal was again at the forefront of change: He married a Western-educated Turkish woman, Latife Hanim, who had studied law in Paris and London. In the first two years of the republic she was prominent in public life as First Lady at Mustafa Kemal's side: She went about bareheaded, eschewing the headdress traditionally worn by Muslim women and encouraging forward-looking Turkish women to follow her example. The couple divorced in 1925, taking advantage of another modern freedom made possible by the new secular government.

Women gained the right to vote for and stand as members of Parliament in December 1934. That same year Western-style surnames were introduced.

FOUNDER OF A MODERN NATION

Mustafa Kemal set Turkey's new secular republic on firm foundations. He established rule by a single party and pursued neutrality in international affairs, reaching largely friendly relations with foreign powers. He was a man of character, modesty, and great foresight. When he died on November 10 1938, there was a vast outpouring of grief in Turkey and tributes poured in from around the world. Winston Churchill called him a "great hero," while US General Douglas McArthur declared him "one of the greatest leaders of our era. He ensured that Turkey got its rightful place among the most advanced nations of the world."

LEADERSHIP ANALYSIS

LEADER TYPE: *Reformer*
KEY QUALITIES: *Revolutionary, foresighted*
LIKEMINDED LEADERS: *Fidel Castro, Mohandas Gandhi*
FACT: *Atatürk won 24 military awards including the French Légion d'honneur (1914) and the German Iron Cross (1915).*

PABLO PICASSO

ENERGETIC AND PROLIFIC ARTIST WHO CONSISTENTLY CHALLENGED THE LIMITS OF ART

NATIONALITY: *Spanish*
ACHIEVEMENT: *Leader of Cubist art movement*
WHEN: *1907–11*

With his French artist friend Georges Braque, the omni-talented Spaniard Pablo Picasso took painting, dismantled it, put it back together, and created modern art—establishing himself as leader of the avant-garde.

In late 1907, several leading artists visited Pablo Picasso's studio in Paris to view his latest and profoundly shocking painting *The Brothel of Avignon* (later known as *Les Demoiselles d'Avignon—The Young Ladies of Avignon*). In *The Young Ladies* Picasso abandoned traditional perspective to produce a stylized, resolutely two-dimensional image in which he represented five prostitutes in a number of jarring and fragmented views. He developed the technique further in works such as *The Reservoir*, *Horta de Ebro*, painted in the summer of 1909 in southern Spain, using geometric shapes to represent buildings and landscapes from a number of perspectives. The profoundly ambitious, endlessly innovative Picasso was at the cutting edge of a new way of representing reality.

Alongside Georges Braque, Picasso became leader of Cubism—arguably the most influential art movement of the twentieth century. Cubist artists rejected techniques such as perspective and foreshortening that are used to give the illusion of a three-dimensional image, instead emphasizing the two-dimensional reality of the canvas, breaking up the objects they represented into geometric forms and using multiple points of view. The movement's name came from a review by critic Louis Vauxcelles of Braque's 1908 oil painting *The Houses at L'Estaque* in which Vauxcelles referred to "bizarreries cubiques" (cubic oddities). Picasso and Braque developed the new style in 1907–11 but did not exhibit in the first formal exhibition by Cubist artists such as Jean Metzinger and Albert Gleizes at the Salon des Indépendants in spring 1911.

Picasso was an arch-innovator. From this early form of Cubism, he and Braque drove on after 1910 to an even more abstract style. First Picasso created paintings that consisted of an arrangement of geometric shapes, in which the object represented was barely if at all discernible—for example, his *Still Life With a Bottle of Rum*, painted in the summer of 1911. Next he introduced papier collé—collage using glued papers, for example his *Man with a Hat and a Violin* of 1912, which incorporates strips of newspaper. He was leading the way in contemporary art; other artists had to take notice of where he went.

ENERGETIC, CREATIVE

Before his engagement with Cubism, Picasso had already demonstrated immense creativity and innovative energy. The son of a professor of drawing, he had studied under his father. He had his first exhibition aged just 13 and in 1900 had the honor of having his painting *Last Moments* shown in the Spanish section of the Universal Exhibition in Paris.

After the suicide of his friend Carlos Casagemas, he entered what is known as his "Blue Period," so called for his use of blue as the predominant color in all his work of 1901–04. This was followed by his "Rose Period" of 1904–1906, the beginning of which coincided with his permanent move to Paris.

OPPORTUNIST

Living in Paris in the early twentieth century, he was at the very heart of modern art and capitalized on every opportunity. Connections paved his path to greatness. Through Dutch writer Tom Schilperoort he met American writer and art collector Gertrude Stein in 1905, and through Stein was introduced to Henri Matisse in 1906. Indeed Picasso was quite the networker, opening himself up to a myriad of opportunities and inspirations.

This readiness to embrace all opportunities led to exciting collaborations for Picasso. Alongside his Cubist work, in 1917, he created sets and costumes for the ballet *Parade* with composer Erik Satie, poet Jean Cocteau, and the Ballets Russes of Sergei Diaghilev. He later carried on his association with the Ballets Russes, creating designs for Igor Stravinky's *Pulcinella* (1920) and others. In the 1920s and 1930s Picasso met the French writer and poet André Breton, pioneer of the artistic movement of Surrealism. This meeting resulted in the development of important links with Surrealism for Picasso who, though he never aligned himself with the movement, was profoundly influenced by its ideas.

INNOVATOR

Throughout his long career Picasso regularly changed style and approach, often taking his cue from events that inspired him. When the Spanish Civil War broke out in 1936 he produced work for sale in support of the Republicans, whom he enthusiastically backed in their struggle against the Nationalists under General Francisco Franco. In 1937 he painted the vast canvas *Guernica*, probably his most celebrated work, to commemorate the suffering caused by the bombing of the Basque town of that name.

PICASSO'S ESTIMATED PORTFOLIO

1 3 5 0 0
PAINTINGS

1 0 0 0 0 0
GRAPHIC PRINTS OR ENGRAVINGS

3 4 0 0 0
BOOK ILLUSTRATIONS

3 0 0
SCULPTURES AND CERAMICS

TIME LINE

October 25 1881
Born in Málaga, Spain.

1894
First exhibition, A Coruña.

1901–04
Blue Period.

1904–06
Rose Period.

1907–11
Develops Cubism.

May 1917
Picasso designs sets and costumes for ballet Parade.

1919
Creates designs for Ballet Russes' Three Cornered Hat.

1923
Meets leading surrealist André Breton.

1935
Devotes his time to writing poetry and making prints.

1937
Produces The Dream and Lie of Franco *to support Republicans in Spanish Civil War.*

April 26 1937
Bombing of Guernica inspires his painting of that name.

1941
Writes Surrealist play Desire Caught by the Tail.

1944
Joins Communist Party.

1946
Fifty-year retrospective at MOMA, New York City.

1966
Designs Cubist sculpture for Daley Plaza, Chicago.

April 8 1973
Dies at Mougins, France.

After World War II, living mostly in the south of France, he took a new artistic direction again—in the 1950s creating a series of works based on those of historical artists including Francisco Goya, Diego Velázquez, and Eugène Delacroix, and in the late 1960s producing paintings and etchings that pointed the way to the neo-Impressionist style that emerged after his death. Ever productive, Picasso carried on working right to the end of his life in 1973.

UNPREDICTABLE

Many artists, such as Picasso's friend Georges Braque or early rival Henri Matisse, develop a style and stick to it, more or less, for the remainder of their career—to that extent they are predictable. Picasso's changes of approach meant that he stayed consistently ahead of people's expectations and kept his work in the

MULTISTYLING?

Picasso worked on more conventional, naturalist paintings alongside his avant-garde Cubist canvases. Throughout his life he was able to work simultaneously in different styles. He said he was not finding his way toward some perfect form of painting—he chose the style that best suited the subject. Leaders benefit from being open in this way—keeping themselves alive to several opportunities or possible outcomes or ways of leading a group; not closing down options. Likewise leaders will benefit from adapting their style or approach to different challenges.

public eye. It was this freshness of approach and continual innovation that kept Picasso as the forefront of the development of modern art throughout his life.

Picasso was enormously productive producing works across different medias and exploring style, approach, and form. Like another creative powerhouse, William Shakespeare, Picasso was highly ambitious, alert to opportunity—and courageous enough to seize it. He was powerfully engaged with his work. He rarely used professional models, instead working with people with whom he felt a strong connection—often his mistresses. He had the immense creative energy of a William Morris and, like Morris, he worked in several different media. Picasso was most famous as a painter, but also made drawings, ceramics, sculpture, and tapestries, and wrote poetry. Tirelessly creative, Picasso has stubbornly defied categorization due to his phenomenal achievements across so many artistic fields. He is remembered as a towering figure of the twentieth century, pioneer of the mold-breaking movement of Cubism, and, through a whole series of other artistic engagements and innovations, a leader for artists to the modern day.

▲ *Picasso was introduced to many influential people through Gertrude Stein, shown here in her salon which was decorated with artwork from her many protégés.*

LEADERSHIP ANALYSIS

LEADER TYPE: *Innovator*
KEY QUALITIES: *Passionate, creative, brave*
LIKEMINDED LEADERS: *William Shakespeare, William Morris*
FACT: *At his death Picasso owned 50,000 pieces of his own work, which passed to his heirs and to the French state.*

FRANKLIN D. ROOSEVELT

RESILIENT REFORMER WHO PUT AMERICA BACK ON ITS FEET

NATIONALITY: *American*
ACHIEVEMENT: *Four times US president, led his country through the Great Depression and World War II*
WHEN: *1932-45*

President Franklin D. Roosevelt led the United States through the Great Depression and the greater part of World War II—two of his country's darkest periods. He was a gifted communicator and administrator who built and maintained a coalition of support for his sometimes unpopular policies.

In his inaugural address as president on March 4 1933 Franklin D. Roosevelt defied the economic problems of the Great Depression, declaring "This great nation will endure as it has endured, will revive and prosper ... the only thing we have to fear is fear itself." This resilient and serious-minded leader was at his inspirational best as he transmitted his determination and self-confidence to the nation.

Franklin D. Roosevelt—F.D.R.—knew all about recovery. He had come back from a potentially career-ending bout of poliomyelitis that left him unable to walk without a cane or brace to win the presidential election in 1932. He had campaigned on the promise of a "New Deal" for the "forgotten man" who was suffering the consequences of an economic crisis that, by the time of his inauguration, had reduced industrial production to only 56 percent of its level before the depression hit, leaving 13 million people unemployed.

AMBITIOUS AND DRIVEN

F.D.R. was inspired to enter politics by his cousin, Theodore Roosevelt, who served as twenty-sixth president of the United States from 1901 to 1909. Franklin fell in love with and married Theodore's niece, Eleanor, when she was involved in charitable work helping the poor of New York City. After studying at Harvard and Columbia University Law School, F.D.R. began work in a law firm in Wall Street, New York, and then in 1910 at the age of 28 he won a senate seat as a Democrat in a strongly

Roosevelt signs the declaration of war against Germany and Italy on December 11 1941—three days after declaring war on Japan. ▶

TIME LINE

January 30 1882
Born, Hyde Park, New York.

1910
Elected to New York state senate.

1913
Assistant Secretary to the Navy.

1920
Runs unsuccessfully as vice-president.

1928
Elected Governor of New York.

November 1932
Elected US president.

1933
First "fireside chat" radio broadcast.

1933–39
New Deal.

November 1936
Re-elected US president.

November 1940
Elected US president for a third time.

December 1941
Japan attacks Pearl Harbor. US enters World War II.

November 28–December 1 1943
Tehran Conference of F.D.R., Churchill, and Stalin.

November 1944
Elected US president for fourth time.

February 4–11 1945
Yalta Conference of F.D.R., Churchill, and Stalin.

April 12 1945
Dies, Warm Springs, Georgia.

Republican area of New York state. He was tall and handsome, with immense vitality—and already appeared to have a great political future. His friends talked of him as a future US president, and he himself expressed this ambition as early as 1907.

He had a good political education in the New York senate and proved himself an effective administrator as Assistant Secretary to the Navy under President Woodrow Wilson. Then in 1921 polio struck while he was on vacation in New Brunswick, Canada. For a while he was completely paralyzed, but while his mother urged him to retire from public life he and his wife Eleanor were determined to maintain his career.

REFORMER

By 1928 he was back. He won election as governor of New York state, again succeeding as a Democrat in the face of strong pro-Republican feeling. F.D.R. was re-elected state governor in 1930 and as the economic depression worsened he anticipated the New Deal reforms he would introduce as president by taking steps as governor to provide relief and stimulate economic recovery.

The New Deal itself was implemented from 1933 to 1939 and greatly increased the role of the federal government. The Public Works Administration unleashed $3.3 billion to fund public works and the Civilian Conservation Corps created temporary jobs in reforestation and flood control. The Agricultural Adjustment Administration set out to raise prices for staple products by paying farmers cash subsidies to limit production.

A social security program delivered payments in old age and for widows, disability insurance, and help for the unemployed. The Works

THE GREAT DEPRESSION

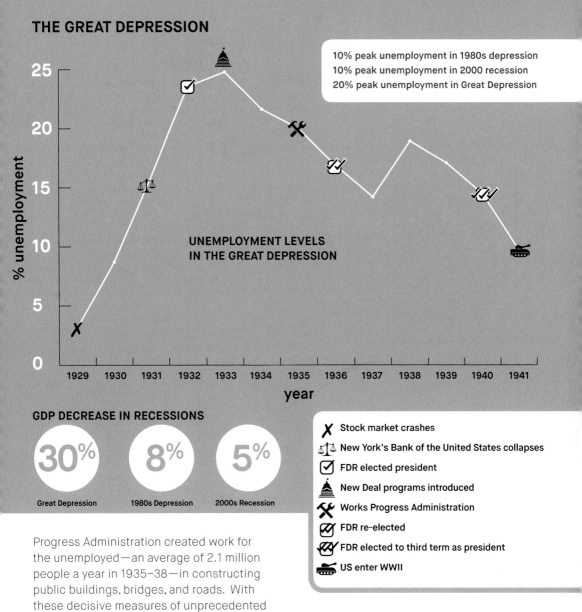

10% peak unemployment in 1980s depression
10% peak unemployment in 2000 recession
20% peak unemployment in Great Depression

% unemployment

25

20

15

10

5

0

1929 1930 1931 1932 1933 1934 1935 1936 1937 1938 1939 1940 1941

year

UNEMPLOYMENT LEVELS
IN THE GREAT DEPRESSION

GDP DECREASE IN RECESSIONS

30%
Great Depression

8%
1980s Depression

5%
2000s Recession

X Stock market crashes

⚖ New York's Bank of the United States collapses

☑ FDR elected president

🏛 New Deal programs introduced

✖ Works Progress Administration

☑ FDR re-elected

☑☑ FDR elected to third term as president

🚂 US enter WWII

Progress Administration created work for the unemployed—an average of 2.1 million people a year in 1935–38—in constructing public buildings, bridges, and roads. With these decisive measures of unprecedented federal intervention, F.D.R. helped to reinvigorate the US economy, and encouraged Americans across the country that they were on the road to recovery.

COMMUNICATOR OF COURAGE

F.D.R. was a skilled communicator. In a series of evening radio broadcasts from 1933–44—later known as fireside chats—F.D.R. explained his pioneering policy and, with a cheery voice and upbeat manner, inspired ordinary Americans. For his easy camaraderie with the general public he was likened to the great Abraham Lincoln (see page 108).

A *New York Times* editorial on his death highlighted his ability to inspire "free men ... with greater hope and courage" and praised the "fresh and spontaneous interest which this man took, as naturally as he breathed air, in the troubles and the hardships and the disappointments and the hopes of little men and humble people." F.D.R. was seen as a man of the people. It was this quality that secured his crashing victories in an historic four successive presidential elections.

POLITICAL OPERATOR

By 1939 the main focus of F.D.R.'s presidency was foreign policy and the threat of global war. In the 1930s a strong strain of American opinion was virulently opposed to American involvement in any European conflict. After war broke out in September 1939 F.D.R. pushed against this isolationist block and in summer 1940, after the Nazi conquest of northern France left Britain isolated and apparently facing invasion, he won Congress' approval of an increase in defense preparations and an agreement to back Britain with "all aid short of war."

At this critical time F.D.R. was in the midst of a presidential campaign. He had been re-elected in 1936, and then in 1940 was nominated by the Democrats for a third term—despite the tradition, honored since the time of George Washington, that presidents should serve no more than two terms. Nonetheless, he triumphed once more, soundly defeating Republican nominee Wendell L. Willkie.

ADAPTABLE

F.D.R. was always willing to experiment. He tried many cures for polio and a range of remedies for the intransigent problems of the Great Depression. In this he was similar to his great ally of the war years, British Prime Minister Winston Churchill who was famous for a pragmatic wartime strategy. F.D.R. was also a great builder of consensus: Like Churchill's successor in Britain, Clement Attlee, he was able to persuade others to buy into his ideas and convinced potentially incompatible people to work effectively for him (see page 164).

Another trait shared with Attlee was F.D.R's capacity to make a decision and then put it aside. As wartime leader he often went to bed late after making important judgments. Of dealing with such responsibility he simply said: "I think of the things that have come before me during the day and the decisions that I have made, I say to myself—well, I have done the best I could and turn over and go to sleep."

WAR LEADER

Back in office he did what he could to support beleaguered Europe, in March 1941 overseeing the passage of the Lend-Lease Act, under which the United States provided weapons and military equipment to the Allies without requiring cash payment and in return for "direct or indirect benefit which the President deems satisfactory." Then in August 1941 he met British leader Winston Churchill on a battleship moored off Newfoundland and agreed The Atlantic Charter that committed the United States and Britain to "the final destruction of Nazi tyranny." By the end of the year, the United States was at war with Japan, Germany, and Italy following the Japanese attack on Pearl Harbor, Hawaii, on December 7 1941.

▲ *In 1945 F.D.R. laid the foundations for postwar US relations with Saudi Arabia, meeting Saudi king Adbulaziz on board USS Quincy in Egypt.*

At war, F.D.R. was at the forefront of the international alliance against the Axis powers. He held a series of conferences with British Prime Minister Winston Churchill and Soviet leader Joseph Stalin. In the midst of the conflict he won a fourth straight election victory, despite failing health, conducting a energetic campaign and defeating Republican candidate Thomas E. Dewey in 1944.

However, Roosevelt did not live to see victory in World War II. He died after suffering a cerebral hemorrhage on April 12 1945. Grief swept the nation. His successor Harry S. Truman dedicated Victory in Europe celebrations to his memory and said his greatest wish was that Roosevelt had lived to see and celebrate the victory. This extraordinary politician—the only president to be elected four times and the man who had carried the country through the profound challenges of the Great Depression and World War II—was hailed immediately as one of the United States' greatest ever leaders. The *New York Times* wrote: "Men will thank God on their knees a hundred years from now that Franklin D. Roosevelt was in the White House."

LEADERSHIP ANALYSIS

LEADER TYPE: *Collaborative*
KEY QUALITIES: *Courageous, charismatic*
LIKEMINDED LEADERS: *Winston Churchill, Clement Attlee*
FACT: *"I have no expectation of making a hit every time I come to bat,"* F.D.R. said. *"What I seek is the highest possible batting average."*

CLEMENT ATTLEE

CONSENSUS BUILDER WHO CREATED A WELFARE STATE AND STEERED BRITAIN INTO THE POSTWAR WORLD

NATIONALITY: *British*
ACHIEVEMENT: *Oversaw the creation of the welfare state, including the NHS*
WHEN: *1945-51*

British Prime Minister Clement Attlee oversaw the creation of the National Health Service (NHS) and the breaking up of the empire in six postwar years. A highly effective if sometimes unglamorous leader, he managed sweeping change and delivered a political consensus that lasted decades.

Prime Minister Clement Attlee spoke clearly into the microphone as he explained the operations of the new Social Services scheme, on July 4 1948. He declared "Tomorrow there will come into operation the most comprehensive system of social security ever introduced into any country." The scheme, which incorporated the new National Health Service, was "available to every citizen ... designed to cover you and your family throughout your life."

Some leaders are charismatic figures or have a gift for publicizing themselves and their achievements. Others are simply good at delivering results. They have a gift for getting people to work together and for getting things done. Clement Attlee was of the second type. One of his principal gifts was an ability to build and maintain consensus.

In his 1948 broadcast he emphasized a need for political unity, declaring that in building up the social security scheme "all parties in the state have borne their part." In this way, he claimed, the new scheme was brought in with "the approval of the nation." He continued, "We may be proud that Britain, which has given the lead in so many things to the world, is still in the forefront of social advance."

LOYAL, SELF-EFFACING
Attlee said of himself that he had "none of the qualities that create publicity." The son of a solicitor, he was from a comfortably off middle-class family and he did not try to reinvent himself. His political views were shaped, after an education at British public school Haileybury College and University College, Oxford, by the years he spent working in Stepney, in the impoverished East End of London, from 1905 onward. He joined the Independent Labour Party, and after serving in Gallipoli, Iraq, and France in World War I, he was elected MP for the East End Limehouse constituency in 1922.

His experience in Stepney and the army gave him confidence in his ability and his judgment. He was patriotic and dutiful, loyal, self-sufficient, never impulsive—a

▲ Attlee with US President Harry S. Truman and Soviet leader Joseph Stalin at the Potsdam Conference, 1945.

man of measured judgments. This enabled him to function effectively, even under the high pressure of being prime minister in a country devastated by war, to drive through the establishment of the welfare state and to deftly manage the dismantlement of the empire. Asked how he coped, he replied "By not worrying ... You take a decision and have done with it. No good keeping on asking yourself if you've done the right thing." An approach he shared with US President Franklin D. Roosevelt (see page 158), this ability to set work aside, even while taking responsibilities very seriously, can be immensely valuable for leaders: It allows them to keep a clear head and make considered decisions.

LUCKY?

Attlee had good judgment—and timing. He knew when to hold back and when to deliver. He believed that an essential quality needed in a good prime minister was "a sense of the time and the occasion and the atmosphere of the country." Attlee understood that the ability to gauge the response of your counterparts in a meeting or negotiation can make the difference between success and failure. He regarded this kind of political judgment as distinct from "intellectual power" and "often quite divorced from it." He added: "A lot of clever people have got everything except judgment."

In addition to his impeccable timing and sensitivity to the mood of the room, Attlee seems to have had another quality that is often found in great leaders—a degree of good fortune. In the election of October 1931 the Labour Party suffered a collapse. Attlee kept hold of his seat in Limehouse by a slim margin of 550 votes, but other notable politicians such as Arthur Greenwood and Herbert Morrison lost their seats. Their removal probably eased his rise to the leadership of the party. He became deputy leader to George Lansbury in 1931 and leader in 1935 when Lansbury

TIME LINE

January 3 1883
Born, Putney, London.

1919
Mayor of Stepney.

1922
Elected MP for Stepney.

1924
Undersecretary of State for War.

1931
Labour Party deputy leader.

1935
Labour Party leader.

1940
Lord Privy Seal in war government.

1942
Deputy prime minister.

1945
Prime minister.

August 15 1947
Indian independence is granted.

January 4 1948
Burma becomes independent.

July 4 1948
Explains Social Service and NHS in radio broadcast.

July 5 1948
Launch of National Health Service.

1951
Leader of the opposition.

1955
Enters House of Lords.

October 8 1967
Dies, Westminster, London.

resigned; Morrison or Greenwood might have been chosen ahead of him at this point if they had been members of Parliament.

MAKING AND MAINTAINING LINKS

After serving in the coalition government led by Winston Churchill in World War II, Attlee delivered a crushing victory for the Labour Party in 1945, winning 393 seats in the House of Commons, a majority of 145. Even in the face of this electoral victory, this consensual leader notably avoided triumphalism in his behavior and speeches as prime minister. In his new role he was measured and reliable—as his performance had been in World War II coalition. He took great care to maintain good relations across the Atlantic, reassuring the United States that the Labour government's social welfare program was a long way away from communism.

The political consensus Attlee and his government built lasted from the immediate postwar period right through the 1950s, 60s, and 70s until it was partly dismantled by the divisive government of Margaret Thatcher. Yet even then the NHS has remained a much-cherished product of his administration in Britain. His kind of consensual leadership was exhibited in the United States by the great war leader Franklin D. Roosevelt. Winston Churchill famously dismissed Attlee as "a modest man ... with plenty to be modest about," yet Attlee was a tremendously effective leader whose government oversaw major change that transformed the face of postwar Britain.

ATTLEE'S ROUND TABLE POLITICS

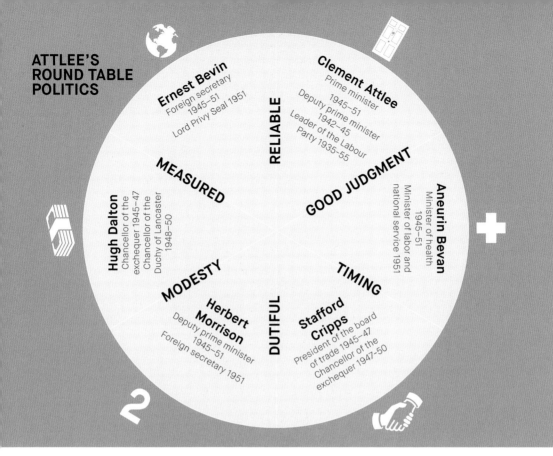

Ernest Bevin
Foreign secretary
1945–51
Lord Privy Seal 1951

Clement Attlee
Prime minister
1945–51
Deputy prime minister
1942–45
Leader of the Labour
Party 1935–55

RELIABLE

MEASURED

GOOD JUDGMENT

Hugh Dalton
Chancellor of the
exchequer 1945–47
Chancellor of the
Duchy of Lancaster
1948–50

Aneurin Bevan
Minister of health
1945–51
Minister of labor and
national service 1951

MODESTY

TIMING

DUTIFUL

Herbert Morrison
Deputy prime minister
1945–51
Foreign secretary 1951

Stafford Cripps
President of the board
of trade 1945–47
Chancellor of the
exchequer 1947–50

MANAGING ABILITY

Attlee was skilled at managing and getting the best out of very able colleagues—men such as Aneurin Bevan, Ernest Bevin, Hugh Dalton, Herbert Morrison, and Stafford Cripps. Good team management is central to effective leadership. Attlee had firm control of discussions in the Cabinet and an ability to come to decisions quickly. During World War II, indeed, he was known for much better management of committees than Churchill—where Churchill often oversaw thrilling debates with no clear outcome, Attlee led his committees to quick and clear decisions.

LEADERSHIP ANALYSIS

LEADER TYPE: *Collaborative*
KEY QUALITIES: *Modest*
LIKEMINDED LEADERS: *Harry S. Truman*
FACT: *Gandhi said Attlee was a good example of "the understatement which characterizes the best in Britain."*

LORD REITH

A FORCE TO BE RECKONED WITH, THE STERN LEADER WHO STEERED BBC RADIO TO INTERNATIONAL SUCCESS

NATIONALITY: *Scottish*
ACHIEVEMENT: *First Director General of the British Broadcasting Corporation; established BBC World Service Radio*
WHEN: *1927-38*

The forbidding son of a Scottish church minister, Lord Reith combined a brusque manner with boundless energy in overseeing the establishment of the British Broadcasting Corporation (BBC) in the 1920s and 30s. But the defining characteristic of his leadership and management was his high-minded approach that demanded broadcasters inform and educate as well as entertain.

The first issue of *Radio Times*, dated September 28 1923, was a triumphant success—its print run of 285,000 completely sold out. John Reith had been in his position as General Manager of the British Broadcasting Company for less than a year. When he discovered that newspapers refused to carry free listings of the timings of radio programs—the newspaper magnates were nervous of the upstart medium of radio—Reith came up with the idea of publishing a standalone magazine: The *Radio Times* was born.

The British Broadcasting Company was set up by a group of radio manufacturers to make programs that would boost popularity of their equipment. Reith had known nothing of broadcasting when he applied for the job of General Manager the previous year. But with steely determination he set about making the job his own and ensuring success.

FULL OF DRIVE

After appointing a highly able personal secretary, Isobel Shields, Reith hit the ground running, full of energy and drive. He made quick decisions and managed problems effectively. The directors of the BBC gave him a free hand—Reith reported that he was told at his interview, "We're leaving it all to you. You'll be reporting at our monthly meetings and we'll see how you're getting on."

Reith was a somewhat stern figure. His religious upbringing fed into the view he quickly formed of radio broadcasting—that it should not only entertain, but also educate and inform. The approach worked. Listener numbers were rising fast and sales of wirelesses (radio sets) were making money for the manufacturers.

Central to the success of this approach was the fact that the British Broadcasting Company was a monopoly. With its licence coming to its end (at the close of 1926), Reith proposed the creation of the British Broadcasting Corporation, a public corporation run on a day-to-day level by its managers, but overseen by a board of governors who would

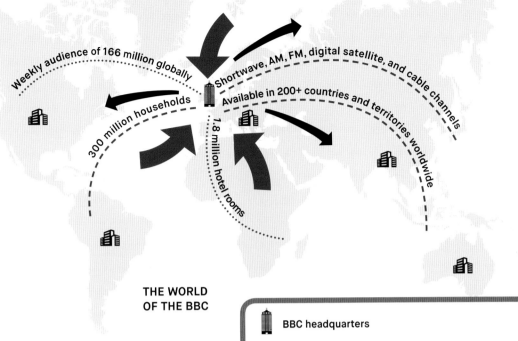

**THE WORLD
OF THE BBC**

🏢	BBC headquarters
🏢	BBC Worldwide: Offices in North & South America, Europe, Asia and Australasia
·········	BBC World Service
– – –	BBC World News
◀	⅔ of revenue comes from outside the UK
◀	Broadcasts in 28 languages

put the public interest above commercial considerations. This plan came to fruition in 1927 and Reith was made Director General of the new corporation; he also received a knighthood for his endeavors.

His performance—and that of the British Broadcasting Company—during the General Strike of 1926 had played an important role in bringing about this outcome. Reith had to fight against Winston Churchill, then chancellor of the exchequer, to maintain the broadcaster's independence from government influence; he had the support of Prime Minister Stanley Baldwin, who trusted Reith to follow the right path, and in the course of the dispute the BBC was established as the source of impartial news.

FORCE COMMANDS LOYALTY

The Director General was a force to be reckoned with at the corporation. He had an often difficult relationship with the governors and he gained a reputation for ruling, in the words of Clement Attlee "a little by fear." In the 1930s—as dictators arose in continental Europe—this led to unflattering comparisons: Nancy Astor, MP, referred to Reith's "Mussolini tendencies," while her fellow Member of Parliament George Lansbury suggested that Reith would have been "a very excellent Hitler for his country."

Yet in 1934 when Reith appeared before a committee of Conservative MPs and came under attack from the press, 800 members of BBC staff signed an official letter

July 20 1889
Born John Charles Walsham Reith in Scotland.

1914–15
Serves in Fifth Scottish Rifles, World War I.

1915–17
Supervises armament manufacture in United States.

1920–22
General manager of an engineering firm in Glasgow.

1922–27
General Manager, BBC.

1927–38
Director General, BBC.

1936
Launches BBC World Service.

1938
Chairman of Imperial Airways.

1940
Made Baron Reith of Stonehaven.

1940
Government minister of information.

1943–45
Director Combined Operations Material at the Admiralty.

1946–50
Chairman Commonwealth Telecommunications Board.

1948
BBC Reith Lectures founded.

1965–68
Lord Rector, Glasgow University.

1967–68
Lord High Commissioner to General Assembly of Church of Scotland.

June 16 1971
Dies, Edinburgh.

stating they were "disgusted" by "false and malignant statements" in the press and wanted "to reaffirm their loyalty and gratitude to the Director General." His forceful management style commanded utter devotion.

PRODIGIOUS ENERGY

In 1938 Reith was offered a new job as General Manager of Imperial Airways by Prime Minister Neville Chamberlain; he did not put up a struggle to stay at the BBC and indeed had previously made comments suggesting he was looking for a new challenge. But Reith appears to have regretted leaving the BBC for the rest of his life. In 1960 after appearing on BBC interview show *Face to Face* he signed

MORAL LEADER

Reith's values were strict. After the success of Radio Times *in 1923, the directors of the BBC offered Reith a share in its financial profits but he refused, saying that he had a moral responsibility not to make money from the publication. Later, when Director General, he terminated the contract of BBC chief engineer Peter Eckersley because he had conducted marital infidelities in public. Eckersley later commented: "I happened to come under the control of that rare individual who acts according to his spiritual convictions." Under Reith's rule, BBC radio did not start broadcasting on Sunday until 12:30pm, so that it would not prevent people from going to church; and for the rest of the day avoided light-hearted distractions, concentrating on classical music and religious programming.*

John Reith carried the strict Presbyterian values of his upbringing into adult life as a leader in the world of broadcasting.

the visitors' book, "John Charles Walsham Reith, late BBC and regrets he ever left it."

Although he had a series of important and high-ranking positions, he never fully found an outlet for his prodigious energy that suited him as well as being Director General. In 1950 he wrote to Prime Minister Clement Attlee, "Isn't there some big job you would like me to do? I could do such a lot, you know."

His lasting legacy lay in his work at the BBC. The approach he established—that broadcasters should combine education and information with entertainment—became enduringly associated with his name. The "Reithian values" have informed public service broadcasting and remain an important element of debates about the future of television, radio, and other broadcast media.

LEADERSHIP ANALYSIS

LEADER TYPE: *Combative*
KEY QUALITIES: *Prodigiously energetic, high-minded*
LIKEMINDED LEADERS: *Queen Victoria.*
FACT: *He likened rival (commercial) channel ITV to the "bubonic plague."*

CHARLES DE GAULLE

DETERMINED FRENCH PATRIOT WHO FOUGHT ON AFTER THE FALL OF FRANCE IN WORLD WAR II

NATIONALITY: *French*
ACHIEVEMENT: *Led Free French government in exile in World War II*
WHEN: *1940–44*

Charles de Gaulle was the proud and driven leader of the Free French forces in exile during World War II, and brought military toughness and independence of mind to his later life as statesman and president of the Fifth French Republic.

French Brigadier General Charles de Gaulle sat before a BBC Radio microphone on June 18 1940 and called on his countrymen not to give up after the previous month's German occupation of France. He showed all the combative self-confidence that typified his later career in getting this speech—one of the most celebrated in French history—on air at all.

De Gaulle had secretly flown from France to London on June 17 determined to establish himself as leader of the "Free French" in opposition to his country's new government. Nazi Germany's Blitzkrieg assault had brought France to its knees. A government under World War I hero Marshal Philippe Pétain was formed on June 16 and was set to sign an armistice with the Germans. Under the eventual agreement the part of France unoccupied by the Nazis was controlled by the Vichy administration (named after the town in central France in which it was based) under Pétain.

De Gaulle did not have much to support his claim to be leader of all Frenchmen outside France—he was little known either in Britain or in France; he was already 50 years old and his military record, while satisfactory, was not outstanding. But with unflinching confidence he presented himself as the ideal man. He had made sure he was in the right place and he persuaded British Prime Minister Winston Churchill that this was the right time.

INSPIRATIONAL

Before his speech, according to eyewitnesses, de Gaulle appeared tense, as if summoning all his powers to concentrate them in this historic moment. He spoke loudly, in the tone of a general addressing troops before battle. In the speech de Gaulle declared, "Is defeat complete? No! ... For France is not alone! She is not alone! She is not alone!" He called on French soldiers, engineers, and armaments workers who were outside France to make contact with him. He added, "the fire of French resistance must not be stamped out and will not be stamped out." Churchill had given permission for one broadcast, but de Gaulle finished with a promise to

▲ Banners celebrating de Gaulle can be seen among the crowds celebrating the liberation of Paris.

make another the next night. There was little that Churchill or other government members—who were nervous of alienating the Vichy government while they still had hopes of gaining access to the French navy—could do to prevent it.

As promised, De Gaulle spoke again on June 19. Declaring that he was speaking for France he urged that armed Frenchmen had a duty to fight. He made a third, even bolder speech on June 22. In a feat of bravado de Gaulle had commandeered the airwaves and confirmed himself as leader of the Free French.

PRAGMATIC

Little by little the Free French—later known as Fighting France—became established and de Gaulle cemented his position as leader. Having made his home in London he was proud and often prickly, refusing to ingratiate himself with his British hosts. He once told Winston Churchill over the telephone that the French thought de Gaulle to be a reincarnation of Joan of Arc, the fifteenth-century French freedom fighter against the English. This was part of a successful strategy to maintain as strong a position as possible in his role of leader. He presented his presence in London as leader of the French as a simple fact, not a negotiable proposition.

In May 1943 the base of the Free French was moved from London to Algiers. Initially de Gaulle had to share power with General Henri Giraud, but when Giraud left for a visit to the United States de Gaulle showed considerable political maneuvering skills in ousting Giraud and re-establishing himself in sole charge of the newly created French Committee of National Liberation—the provisional government of a future liberated France.

TIME LINE

November 22 1890
Born Charles André Joseph Marie de Gaulle, in Lille.

1932
Lectures on leadership, "The Edge of the Sword."

June 18 1940
Broadcasts first appeal to Free French from London.

August 2 1940
In his absence sentenced to death by French military court.

1943
Free French headquarters is moved to Algiers.

August 1944
Paris liberated. De Gaulle makes triumphant return.

January 20 1946
Resigns as provisional president.

November 1946
Fourth French Republic.

1947
Forms Rassemblement du Peuple Français.

June 2 1958
Invested as prime minister.

December 21 1958
Elected president.

1962
Algeria becomes independent.

December 21 1965
Re-elected president.

1968
Crushes "student revolution."

April 28 1969
Resigns presidency.

November 9 1970
Dies, Colombey-les-deux-Églises.

LIBERATOR

As the tide of the war in Europe turned, Free French troops took part in the liberation of their country alongside Allied forces. On August 26 1944 de Gaulle rode in triumph down the Champs-Élysées in central Paris as the city was liberated. Some survivors of the Vichy regime who were still in the city shot at him both during this procession near the Place de la Concorde and as he entered Notre Dame Cathedral to be presented as head of a provisional government. Eyewitnesses described how he walked tall down the aisle despite several shots being fired—as if he had utter faith that he could not now be killed.

Afterward in the Hôtel de Ville a cheering crowd heard him make a grand speech:

> Paris! Paris outraged, Paris broken down, Paris made a martyr, but Paris set free! Set free by herself, set

LEADER OF ALL

Leaders like de Gaulle who have to control groups with diverse membership need particular skills in presenting themselves. De Gaulle's appeal was "À Tous les Français" ("To All Frenchmen") and while he himself was conservative and a practicing Roman Catholic he had to exercise command over communists. In this his insistence on the independence of his Free French movement from Britain and the United States was key, building unity among the French by emphasizing separateness from others fighting in largely the same cause.

free by her people with the help of the armies of France, with the backing and help of the whole of the country.

As he had done in London earlier in the war, he did his utmost to present the French as equals to the other Allies, far from a junior partner or grateful recipient of help, so he made no mention of the role of the British, Americans, and other Allies in the freeing of France.

DEFENDER OF FRANCE

In his postwar life as president of the Fifth French Republic from 1958 he exhibited much the same outspoken determination to exercise power on his own terms. His goal was to strengthen France's international position, opposing "Anglo-Saxon" influence, and to rule with presidential authority at home. He was, as always, unafraid of making enemies— twice vetoing Britain's membership of the European Economic Community in 1963 and 1967; withdrawing French troops from the NATO military alliance in 1966; and calling for neutrality with regard to the Vietnam War in 1966 and the Arab–Israeli War in 1967. By the late 1960s his stance began to cause unease in France and on April 28 1969 he resigned the presidency after defeat in a referendum on constitutional reform.

His bravery and confidence in so quickly establishing a base for resistance to the Vichy government in 1940 and his determined efforts to maintain the pride and status of France on the international stage will be forever remembered and celebrated—especially in France, where he is honored as one of the greatest national leaders in the country's history, a leader on a par with Napoleon Bonaparte or Charlemagne.

▲ *Charles de Gaulle strikes a defiant pose as leader of the "Free French" resistance in London in June 1940.*

LEADERSHIP ANALYSIS

LEADER TYPE: *Combative*
KEY QUALITIES: *Confident, combative, proud*
LIKEMINDED LEADERS: *Simón Bolívar, Fidel Castro, Margaret Thatcher*
FACT: *So many foreign dignitaries wanted to attend his funeral that a separate memorial was arranged to be held at the same time.*

41 MOTHER TERESA

THE NOBEL PEACE PRIZE WINNER WHO TOOK HER COMPASSION TO THE SLUMS OF KOLKATA

NATIONALITY: *Albanian*
ACHIEVEMENT: *Founded Missionaries of Charity to enable the sick, destitute, and dying to maintain dignity*
WHEN: *1948-97*

Mother Teresa—awarded the 1979 Nobel Prize for her work caring for the sick, dying, orphaned, and destitute—combined strongly-felt compassion with utmost determination. In founding and maintaining the Missionaries of Charity and opening schools, leper homes, and hospices for the "poorest of the poor," she demonstrated the power of selfless action driven by conviction.

On September 10 1946 Sister Teresa, an Albanian-born nun working as a teacher at a convent school in India, had a life-changing experience when she felt a call from God to leave her convent and help the poor while living among them. She recalled of the experience, "It was an order."

In 1948 she embarked on this work, initially following basic medical training then taking to the slums of Kolkata. She put away her nun's habit and began to wear a simple white cotton sari with a blue border that would eventually become the uniform of her order, the Missionaries of Charity.

SELF-BELIEF

In early 1949 her first followers joined her. They had to beg on the streets for food and supplies. Experiencing firsthand how hard poverty must be for the poor, Teresa wrote in her diary: "I thought how much they must ache in body and soul, looking for a home, food, and health." Though tempted to return to the relative comfort of her convent, full of conviction she chose to remain: "I did not let a single tear come." From the municipal authorities she gained possession of a former pilgrim hostel to use as her headquarters.

In these first months and years Teresa demonstrated the irrepressible self-belief and inner toughness so often required of those getting a new venture off the ground. In such challenging times, developing leaders have to determine whether they feel sufficiently committed to continue the project they are building: Teresa did so. Her commitment was to Jesus and to the poor. She showed the determined compassion that would be the hallmark of her leadership over decades. It was this strength of conviction that carried her to greatness.

On October 7 1950 she gained the approval of the pope to establish her venture as a diocesan congregation with a mission to care for "the hungry, the naked, the homeless,

▲ Mother Teresa with some of the children her establishment helped in Kolkata. She wears the blue-bordered cotton sari that identifies her missionaries.

the crippled, the blind, the lepers, all those people who feel unwanted, unloved, uncared for throughout society, people that have become a burden to society and are shunned by everyone." In 1952 she opened her first hospice for the dying, the Nirmal Hriday ("Home of the Pure-hearted") in Kolkata. As in treating the destitute and sick, her focus here was on the dignity of the human being. In the hospice people of different faiths—Christians, Muslims, and Hindus—were given access to their own rites. In Mother Teresa's words: the home was "for people who [had] lived like animals to die like angels—loved and wanted."

PRACTICAL OPTIMISM

As the Missionaries of Charity grew, Teresa pursued new ventures, opening a leper house, Shanti Nagar (Place of Peace) and several leprosy clinics, as well as a children's home, Nirmala Shishu Bhavan (Immaculate Heart Children's Home). In her work she was inspired by the compassionate outlook of Jesus and Saint Francis of Assisi, who himself worked tirelessly with lepers and the poor (see pages 30 and 62). Teresa also started to expand her work from Kolkata, throughout India and then around the world. The order

TIME LINE

August 26 1910
Born Anjezë Gonxhe Bojaxhiu in Skopje.

August 15 1928
Resolves to become a nun.

May 24 1931
Takes first religious vows as a nun.

1928–45
Teaches at order's school in Kolkata.

May 14 1937
Takes solemn vows as a nun.

1946
Experiences God's call to care for sick and poor.

1948
Founds Order of the Missionaries of Charity.

1952
Order opens first home for the dying, in Kolkata.

1955
Opens orphanage and home for homeless youth.

1963
Missionaries of Charity Brothers established.

1965
Order opens first house outside India, in Venezuela.

January 6 1971
Awarded Pope John XXIII Peace Prize.

1971
First house in the United States opens in the South Bronx.

1979
Receives Nobel Peace Prize.

September 5 1997
Dies in Kolkata, India.

October 19 2003
Beatified by Roman Catholic Church.

opened homes in many countries in Europe and Africa and in the United States.

The success of her work was an inspiration to many, not least Pope John Paul II. On February 3 1986 John Paul began a visit to Kolkata with a stop at the Nirmal Hriday, which he said bore witness to "the primacy of love." On October 19 2003 on the occasion of Teresa's beatification (her establishment among the "blessed," a precursor to being declared a saint), the same pope said, "I am personally grateful to this courageous woman whom I have always felt beside me ... Her life is a testimony to the dignity and the privilege of humble service."

INTERNATIONAL OUTLOOK

Like many committed to international work Teresa presented herself as standing in opposition to national boundaries. She declared "By blood, I am Albanian. By citizenship, an Indian. By faith, I am a Catholic nun. As to my calling, I belong to the world. As to my heart, I belong entirely to the Heart of Jesus." She was known to be a fluent speaker of five languages: Albanian, Serbian, English, Bengali, and Hindi. On her death Peruvian diplomat Javier Pérez de Cuéllar, former United Nations secretary general, said "She is the United Nations. She is peace to the world."

Always a devout Roman Catholic, Teresa provoked opposition in some quarters due to her unflinching loyalty to church doctrines that condemned divorce, contraception, and abortion. She exhibited a practical optimism in the face of such criticism: "No matter who says what, you should accept it with a smile and do your own work."

Teresa's health declined from 1983 after she suffered her first heart attack. She resigned as head of her order in 1990 but was near-unanimously re-elected—

MOTHER TERESA'S LEGACY

1948 **Works alone**

1949 **13 Followers**

number of
countries in which
Missionaries of
Charity are active

1997 **Missionaries of Charity has 4,000 sisters and an associate male order of 300 brothers**

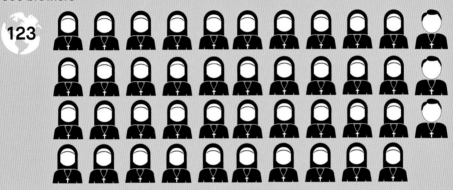

123

with her own vote the only dissenting one. Finally, on March 13 1997, just months before her death, her nuns finally had to accept her need to step down and she passed leadership of the order to Sister Nirmala Joshi.

DETERMINATION DESPITE DOUBT

After her death, the publication of Teresa's diaries revealed that she suffered a prolonged period of doubt and spiritual drought. She wrote "Where is my faith? Even deep down ... there is nothing but emptiness and darkness ..." Despite this she labored tirelessly in the service of the destitute and abandoned, demonstrating the force of her determination and the power of her compassion.

LEADERSHIP ANALYSIS

LEADER TYPE: *Leader by example*
KEY QUALITIES: *Self-confidence, empathy*
LIKEMINDED LEADERS: *Jesus of Nazareth, Saint Francis of Assisi, Mohandas Gandhi.*
FACT: *She took the name Teresa in 1928 to honor Saint Thérèse of Lisieux.*

42

VINCE LOMBARDI

CHARISMATIC LEADER WHO WAS THE ULTIMATE EXPONENT OF TEAMWORK AND DETERMINATION TO SUCCEED

NATIONALITY: *Italian-American*
ACHIEVEMENT: *Greatest American football coach*
WHEN: *1948–69*

Widely accepted as the greatest American football coach of all time, Vince Lombardi was famed for his single-minded determination to win, with a forceful emphasis on teamwork and the execution of simple plays. He made the Green Bay Packers the most successful team of the 1960s, winning five National Football League (NFL) championships in seven years in 1959–67.

On January 15 1967 the Green Bay Packers stormed to a 35–10 victory over the Kansas City Chiefs at the Los Angeles Memorial Coliseum. This was the first playoff between the American Football League and the National Football League: The original Super Bowl game that is now such a well-loved feature of American life.

Green Bay's triumph—built on the performance of veteran quarterback Bart Starr—was another feather in the cap of coach Vince Lombardi who had completely turned around the fortunes of the Packers when he was appointed head coach in 1959 after a disastrous 1958 season in which they had finished 1–10–1 (one win, ten losses, and one tie). Since then, he had led them to be NFL champions in 1961, 1962, 1965, and 1966.

WORKING TOGETHER FOR VICTORY

Lombardi's Italian-American background, devout Catholicism, and seemingly miraculous way with results won him the nickname "the pope." He declared that religious faith was liberating: "When we place our dependence in God, we are unencumbered ... This confidence, this sureness of action, is both contagious and an aid to the perfect action." In the individual he stressed the importance of character, toughness, and the will to win. Victory depended on individuals who embodied these characteristics coming together according to a well-executed plan—it depended on teamwork. Lombardi's whole coaching style was underpinned by the mantra: "People who work together will win."

The son of immigrants to the Bronx from Salerno, Italy, Lombardi was a devout child, and as a young man followed four years of a six-year training to become a Catholic priest. However, he decided against following that path and instead won a football scholarship to Fordham University, where in 1936 he was part of the "Seven Blocks of Granite," the Fordham's football team's formidable offensive unit.

He excelled in his first coaching job, at Saint Cecilia's Roman Catholic High School in Englewood, New Jersey, where he led the team to victory over Brooklyn Prep, a Jesuit school known to be one of the best school football teams on the US East Coast. After a brief stint coaching back at Fordham, he took what turned out to be a transformational step, accepting a position as assistant football coach at the United States Military Academy in West Point. Here he learned from head coach Earl Henry "Red" Blaik—always addressed as "the Colonel," Blaik imposed military discipline while also stressing the importance of organization.

PERFECT DISCIPLINE

Following in his mentor's footsteps Lombardi built the success of his teams on discipline—allied to drive and planning. He declared "There is only one kind of discipline, and that is the perfect discipline. As a leader, you must enforce and maintain that discipline; otherwise, you will fail at your job." He argued that the toughness needed for success was built on "a perfectly disciplined will that refuses to give in." His experience, he said, was that deep down people appreciated discipline—and its fruits.

▲ *Teaching tactics—Lombardi takes his players through the game during a team meeting, early 1960s.*

After West Point, Lombardi broke into professional football with a job as an assistant coach at the New York Giants in 1954–58, before being appointed as head coach of the Green Bay Packers in February 1959 and embarking on his dazzlingly successful career there. Once he had achieved pre-eminence as a coach, he spoke widely about the qualities and level of application necessary for success. His inspirational statements bear the mark of hard-won experience and are frequently quoted by business leaders and trainers even today.

COMMITMENT TO EXCELLENCE

Lombardi believed that the qualities needed to prevail were not innate: They could be developed. To be successful, a person had to make "a personal commitment to excellence and to victory"; you might never win the ultimate victory, but could work toward it with enthusiasm and perseverance day by day—"each week, there is a new encounter; each day, there is a new challenge." To win, players—and people in everyday life—needed to "give it everything."

TIME LINE

June 11 1913
Born in Brooklyn, New York.

1928
Aged 15, begins study for the priesthood.

1932
Quits training to be a priest.

1933
Wins football scholarship to Fordham University, the Bronx.

1939
Teacher and sports coach at Saint Cecilia High School in Englewood, New Jersey.

1947–48
Football and basketball coach at Fordham University.

1948–53
Assistant football coach at United States Military Academy in West Point. He learns from gifted coach Earl Henry "Red" Blaik.

1954–58
Assistant coach at New York Giants.

1959–67
Head coach, Green Bay Packers.

September 27 1959
First regular season Packers' game is a 9-6 win over Chicago Bears.

1959
NFL Coach of the Year.

1969
Head coach, Washington Redskins.

September 3 1970
Dies of colon cancer, Washington, D.C., aged 57.

1971
Inducted into Pro Football Hall of Fame.

At the Green Bay Packers Lombardi's remarkable record was 105–35–6 (105 wins, 35 losses, 6 ties) in 1959–67. He lost only one championship playoff game—in 1960 when the Packers were defeated 17–13 by the Philadelphia Eagles. This game ended as the Packers were just a few yards short of the goal line in a drive that would have won the match. After the game, Lombardi famously told his players, "This will never happen again. You will never lose another championship." A master at building team spirit, he exuded confidence and passed it on to his players.

After his stint at the Packers he became head coach and general manager of the Washington Redskins. Here he is widely regarded as having laid the groundwork for the success enjoyed by the Redskins in the 1970s, but he himself was not there to see it. He died on September 3 1970 aged just 57 and only months after learning that he had colon cancer. While on his sickbed he received a call from President Nixon, who promised that all America was behind him, in typical fashion Lombardi replied that he would never give up his fight against the illness. However, this was one fight he could not win.

Lombardi's name has lived on in the American business world, where his inspirational quotes are often displayed in offices and his emphasis on teamwork, simplicity, and execution has been profoundly influential. In American football his astonishing achievements also won him immortality—the Vince Lombardi trophy is awarded each year to the victors in the annual Super Bowl championship game.

LOMBARDI'S COACHING TRIUMPH

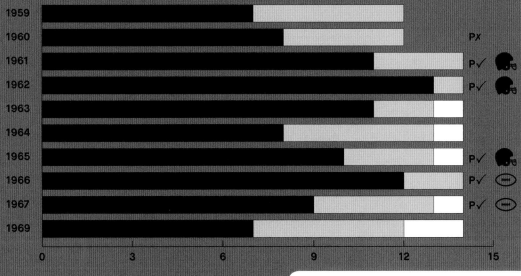

1959		PX
1960		PX
1961		P✓
1962		P✓
1963		
1964		
1965		P✓
1966		P✓
1967		P✓
1969		

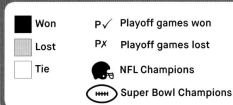

■	Won	P✓	Playoff games won	
▨	Lost	PX	Playoff games lost	
□	Tie		NFL Champions	
			Super Bowl Champions	

LEADERS ARE MADE

Another giant of the sporting world, soccer manager Alex Ferguson, claimed "I think self-confidence—to stand up and lead—is probably just within me." But Lombardi disagreed. He argued for self-determination: "Leaders are made, they are not born. They are made by hard effort ..."

Lombardi believed that this applied both on and off the football field. Football, he suggested, contained valuable life lessons: It taught people that "work, sacrifice, perseverance, competitive drive, selflessness, and respect for authority is the price that each and every one of us must pay to achieve any goal that is worthwhile." His philosophy of hard work and dedication was one that he embodied throughout his glittering career.

LEADERSHIP ANALYSIS

LEADER TYPE: *Talent promoter*
KEY QUALITY: *Disciplined, confident*
LIKEMINDED LEADERS: *Nelson Mandela*
FACT: *His grandson Joe Lombardi is a successful football coach, with Atlanta Falcons (2006), New Orleans Saints (2007-13) and Detroit Lions (from 2014).*

43 INDIRA GANDHI

AMBITIOUS PRIME MINISTER WHO TOOK A TOUGH LINE IN FIGHTING HER WAY TO THE TOP IN INDIAN POLITICS

NATIONALITY: *Indian*
ACHIEVEMENT: *First female prime minister of India*
WHEN: *1966-77; 1980-84*

Indian stateswoman Indira Gandhi, the only woman to have been prime minister of India, maintained a firm grip on power as she set her country on course toward becoming a world economic force.

In 1975 Prime Minister Indira Gandhi defied Indian courts that had found her guilty of malpractice and ruled by decree under a state of emergency. Four times elected prime minister of India, Gandhi was a strong-willed leader and highly effective operator under pressure who used centralized power to achieve results.

The state of emergency lasted from June 25 1975 to March 21 1977. In this time Gandhi launched a 20–point program to boost industrial and agricultural production. She cracked down on opponents, banning organizations and imprisoning individuals. She also delivered amendments to the Constitution that freed her from the charges of malpractice, which centered on her sweeping victory in the election of 1972. Gandhi was ruthless in wielding authority. She embodied power. Dev Kant Barooah, President of her National Congress Party, declared "India is Indira, Indira is India."

BORN TO GREATNESS?

Gandhi's family background and education inspired her to seek political office. She was the only daughter of Jawaharlal Nehru, the first prime minister of India after it achieved independence from Britain in 1947. Born in 1917, she witnessed patriotism and public service at first hand in the struggle for independence. She was educated at the institution in Shantiniketan in Bengal founded and led by the great mystic and writer Rabindranath Tagore, winner of the 1913 Nobel Prize for Literature, then at Somerville College, Oxford University in England.

Indira returned to India in 1941 and the following year married journalist Feroze Gandhi, a fellow member of the National Congress Party (no relation to Indian nationalist leader Mohandas Gandhi). Her motivation to make her mark in the service of India can only have been strengthened when, soon after their wedding, the couple were imprisoned by the British for subversion in September 1942–May 1943.

RISE TO POWER

When Jawaharlal Nehru became prime minister after independence, Indira gained solid political experience serving as her father's assistant and host. She became a member of the Congress Party's ruling committee, then the party president in 1959. When her father died in 1964 he was replaced as prime minister by Lal Bahadur Shastri, who appointed Gandhi minister of information and broadcasting in his government. Following Shastri's sudden death from a heart attack, Indira took his place as party leader and prime minister. She was sworn in on January 24 1966—India's first female prime minister. Her appointment was a compromise between the two opposing wings of the party.

As prime minister she began to establish strong personal and central control. She got the better of her rivals in the Congress Party, appointing as ministers allies on whose loyalty she could rely, and concentrated power within the prime minister's office. She promoted herself as standing for the disadvantaged, for socialism and secularism, and won enthusiastic support among women, the poor, and the dalits (those outside the traditional caste system, often referred to as "the untouchables"). In the election of 1971, fighting with the slogan "Get rid of poverty!," she won 352 seats, a vast parliamentary majority. In December of the same year she oversaw India's swift military victory over Pakistan in a war that resulted in the independence of East Pakistan as Bangladesh.

▲ Recently elected as prime minister, Mrs Gandhi visits the United States and spoke at the National Press Club, Washington D.C., in 1966.

Following this success Gandhi once again triumphed in the parliamentary elections of 1972. This time her victory provoked an accusation of violation of electoral law, resulting in Gandhi's declaration of a state of emergency.

In 1977, after the end of the state of emergency, Gandhi and the Congress Party suffered a heavy defeat in the new elections. Not one to be put down she began her fightback at once, splitting from the Congress Party to form a new organization Congress (I)—where "I" was for "Indira"; in November 1978 she won a new parliamentary seat and a landslide victory in the election of January 1980.

INDIA ON THE INTERNATIONAL STAGE
In her time as prime minister Gandhi greatly boosted India's standing internationally, building connections with China and the Soviet Union and overseeing India's first

TIME LINE

November 17 1917
Born, Allahabad.

1942
Marries Feroze Gandhi.

1959
President of Indian Congress Party.

1964
Appointed minister of information.

January 1966
Leader of Congress Party and prime minister.

1967
Wins small majority in election.

1971
Wins large majority in election.

December 1971
India defeats Pakistan in Bangladesh Liberation War.

March 1972
Wins third election.

1975
Declares state of emergency.

1977
Defeated in general election.

November 1978
Wins new seat in parliament.

January 1980
Landslide election victory makes her prime minister a second time.

June 1980
Sanjay dies in air crash.

June 1984
Orders attack on Golden Temple, Amritsar.

October 31 1984
Assassinated, New Delhi.

satellite, named after the great fifth-century Indian mathematician and astronomer Aryabhata, which was launched from the Soviet Union on April 19 1975. The previous year, in May 1974, India had tested its first nuclear weapons, at a site in Rajasthan.

One aspect of Indira's desire for central control was her plan to build a dynasty. She had intended for her son Sanjay to take power in her wake, but he was tragically killed in an aeroplane crash in June 1980. She turned instead to her older son, Rajiv, whom she persuaded to lay aside his career as an airline pilot to enter politics. In the event he became prime minister (1984–89) after his mother's assassination.

UNDONE BY RUTHLESSNESS

In 1971, at the time of the war with Pakistan, Gandhi was described in some quarters as Durga, the warlike Hindu goddess dubbed "the invincible." In

MANAGING CHANGE

Mrs Gandhi showed profound resilience to survive four terms as prime minister and fighting spirit to bounce back from the low point of imprisonment in 1977-78. In a speech in 1980 she identified an ability to stay calm amid change and when faced with setbacks as a characteristic of India and of Indian women. They "have the genius of synthesis, to adapt and to absorb" and then added that this "gives them resilience to face suffering and to meet upheavals with a degree of calm, to change constantly and yet remain changeless."

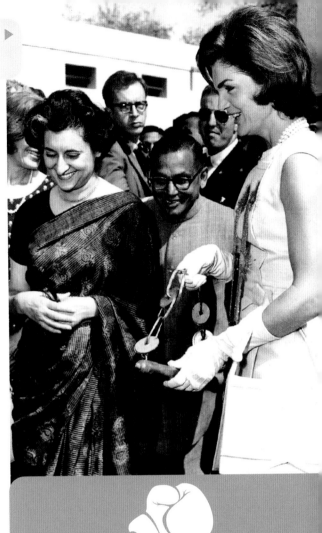

In 1962, Mrs Gandhi accompanies Jackie Kennedy on a visit to New Delhi during the First Lady's tour of India and Pakistan.

later years she came to be known as the "Iron Lady," after the formidable British Prime Minister Margaret Thatcher, who exhibited a similar ruthlessness in her use of power. Like Thatcher, Gandhi was in a sense a victim of her own determination and single-minded drive. Gandhi's severe reaction against Sikh agitation for an autonomous state in the Punjab caused outrage among the wider Sikh community. On June 1984 Indira Gandhi ordered an attack on the Golden Temple, in Amritsar, the Sikhs' holiest shrine. More than 450 Sikhs were killed. On October 31 1984, two Sikh members of her bodyguard turned their guns on her in her own garden.

FEMALE PIONEER

In 1980 in a speech at the opening of the All India Women's Conference Building Complex in New Delhi she declared, "To be liberated, woman must feel free to be herself, not in rivalry to man but in the context of her own capacity and her personality." Indira Gandhi broke new ground for women in international politics—when she came to power in 1966 she was not the world's first female prime minister but her three consecutive election wins in 1967, 1971, and 1972 followed by her return to power in 1980 made her the world's longest-serving female prime minister. This was a remarkable achievement for the woman who declared in October 1984 just the day before her assassination:

I have lived a long life and I am proud that I spent the whole of my life in the service of my people ... when I die, I can say that every drop of my blood will invigorate India and strengthen it.

LEADERSHIP ANALYSIS

LEADER TYPE: *Combative*
KEY QUALITIES: *Ruthless, centralizer*
LIKEMINDED LEADERS: *Margaret Thatcher*
FACT: *As a girl Indira use to play at being Joan of Arc.*

44 NELSON MANDELA

COURAGEOUS LEADER WHO LED THE PROTEST AGAINST APARTHEID AND THEN UNIFIED SOUTH AFRICA

NATIONALITY: *South African*
ACHIEVEMENT: *Defeated apartheid and promoted reconciliation*
WHEN: *1994–99*

South African lawyer and campaigner Nelson Mandela fought against the racially divisive apartheid system and endured a grueling 27-year imprisonment before becoming president of South Africa in 1994. As leader of his country, he inspired his country—and the world— by promoting reconciliation.

At his inauguration as president of South Africa on May 10 1994, Nelson Mandela declared "The time for the healing of the wounds has come ... The time to build is upon us." Putting his natural authority to work alongside the hard-won wisdom of his long imprisonment, he directed his nation toward a future free of bitterness.

As a potent symbol of his desire to achieve reconciliation Mandela invited to his inauguration former president P.W. Botha, who for years had enforced the apartheid system that denied blacks equal rights with whites, and lawyer Percy Yutar who had argued for Mandela's execution when he was on trial in 1963–64. Similarly, guests to his first dinner as president included warders who had been his often brutal jailers during his long imprisonment. He also put his weight as president behind the Truth and Reconciliation Commission chaired by Archbishop Desmond Tutu, under which those who confessed acts committed under the apartheid regime would be granted amnesty.

As president, Mandela refused to dwell on the wounds caused by the racially divisive system of apartheid. Like the Indian nationalist leader Mohandas Gandhi, who worked so hard to bring Muslims and Hindus together in India, Mandela was determined to build bridges between opposing groups. Mandela aligned these grand ideals for a healed and united South Africa with a focus on practical steps to effect change. It would be by "our daily deeds as ordinary South Africans" that his vision for post-apartheid South Africa would become reality.

Mandela was carried to greatness by his dedication to the cause of black nationalism, the natural authority he possessed, and the inner strength he developed during 27 years' imprisonment. His goal as president was to inspire former enemies to work together, as partners, for the greater good, for the future of South Africa. He said, "If you want to make peace with your enemy, you have to work with your enemy. Then he becomes your partner." This was the attitude that inspired people around the world.

THE APARTHEID IN NUMBERS

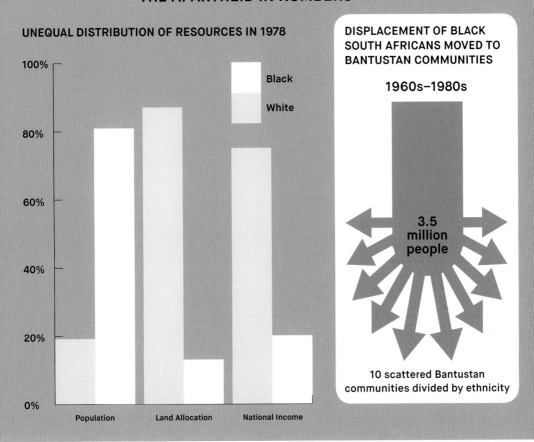

UNEQUAL DISTRIBUTION OF RESOURCES IN 1978

Black

White

Population · Land Allocation · National Income

DISPLACEMENT OF BLACK SOUTH AFRICANS MOVED TO BANTUSTAN COMMUNITIES

1960s–1980s

3.5 million people

10 scattered Bantustan communities divided by ethnicity

DEDICATED, FEARLESS

By the time Mandela became president he had been at the forefront of the struggle against apartheid for 50 years. He joined the African National Congress (ANC), a black nationalist organization, in 1944 and had become one of its leaders by 1949. After studying law he set up South Africa's first black law firm, with fellow ANC member Oliver Tambo in 1952.

Following the Sharpeville Massacre of 1960, in which 69 unarmed South African blacks were shot dead by police, and the banning of the ANC by the government, Mandela and the ANC turned to violent means to effect change. He later recalled, "All lawful modes of expressing opposition had been closed by legislation, and we were placed in a position in which we had either to accept a permanent state of inferiority, or to defy the government." In 1961 he became leader of the ANC's armed wing Umkhonto we Sizwe (Spear of the Nation), whose members undertook acts of sabotage against South African military and government targets. He traveled in Africa and to England to raise support for the anti-apartheid struggle.

On his return to South Africa in 1962 Mandela was arrested and imprisoned, and in 1963–64 he was tried for sabotage. Even from the dock, facing the death penalty,

July 18 1918
Born Umtata, Cape of Good Hope.

1944
Joins African National Congress (ANC).

1949
Becomes leader of ANC.

1960
Sharpeville massacre.

1960
ANC banned.

March 29 1961
Acquitted at 1956–61 Treason Trial.

December 16 1961
Launches Umkhonto we Sizwe (Spear of the Nation).

June 12 1964
Sentenced to life imprisonment.

February 2 1990
Ban on ANC is lifted.

February 11 1990
Freed from prison.

1991
Elected ANC president.

1993
With South African President F.W. de Klerk wins Nobel Peace Prize.

April 1994
Elected President of South Africa.

1997
Stands down from ANC.

1999
At end of presidential term, retires from politics.

December 5 2013
Dies, Johannesburg.

he had utter dedication to the cause. He declared: "I have cherished the ideal of a democratic and free society in which all persons live together in harmony and with equal opportunities. It is an ideal which I hope to live for and to achieve. But if needs be, it is an ideal for which I am prepared to die."

Mandela was sentenced to life imprisonment and was held from 1964–82 in the notorious Robben Island prison, off Cape Town's coast. In jail he suffered terrible treatment: At one point, each Thursday he and other prisoners were made to dig a big trench and then climb down into it. Their wardens then urinated on them, before instructing them to fill in the trench and return to their cells. A leader among

DON'T HOG THE LIMELIGHT

Over years as a leading figure in the ANC, as a leader among the men incarcerated with him as prisoners of the state, and as president of South Africa, Mandela developed a solid philosophy of how to get the best out of others. He said: "It is better to lead from behind and to put others in front, especially when you celebrate victory when nice things occur." If a person has established authority, he or she will benefit from taking a step back and allow celebrations of success to include all who contributed. Mandela went on: "You take the front line when there is danger. Then people will appreciate your leadership." People prove they deserve to be leaders when they step forward in times of difficulty.

After stepping down from the presidency, Mandela remained an international figure. Here he swaps opinions with a schoolchild.

the prisoners, he often protested at their ill treatment and was locked in solitary confinement as a punishment. When his mother died and then his eldest son was killed in a car crash his application to attend the funerals was denied. Yet Mandela also managed to develop a positive relationship with some of his jailers. In these years in prison Mandela transformed anger into the practical forgiving outlook that made his leadership as president so inspirational. Archbishop Desmond Tutu commented "The suffering of those 27 years helped to purify him and grow the magnanimity that would become his hallmark."

Meanwhile in the outside world the anti-apartheid movement made Mandela the world's most celebrated political prisoner. This together with his evident suffering meant that he had unchallengeable authority when he was released by South African President F.W. de Klerk on February 11 1990.

As the figurehead for the anti-apartheid movement and the first black president of South Africa Nelson Mandela was one of the towering figures of the twentieth and early twenty-first centuries, whose life and work truly changed history. His most enduring legacy was his commitment to peace and reconciliation in a country where bitterness and wounds inflicted during decades of racist repression might have created a bloodbath. He possessed natural authority but also learned a great deal about his own character and how to lead others during more than a quarter of a century in jail. "Men of peace," he said, "must not think about retribution and recriminations. Courageous people do not fear forgiving for the sake of peace."

LEADERSHIP ANALYSIS

LEADER TYPE: *Unifier*
KEY QUALITIES: *Humanity, magnanimity*
LIKEMINDED LEADERS: *Mohandas Gandhi, Martin Luther King, Jr*
FACT: *His birth name Rolihlahla means "troublemaker" in the language of his Xhosa tribe.*

EVA PERÓN

EVITA ACHIEVES GLOBAL FAME AS CHAMPION OF THE "SHIRTLESS" POOR IN ARGENTINA

NATIONALITY: *Argentinian*
ACHIEVEMENT: *Iconic leader and force for change*
WHEN: *1946-52*

Eva Perón was a powerful force for change in the government of her husband, Argentine president Juan Perón, and was revered as a saintly figure for her work with the poor. A former actress, she expertly managed her public persona and legacy.

On August 22 1951, a mass rally of two million people in Buenos Aires called on Eva Perón—popularly known as "Evita"—to run as candidate for vice-president of Argentina. Her husband Juan Perón was campaigning for reelection as president and Evita's millions of passionate supporters, thrilled by her unofficial role as a supporter of the poor in his first administration (since 1946), wanted her to stand in an official capacity. They wanted her as their leader in government.

On that day she and her husband addressed the crowd from a huge scaffolding erected on the Avenue of 9 July (named after Argentina's independence day) in the center of the city. Huge posters bearing the likenesses of the presidential couple rose above the stage beneath giant letters spelling out "PERÓN—EVA PERÓN." She asked the crowd for time to decide, but they impatiently replied "Now, Evita, now!" Evita promised she would give her decision in her regular radio broadcast a few days later.

In the end Evita announced she would not stand. She declared she hoped that history would remember her as a footnote in the large chapter written on the achievements of her husband, and that people would remember that "there was a woman alongside General Perón who carried to him the hopes and needs of the people so he could satisfy them, and her name was Evita." The decision was presented by the Perón camp as an act of selfless renunciation. However, historians suggest that the Argentine upper classes and the military establishment—threatened by her success as a champion of the needy—forced Evita to turn down the invitation to stand alongside her husband.

GIFTED, IMAGE-CONSCIOUS

Evita was ambitious and clever. A former actress, she was skilled in self-presentation. She used all these qualities to rise from humble beginnings to become the First Lady of Argentina and, by 1951, one of the most influential women in the Western world.

Eva demonstrated her immense drive early in life when, aged 15, she made her way to Buenos Aires to seek fame. Her poverty-stricken background and the snobbery she encountered as someone born out of wedlock and with no formal education were great

motivations throughout her life. In Buenos Aires Eva established herself as a model and actress. In 1944 she met and married Colonel Juan Perón, who had played an important part in the 1943 coup that ushered in a military government in Argentina. Together they formed a powerful alliance as he prepared a bid for political power.

Evita was far from a passenger in this partnership. She set up and was elected president of a radio employees' union and began her first campaigns for the poor. She also presented a daily radio program, "Towards a Better Future," that promoted her husband's achievements in the build-up to his presidential bid.

CHARISMATIC CAMPAIGNER

She campaigned tirelessly at Juan Perón's side when he ran for president in 1946—the first woman to appear on the campaign trail in Argentina. As they traveled the length and breadth of the country, she made a powerful connection with the Argentine people—most of all the poorly paid working class or *descamisados* ("shirtless ones"). It was on the campaign trail that she first encouraged the people to call her "Evita" (an informal version of Eva). After Juan Perón's landslide election victory, Evita exercised substantial power in his administration, effectively working as minister of health and labor.

She achieved all this in a conservative and male-dominated society that did not easily accept women in public life or roles of authority. She played a significant part in winning the vote for women in her country in September 1947, making radio addresses and publishing newspaper articles in support of female suffrage, and she founded the Female Peronist Party, the first significant political party for women in Argentina.

Evita's position of influence was not uncontroversial. She had many opponents in the Argentinian military and upper social classes who denounced Peronist politics

TIME LINE

May 7 1919
Born in Los Toldos, Argentina.

January 2 1944
Meets Colonel Juan Domingo Perón.

1945
Marries Juan Perón.

1946
Perón elected president.

1947
Establishes the Maria Eva Duarte de Perón Welfare Foundation.

September 1947
Bill giving women right to vote.

1948
Launches weekly newspaper column, "Eva Perón Says."

1949
Forms Female Peronist Party.

1951
Nominated for vice president, but declines.

1951
Publishes book, The Purpose of My Life.

July 26 1952
Dies aged 33, Buenos Aires.

1955
Her embalmed body is stolen and taken to Italy.

1971
Her body is returned to her exiled husband in Spain.

1973
Juan Perón returns as president.

1974
On Juan Perón's death, his third wife, Isabel, succeeds as president. She returns Evita's body to Argentina.

as undemocratic and alleged that she used her populist appeal to achieve her own private ends. She particularly made enemies in these ranks when she abolished the Society of Beneficence, a charitable organization traditionally headed by the First Lady, and established the Maria Eva Duarte de Perón Welfare Foundation (later the Eva Perón Foundation) in its place.

The foundation became a major force for change that employed 14,000 workers, built hospitals and schools, and distributed much-needed practical help to the poor.

ICON AND CELEBRITY

Evita was a celebrity leader. She was an actress and radio name before she ever became First Lady. She never held a formal government position, but was powerfully in the public eye throughout her husband's government. Some authorities suggest that she knowingly aligned elements of her carefully managed public persona with the Roman Catholic images of the Virgin Mary and Mary Magdalene—notably in her work with the poor and sick through the Eva Perón Foundation. Her untimely death (like that of Princess Diana in 1997) increased the force of mourning and the power of her memory. Eva Perón's celebrity has endured long after her death, not only in Argentina but around the world—in no small part due to the success of Evita, first a rock concept album by Andrew Lloyd Webber and Tim Rice in 1976, then a hugely successful London and Broadway musical theater show from 1978 and then a movie starring Madonna and Antonio Banderas in 1996.

Evita gave several hours daily to her work for the foundation, meeting the poor and helping the sick including lepers and those with syphilis. This aspect of her life gave rise to the subsequent idealization of her name and image as a saintly figure.

INTERNATIONAL FAME AND APPEAL

Evita was an adept manager of both her own image and that of her husband. In 1947 she embarked on a highly publicized goodwill tour of Europe. During this trip she was featured as cover star for *Time* magazine under the title "Eva Perón: Between Two Worlds, An Argentine Rainbow." The article included the first published mention of Eva's illegitimate birth. Evita's response shows her ruthless management of the Perón image: She took revenge by banning the publication for four months in Argentina. The following year, 1948, she launched her own weekly newspaper column: "Eva Perón Says."

"SPIRITUAL LEADER OF THE NATION"

By August 1951, when she turned her back on running for vice-president, Evita was seriously ill. Since January 1950 she had known that she had advanced cervical cancer; despite treatment she was unable to beat the disease. Nevertheless the 1952 election was another triumph for Juan Perón: When on June 4 1952 Evita rode with her husband through the capital to celebrate his reelection, she was so ill she could not stand unaided—and needed a frame to support the weight of her fur coat. She died the following month, aged just 33, on July 26.

The news was broadcast across the country and the government declared a two-day mourning period. Over the following days crowds packed the streets near the Ministry of Labor building where her body was held—in the resulting crush, eight people died and more than 2,000 were injured. Evita was granted a state funeral—an honor generally reserved for a head of state—and a Roman Catholic Requiem Mass. She was remembered in the title she had been given in the month before her death: "Spiritual Leader of the Nation."

Evita continues to exert a powerful hold over the imagination of Argentines. On the fiftieth anniversary of her death, in 2002, a museum in her honor was opened in Buenos Aires, and two vast murals of her were unveiled in 2011 on buildings overlooking 9 July Avenue. Moreover, Cristina Kirchner, the first woman elected Argentine president in 2007, declared that women like her who grew up in the 1970s owed a great debt to Evita for "her example of passion and combativeness." She added: "Eva was a unique phenomenon in Argentine history."

LEADERSHIP ANALYSIS

LEADER TYPE: *Reformer*
KEY QUALITIES: *Charismatic, energetic*
LIKEMINDED LEADERS: *Elizabeth I, Fidel Castro, Nelson Mandela*
FACT: *Mourners bought so many wreaths after Evita's death that the florists of Buenos Aires ran out of flowers.*

MARGARET THATCHER

FORCEFUL LEADER FAMOUS FOR HER DIVISIVE POLITICS, ECONOMIC LEGACY, AND IRON WILL

NATIONALITY: *British*
ACHIEVEMENT: *Europe's first female prime minister*
WHEN: *1979-90*

Dubbed the "Iron Lady" for her forthrightness, Margaret Thatcher broke new political ground when she became the first female prime minister in Europe in 1979. In eleven often highly controversial years in power, she made many enemies while transforming Britain's fortunes.

In her moment of triumph, having been elected prime minister in 1979, Margaret Thatcher chose to quote a prayer attributed to Saint Francis of Assisi: "Where there is discord, may we bring harmony." Yet she was a highly combative leader—and for all her achievements she did not build consensus or convince her opponents that she was right.

Thatcher fought every battle fiercely and to the bitter end. She needed toughness to make her way into the top level of national politics from relatively modest beginnings as a grocer's daughter, to overcome resistance to having a woman as leader in the Conservative Party, and to establish herself as a respected stateswoman on the international stage. As a leader Thatcher was autocratic—in spite of her prayer selection she had no desire to build consensus.

Tough, determined, and convinced of her policies, her style was unbending. This was a trait encapsulated in the nickname the "Iron Lady," and in the celebrated line she delivered in a speech to the 1980 Conservative Party conference: "To those waiting with bated breath for that favorite media catchphrase, the U-turn, I have only one thing to say: You turn if you want to. The lady's not for turning." This no-nonsense approach may be viewed positively or indulgently by members of a group or by outsiders when things are going well, but become a millstone around a leader's neck when circumstances turn against the leader or the group.

BENEFITS OF TAKING A HARD LINE
More than once taking a tough position boosted Thatcher's standing: In 1982 her dwindling popularity looked to be leading toward a defeat in the upcoming election,

Mrs Thatcher walks with the newly elected President Ronald Reagan ▶
during her visit to the United States in February 1981. The two
leaders enjoyed a genuine friendship and were firm allies.

TIME LINE

October 13 1925
Born, Grantham, UK.

1950
Conservative candidate, Dartford.

1951
Conservative candidate, Dartford.

1955
Defeated in Orpington by-election.

1959
Elected member of Parliament for Finchley.

1970
Education Secretary.

1975
Leader of Conservative Party.

1976
Article in Red Star *newspaper dubs her the "Iron Lady".*

May 4 1979
Becomes Prime Minister.

1982
Wins Falklands War against Argentina over British dependency on South Atlantic.

1983
Wins second term in office.

1984
Unemployment hits three million; miners' strike.

1986
"Big Bang" deregulates financial services.

1987
Wins third term in office.

1990
Poll tax riots; replaced as leader by John Major.

April 8 2013
Dies, London, UK.

but she was given a great lift by victory in the Falklands War, fought against Argentina over the Falkland Islands, a British dependency in the South Atlantic. Thatcher was a staunch opponent of the Soviet Union—it was in response to a 1976 speech in which she declared "the Russians are bent on world dominance, and they are rapidly acquiring the means to become the most powerful imperial nation the world has seen" that the Soviet *Red Star* newspaper first gave her the nickname of "Iron Lady." In this she was a firm ally of the United States and its president Ronald Reagan.

Very few of her policies and achievements were uncontroversial, but for her supporters her major strength was her willingness to take on entrenched opinion. Thatcher came to power in 1979 after the so-called "winter of discontent" in which a series of major strikes had disrupted the country. In response, she set out to limit the power of the trades unions and in the bitterly divisive miners' strike of 1984—fought over plans to close 20 pits that the government deemed unproductive—labeled the miners and unionists "the enemy within." She was unapologetic and firm in her approach.

SELF-RELIANCE

Margaret Thatcher placed great emphasis on self-reliance. As a leader she was driven by conviction. She could be pragmatic, but was not in favor of compromise. She certainly did not court popularity. She said "If you set out to be liked, you would be prepared to compromise on anything at any time, and you would achieve nothing."

PUBLIC PERCEPTION OF THATCHER

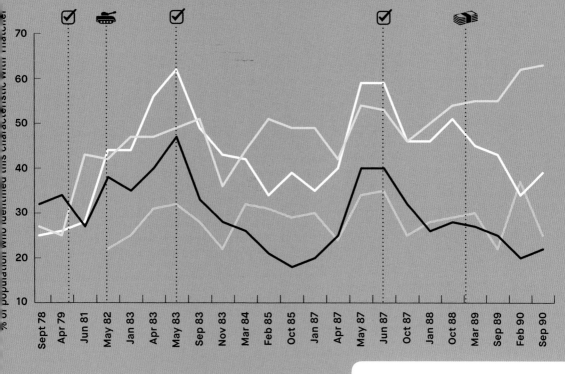

Legend:
- Too inflexible
- Problems facing Britain
- Out of touch with ordinary people
- Capable leader
- ☑ General elections
- 🛺 Falklands war
- 💵 Poll tax introduced

She won: After a strike of almost a year the miners were defeated and returned to work having failed to win any concessions.

This resolute attitude won admiration from some quarters and many praised her for taking difficult but necessary steps in the remaking of Britain. Her government privatized Britain's state-owned industries and public services, including electricity, water, and gas suppliers as well as the national airline and British Steel. She sold publicly owned council houses (a form of social housing) to their tenants. An effect of her industrial policy, which involved the cutting of regulations and subsidies, was the failure of a number of British manufacturing industries and widespread unemployment, which rose to three million—12 percent of the workforce—by 1986. At the same time cuts were made in spending on social security benefits. Her endeavor in these measures—as she put it in a 1988 speech—was to "roll back the frontiers of the state."

NO COMPROMISE
Thatcher's re-election in 1983 and 1987 made her the only British prime minister in the twentieth century to win three consecutive terms of office. The Conservative Party's

Feelings against the poll tax were immensely strong. Riots in March 1990 left a cloud of smoke hanging over Trafalgar Square, London.

1987 election manifesto contained a proposal for local taxation that would prove highly controversial. The document outlined plans to replace the rates system, which was based on rental value of property, with a new personal tax that had no provision for poorer people to pay less.

Once legislation was passed, the new tax—officially called the community charge but quickly dubbed the "poll tax"—was introduced in Scotland in the 1989–90 financial year and in England and Wales in 1990–91. Many people—in some areas as many as 30 percent—refused to pay, deeming the tax unfair, and there were widespread protests. One protest in London on March 31 1990 attracted 200,000 people and ended in rioting that resulted in 400 arrests and 100 injuries.

Despite this and in the face of opposition from notable Cabinet ministers who warned her against proceeding, Thatcher once again refused to back down. She pressed ahead with the tax, but this time her tenacity was ill-judged. The sense grew that she was out of touch with the popular mood and senior Conservatives mounted a leadership challenge in November 1990. She was replaced as leader of the Conservative Party and prime minister by John Major who, as one of his first acts in power, replaced the community charge.

STRENGTH BECOMES A WEAKNESS?

Thatcher's unbending, autocratic, and combative style may have been what carried her to power and pre-eminence, but it seems also to have contributed to her political downfall. After her ousting as prime minister, Thatcher cast a long shadow. She remained an MP until 1992, when she was made a life peer and elevated to the House of Lords. Her legacy was as divisive as her period in office and at her death after a stroke in April 2013 the conflict was still raging, with admirers and opponents either denouncing or enthusiastically praising the results of her time as prime minister.

LEADERSHIP ANALYSI

LEADER TYPE: *Combative*
KEY QUALITIES: *Autocratic, decisive*
LIKEMINDED LEADERS: *Queen Victoric Indira Gandhi*
FACT: *Thatcher famously claimed she slept only four hours each night.*

FIDEL CASTRO

THE CHARISMATIC REVOLUTIONARY WHO CREATED COMMUNIST CUBA

NATIONALITY: *Cuban*
ACHIEVEMENT: *President of communist Cuba*
WHEN: *1961-2006*

Firebrand leader Fidel Castro led a revolution that made Cuba the Western Hemisphere's first communist state. As prime minister and then president of his country, he was a persistently troublesome thorn in the side of the much mightier United States for several decades from 1961 onward.

Fidel Castro exhibited the provocative independence of mind for which he became famous when, in January 1961, he demanded that the United States embassy in Havana reduce its 300 staff. His reason: He suspected many of the staff were spies. In response the United States promptly broke off diplomatic relations. For half a century afterward Castro's continued defiance of the United States made him a hero to countries and peoples in the developing world.

That same month, January 1961, Castro celebrated the second anniversary of the Cuban revolution he had led to oust dictator Fulgencio Batista. In his speech to mark the occasion he declared "A revolution is not a bed of roses. A revolution is a struggle to the death between the future and the past." Castro was a hands-on revolutionary, fighting for the future.

In many countries beyond the United States he was viewed as a heroic anti-imperialist, who dared take on the might of the American military and political machine. He was celebrated as a hero in the mold of Giuseppe Garibaldi, and was an inspiration to figures such Ahmed Ben Bella in Algeria and Nelson Mandela in South Africa (see pages 104 and 188). Right up until the mid-1990s Castro would only appear in public in olive-green military fatigues, presenting himself as a permanent fighter in the revolutionary cause—a leader by example.

REBEL WITH A CAUSE

The son of a Spanish immigrant who became a successful sugar cane farmer, Castro was raised a Roman Catholic and trained as a lawyer. Even while a student he became involved in rebel movements, joining an abortive plot to help exiles from the Dominican Republic oust dictator Rafael Trujillo. In 1953—following the 1952 coup in Cuba that brought former Cuban leader and general Fulgencio Batista to power as dictator—he began to organize rebel forces at home.

TIME LINE

August 13 1926
Born, near Birán, southeastern Cuba.

1945
School of Law, University of Havana.

March 1952
Fulgencio Batista establishes dictatorship in Cuba.

February 26 1953
Leads failed attack on military barracks, imprisoned.

1955
Released from prison, goes into exile in Mexico.

December 2 1956
Failed landing in Cuba, goes into hiding in mountains.

January 1 1959
Batista flees Cuba.

February 1959
Becomes Cuban premier.

February 1960
Trade agreement with Soviet Union.

January 1961
United States breaks off diplomatic ties with Cuba.

April 1961
US-backed Cuban exiles defeated at Bay of Pigs.

1962
Cuban Missile Crisis.

1976
Becomes president.

2004
Launches Bolivarian Alternative for the Americas with Venezuelan president Hugo Chávez.

2006
Provisional transfer of power to brother Raúl.

February 2008
Stands down as president.

Castro's first revolutionary attack, on July 26 1953, was an unmitigated disaster. He led a bold raid against military barracks in Santiago de Cuba that resulted in the death of most of his 165 fighters and his own imprisonment. Whilst in prison he read the works of Karl Marx and Vladimir Lenin, building up a core of inspirational knowledge on which he would draw for the rest of his life as a revolutionary.

PATIENT AND RESILIENT

Released under political amnesty in 1955 Castro went into exile in Mexico, where he set up an anti-Batista revolutionary group, the July 26 Movement (named after their abortive first raid). At this time he met Marxist–Leninist Ernesto "Che" Guevara and Spaniard Alberto Bayo, a veteran of the Spanish Civil War, who pledged to school the rebels in the techniques of guerrilla warfare.

The rebels returned to Cuba in late 1956. Again the initial encounter was a disaster, with most of those who landed

PROTECTOR OF THE POWERLESS

Castro presented himself as a protector of the weak. In his speech to the United Nations in 1979 he asked "Why should some people walk barefoot so others can travel in luxurious cars?" He declared "I speak on behalf of the children in the world who do not have a piece of bread. I speak on behalf of the sick who have no medicine, of those whose rights to life and human dignity have been denied."

▲ *Castro declared that his government were "nationalists and patriots."*

being captured, but a core of the July 26 rebels escaped to the mountains and for the next two years their numbers steadily grew as Castro and his followers waged a highly effective guerrilla and propaganda war against the government. Castro and his fellow rebels were hardy, resilient, and patient in these years living as outlaws. Castro demonstrated his impressive leadership in convincing his followers to build slowly rather than rush a swift assault on their goal. Little by little the rebels edged toward victory. On January 1 1959, in the face of waning political support and a number of miliary defeats at the hand of Castro's rebels, Batista fled the country.

Castro was commander-in-chief of the new government's armed forces. Initially working alongside a moderate named Manuel Urrutia Lleó as president, Castro swiftly took power into his own hands and Urrutia resigned in July 1959.

FRIENDS AND FOES OF FIDEL CASTRO

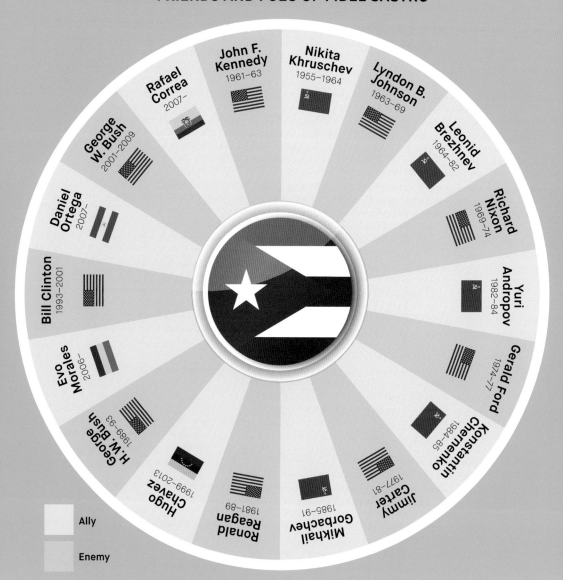

John F. Kennedy
1961–63

Nikita Khruschev
1955–1964

Lyndon B. Johnson
1963–69

Rafael Correa
2007–

Leonid Brezhnev
1964–82

George W. Bush
2001–2009

Richard Nixon
1969–74

Daniel Ortega
2007–

Yuri Andropov
1982–84

Bill Clinton
1993–2001

Gerald Ford
1974–77

Evo Morales
2006–

Konstantin Chernenko
1984–85

George H.W. Bush
1989–93

Jimmy Carter
1977–81

Hugo Chavez
1999–2013

Mikhail Gorbachev
1986–91

Ronald Reagan
1981–89

Ally

Enemy

DEFIANT IN POWER

Castro's government was soon at loggerheads with the United States, especially as he instituted nationalization, land reforms, and a trade agreement with the Soviet Union. Defiant in the face of US might, Castro called on Latin America to rise up in socialist revolution. In April 1961 the US government backed Cuban exiles in an attempt at a coup, but Cuban troops under Castro's command trounced the invasion at the Bay of Pigs. Castro declared with typical defiance, "What the imperialists cannot forgive us, is that we have made a socialist revolution under their noses."

Ties with the Soviet Union became stronger still. The Soviets stationed nuclear missiles with a capability to hit US cities; Castro believed that this would strengthen Cuba's position in relations with the United States while furthering the socialist cause. It was a move that provoked the Cuban missile crisis: The Soviets and the Americans seemed poised to launch nuclear weapons at one another, but eventually both backed down. The Soviets withdrew the weapons from Cuba; one of the clauses in the agreement that brokered peace was that the United States would no longer attempt to overthrow the Castro government in Cuba.

INTERNATIONAL FIGUREHEAD

Castro instituted one-party rule and for decades governed essentially as a dictator. In the face of a continuing United States trade embargo Cuba was increasingly dependent on Soviet support. From the late 1970s Castro became ever more prominent as a leader for the world's less developed countries and in 1979–82 was appointed as president of the Non-Aligned Movement (an organization founded in 1961 for states that are not aligned with any major political power). In this capacity he gave a celebrated speech at the United Nations in New York City. He declared:

> There is often talk of human rights, but it is also necessary to speak of the rights of humanity ... It is not possible to speak of peace in the name of tens of millions of human beings who die yearly of hunger, of curable disease throughout the world. The exploitation of poor countries by rich countries must cease.

When Soviet premier Mihkail Gorbachev initiated his perestroika economic reforms in the 1980s, Soviet subsidies for Cuba were reduced, and after 1990, when the Soviet Union collapsed, conditions in Cuba became more and more difficult. Castro was forced to allow economic liberalization but kept a tight grip on political life. As his health began to fail at the start of the twenty-first century he passed control to his brother Raúl Castro in 2006, before standing down as president in 2008.

Castro was dedicated to the people of Cuba, whom he viewed as his own family, but his legacy is a conflicted one. While he is praised by some as an anti-imperialist and humanitarian, others have accused his regime of human rights abuses and of having devastated the Cuban economy. He was a major figurehead for smaller countries. Bolivian president Evo Morales declared him "the grandfather of all Latin American revolutionaries."

LEADERSHIP ANALYSIS

LEADER TYPE: *Revolutionary*
KEY QUALITIES: *Defiant*
LIKEMINDED LEADERS: *Giuseppe Garibaldi, Ahmed Ben Bella, Nelson Mandela*
FACT: *He claims to have survived 634 assassination attempts.*

48 MARTIN LUTHER KING, JR

PREACHER OF CIVIL DISOBEDIENCE WHO INSPIRED AMERICA WITH HIS DREAM OF A FAIRER SOCIETY

NATIONALITY: *American*
ACHIEVEMENT: *Leader of African-American civil rights movement*
WHEN: *1960s*

American pastor Martin Luther King, Jr, was a profoundly gifted preacher and an intelligent strategist who organized and energized African-Americans in the United States civil rights movement.

"I have a dream," declared Baptist minister Martin Luther King, Jr, "that my four little children will one day live in a nation where they will not be judged by the color of their skin but by the content of their character." With these now widely celebrated words he addressed a crowd of 200,000 at the climax of the civil rights campaigners' March on Washington for Jobs and Freedom on August 28 1963.

King's inspirational rhetoric and spellbinding delivery were to the fore. He declared in characteristically ringing tones:

I have a dream that one day this nation will rise up and live out the true meaning of its creed: "We hold these truths to be self-evident: That all men are created equal." I have a dream that one day on the red hills of Georgia the sons of former slaves and the sons of former slave owners will be able to sit down together at the table of brotherhood.

Like Pericles in ancient Athens, like Abraham Lincoln at Gettysburg, King demonstrated beyond the slightest doubt his gift for making persuasive and powerfully moving declarations. He was a prophetic visionary, summoning a picture of future achievement in clear and unforgettable terms. His great achievements were founded in this ability: He was a preacher of genius.

He was also a strategist, a hugely charismatic and strong-willed leader who galvanized African-Americans into agitating for civil rights. Profoundly inspired by the theories of nonviolent resistance developed by Indian nationalist Mohandas Gandhi, he devised a strategically effective campaign of civil disobedience to bring irresistible

His "I have a dream speech" was unscripted. He was inspired by singer Mahalia Jackson's shout of "Tell them about the dream!" ▶

TIME LINE

pressure for change to bear on the national government in Washington, D.C.

PREACHER—POWERED BY ANGER

Ministry came naturally to King. His grandfather and father were both Baptist preachers and while studying at Morehouse College, Atlanta, he elected to become a minister himself. King was inspired by the college president Benjamin Mays, a gifted preacher and social activist who criticized black churches for doing too little to encourage their members to combat oppression.

He was also motivated by anger at racial segregation, given particular emphasis by his experiences on a pre-college summer stay in Connecticut where he witnessed how African-Americans and whites lived side by side in the northern US states as they were not permitted to do

FORCING THE ISSUE

For King the purpose of nonviolent resistance was to bring about negotiation and change. For African-Americans, the time for patience had passed. Now was the time to force the white community to discuss the problem—to force them without violence. During the 1963 Birmingham campaign he was again jailed. In an eloquent and celebrated "Letter from Birmingham Jail" he explained this core concept: That protests such as sit-ins were designed to bring opponents to the negotiating table. He wrote "Nonviolent direct action seeks to create such a crisis and foster such a tension that a community which has constantly refused to negotiate is forced to confront the issue."

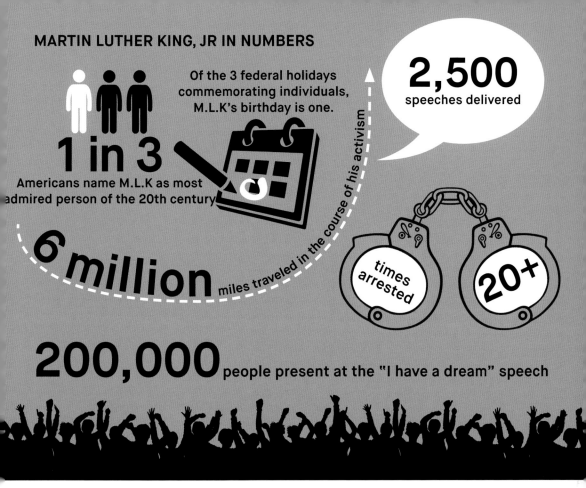

MARTIN LUTHER KING, JR IN NUMBERS

1 in 3
Americans name M.L.K as most admired person of the 20th century

Of the 3 federal holidays commemorating individuals, M.L.K's birthday is one.

2,500
speeches delivered

6 million
miles traveled in the course of his activism

times arrested **20+**

200,000
people present at the "I have a dream" speech

in the segregated south. Like Gandhi in South Africa and India, King provides a powerful example of how anger at injustice can be transmuted into a force for change.

NATURAL AUTHORITY
At Crozer Theological Seminary in Chester, Pennsylvania, King first encountered Gandhi's strategy of satyagraha ("holding to the truth" in nonviolent resistance) that became a central inspiration for his campaigning.

His first taste of social activism was as leader of the bus boycott by African-Americans in Montgomery, Alabama, where he was pastor of the Dexter Avenue Baptist Church. After African-American passenger Rosa Parks refused to give up her seat for a white traveler and was arrested, locals nominated King as leader of the protest campaign. He told them, "We have no alternative but to protest. For many years we have shown an amazing patience ... we come here tonight to be saved from that patience that makes us patient with anything less than freedom and justice."

The boycott gave King an early taste of the violent hatred such civil rights campaigns could provoke when his house was bombed. However, the campaign was a success and after a 385-day boycott segregation was ended on Montgomery buses.

By 1960, while working with his father as a co-pastor of Ebenezer Baptist Church in Atlanta, he was devoting most of his time to the Southern Christian Leadership Conference (SCLC), an organization intended to coordinate and support African-American civil rights activity across the American south. He felt that the time was ripe for change and that African-Americans had reached a "psychological moment ... when a concentrated drive against injustice can bring great, tangible gains." That same year he came to national attention after being arrested while conducting a sit-in to protest against racial segregation at a department store lunch counter in Atlanta—then jailed on the grounds that he had violated probation following a minor traffic offence. The case generated huge publicity and in the end King was freed only after an intervention by Democratic presidential candidate John F. Kennedy—a dramatic act that is thought to have contributed to Kennedy's narrow victory in the election just over a week later.

PUBLICIST
In his campaigns through the 1960s King demonstrated his understanding of the power of publicity and the importance of the young medium of television. His promotion of direct action such as sit-ins and protest marches won support among liberal whites and in the administrations of Presidents Kennedy (1960–63) and Lyndon B. Johnson (1963–69). In 1963 his nonviolent SCLC campaign in Birmingham, Alabama, hit national TV screens after local police chief Eugene "Bull" Connor used dogs and water cannon

King walks in the center of the line of protestors in the March on Washington for Jobs and Freedom, August 28 1963.

against the protestors. Support for King's campaign soared. King himself appeared many times on television and was natural and persuasive in front of the camera.

In the immediate aftermath of these events the March on Washington for Jobs and Freedom was organized. King understood the importance of maintaining as broad a backing as possible for the civil rights campaign. In the celebrated "I have a dream" speech he emphasized how his vision had its roots in the American Dream and told his fellow African-Americans "We cannot walk alone." He held to nonviolence on the grounds of conviction, but he also knew that keeping protests peaceful was crucial to maintaining a broad appeal.

▲ *Martin Luther King Jr was determined to bring people to the negotiating table. Here he and his wife are greeted by New York City Mayor Wagner.*

In 1964 the Civil Rights Act was finally passed, under which racial discrimination was outlawed in employment, voting, and public facilities. That same year King was awarded the Nobel Peace Prize.

MARTYR

He was just 39 when he was assassinated in Memphis, Tennessee, on April 3 1968. His killer was identified as James Earl Ray. He was remembered as a martyr to the cause of African-American civil rights that he championed so passionately and effectively. His great courage, his sound strategic sense, his forthright determination that—like Gandhi's protests—his campaigns must remain nonviolent all marked him out as one of the greatest political and peace campaigners of the twentieth century. His eloquent, passionately delivered sermons and speeches have remained profoundly inspirational and proved him a great prophet of change who pointed the way forward—as he declared on the night before his assassination: "I've seen the promised land. I may not get there with you. But I want you to know tonight that we, as a people, will get to the promised land."

LEADERSHIP ANALYSIS

LEADER TYPE: *Persuasive*
KEY QUALITIES: *Orator, passionate, strategist*
LIKEMINDED LEADERS: *Pericles, Abraham Lincoln, Mohandas Gandhi, Winston Churchill*
FACT: *The Memphis Motel where King was shot was transformed into the National Civil Rights Museum in 1991.*

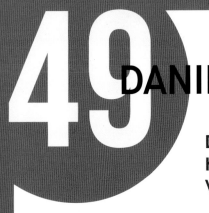

49 DANIEL BARENBOIM

DEDICATED CONDUCTOR AIMING TO HEAL DIVISIONS WITH HIS ORCHESTRA WITHOUT BORDERS

NATIONALITY: *Argentinian*
ACHIEVEMENT: *Founded orchestra that brings together opponents in Arab-Israeli conflict*
WHEN: *1999–*

Profoundly gifted Argentine-Israeli pianist and conductor Daniel Barenboim has been director of several world-renowned opera houses and symphony orchestras, but is celebrated above all for opposing Middle East conflict through the ground-breaking West-Eastern Divan Orchestra, which brings together Arab and Israeli musicians in perfect harmony.

When on August 7 2009 Daniel Barenboim conducted the Arab and Israeli musicians of his West-Eastern Divan Orchestra in Geneva, the concert was dedicated to Edward Said, the Palestinian literary scholar with whom Barenboim had co-founded the orchestra ten years earlier, in 1999. Said and Barenboim opposed conventional thinking on the Arab–Israeli conflict and established the orchestra to promote understanding between Arabs and Israelis. Its first workshop was in Weimar, Germany in the summer of 1999. Said had died in 2003, but Barenboim kept the orchestra going.

Barenboim explained that he set up the Divan orchestra because he saw there could never be a military solution to the Arab–Israeli conflict, which dates back thousands of years, but was brought to a particular focus by the establishment of Israel in the years after World War II. Barenboim has summarized the conflict thus: "Here we have two nations who are absolutely convinced they have equal claims to live on the same little patch of earth, preferably without the other." The conflict might seem uneven, with Israel cast as an occupying power and Palestinians as victims, but in one sense they are what Barenboim calls "symmetrical": Both want what they cannot have. "Each side," he argues, "needs to accept the impossibility of their dream."

At the time of its tenth anniversary in 2009, the orchestra's members hailed from Israel, Palestine, Syria, Lebanon, Jordan, and Egypt—together with players from Iran, Turkey, and Spain. This diverse make-up perfectly reflects Barenboim's aims for the group: "The Divan was conceived as a project against ignorance ... it is absolutely essential for people to get to know the other, to understand what the other thinks and feels, without necessarily agreeing with it." The orchestra project was not, he added, intended to convert Arabs to the Israeli position, or Israelis to the Arab position, but to "create a platform where the two sides can disagree and not resort to knives."

EXPERIENCE OF EQUALITY

Born in Argentina, before moving with his family—of Russian-Jewish descent—to Israel. Barenboim himself stands outside national boundaries: He lives in Berlin, Germany, and holds citizenship of Israel, Palestine, Argentina, and Spain. (He accepted honorary Palestinian citizenship in 2008, and said he hoped it would be seen as a gesture of peace.)

In his orchestra Barenboim aims to use music as a way to break down borders between people and encourage collaboration and unity. Central to the project is his belief that when musicians play together they find common ground in their creative expression: He explains,

> I am not interested in getting the orchestra to play the way I want it to play. What I am interested in is to see how to get 100 people to think and feel alike, to get together and feel one huge common lung. That you breathe the music the same way.

His belief, and hope, is that this experience profoundly alters relations between people who pass through the orchestra. It is an experience of equality and cooperation. Barenboim said of his musicians, "They are here to do things: Make music and learn about the other. This can happen because the orchestra provides something that does not exist on the ground, and that is equality."

PLAYING FOR PEACE

Barenboim's involvement with the politics of Israel and the Middle East has been a thread woven through his long and glittering musical career, but it is the establishment of the West-Eastern Divan Orchestra that has done most in

OPPOSITIONAL STANCE

Daniel Barenboim's leadership of the orchestra and associated campaign depends on a willingness to take his own position whether or not others approve. This can be a key asset for those who lead, in positions where followers cannot yet be convinced of the rightness of a course of action. He holds both Israeli and Palestinian citizenships, which is highly controversial in itself. His response: "Controversial is seen as something very negative because we are so concerned with popularity ... controversial is somebody who has a way of looking at things that is not the usual way, maybe not the accepted, a very singular way." His leadership stance—for peace, for hope—requires bravery in the face of opposition.

November 15 1942
Born in Buenos Aires, of Russian-Jewish descent.

1952
Moves to Israel with his family. Makes international debut as pianist.

1962
Orchestral conducting debut, Israel.

1973
Operatic conducting debut, Edinburgh.

1975–89
Musical director, Orchestre de Paris.

1989–2006
Music director, Chicago Symphony Orchestra.

1992
Music director of Berlin State Opera.

1999
Founds West-Eastern Divan Orchestra.

2002
Orchestra launches annual summer school in Seville.

2004
Establishes Barenboim-Said Foundation in Seville.

2006
Named principal guest conductor, La Scala Opera House, Milan.

July 2012
The orchestra performs the entire cycle of Beethoven symphonies at the BBC Proms, London.

2012
Establishes Barenboim-Said Academy, Berlin, for training of up to 90 musicians from the Middle East.

2012
Orchestra plays in the Gwangju Biennale (arts festival) in South Korea and performs before Pope Benedict XVI.

August 24 2014
Orchestra concludes its summer tour with the Waldbühnenkonzert in Berlin.

promoting the cause of peace in that region. Since 1999 Barenboim has led the West-Eastern Divan Orchestra in concerts around the world demonstrating this unique collaboration, which seeks to dissolve national, religious, and racial barriers.

In the West-Eastern Divan Orchestra and associated projects such as the Barenboim-Said Academy, established in Berlin in 2012, Daniel Barenboim puts his musical genius and natural authority to work in the cause of peace. By promoting cooperation and understanding in this most intransigent of conflicts, Barenboim's groundbreaking artistic venture lays down a challenge to politicians and generals, soldiers and freedom fighters to find an alternative model to that of blame, counter-blame, and violence: A potential legacy that would outshine all his achievements in the opera houses and concert halls of the world.

LEADERSHIP ANALYSIS

LEADER TYPE: *Revolutionary*
KEY QUALITIES: *Visionary, determined*
LIKEMINDED LEADERS: *Jesus of Nazareth, Mohandas Gandhi*
FACT: *German maestro Wilhelm Furtwängler described an 11-year old Barenboim as a "phenomenon."*

STEVE JOBS

VISIONARY INNOVATOR INTRODUCES THE MUST-HAVE TECHNOLOGY OF THE TWENTY-FIRST CENTURY

NATIONALITY: *American*
ACHIEVEMENT: *Founder of Apple, Inc.*
WHEN: *1976-2011*

Through an emphasis on simplicity and ease of use, Steve Jobs made once-forbidding computer technology accessible. The man who brought the Macintosh computer to the world in 1984, he turned Apple, Inc. into one of planet's most respected brands and made skillfully designed products into universal objects of desire.

When Steve Jobs unveiled the iPhone on January 9 2007 he called the touchscreen phone a "magical device" that was "literally five years ahead of any other mobile phone." The phone proved a huge success, and Jobs, a computing pioneer for more than 30 years, again demonstrated his innate gift for anticipating—and often leading—consumer taste.

A little over six months after its unveiling, the iPhone was launched in US shops. Consumers turned up in their thousands to get their hands on this new technology, forming long lines outside stores to purchase one. The revolutionary device, which allows users to operate a touchscreen display with their fingers rather than use buttons, was sold in two models at $499 or $599 each. By September 10 Apple had sold one million iPhones.

The iPhone was just one in a line of innovative products that Jobs and Apple had introduced to the world since 2001. Their portable music player, the iPod, was stupendously successful, selling 100 million in various models in just six years. Then in 2010 Apple unleashed on the market the iPad tablet computer—calling it "the biggest thing Apple's ever done"—and sold one million of the device in 28 days.

With these three must-have products—the iPod, the iPhone, and the iPad—Apple, led by Jobs, achieved a dominant market position with marketing nous and sleek design that delivered ease of use.

RISK-TAKER

By the time of the iPhone launch in 2007 Jobs was a veteran of more than 30 years in the computer industry. After dropping out of college and taking a trip to India, during which time he became a Buddhist, he worked at electronic games manufacturer Atari, then in 1976 established Apple Computer with his friend Steve Wozniak and Atari colleague Ron Wayne. Ambitious and innovative, Jobs, Wozniak,

TIME LINE

February 24 1955
Born in San Francisco.

April 1 1976
Sets up Apple Computer Inc with Wozniak and Wayne.

1976
With Wozniak builds and sells Apple I computer.

1977
Develops prototype Apple II computer.

1984
Apple Macintosh launched.

1985
Ousted from Apple, founds NeXT.

1986
Founds Pixar and launches its first animated film Luxo Jr.

1997
Returns to Apple.

1998
Apple launches iMac.

2001
Apples launches iPod; first Apple retail stores open.

2003
Apple launches iTunes music store.

2006
Disney acquires Pixar for $7.4 billion.

2007
Launches iPhone.

2008
Apple launches the MacBook Air.

2010
Apple launches the iPad.

2011
Resigns as Apple CEO in August. Dies October 5.

and Wayne saw the potential of the home computer market and knew they were on to something big. They aimed their product at early home computer and software hobbyists, but after developing the Apple II in 1977 they realized that their pioneering computer had profound potential. Developed using the profits from the sale of the Apple I, the Apple II was the first computer to work straight out of the box. Until this design all personal computers came in the form of a kit that had to be assembled by the owner. It was a revolutionary design.

After the launch of the Apple Macintosh in 1984, however, Jobs was ousted from the company by the CEO, John Scully, whom he himself had helped bring in. For 11 years, 1985–1996, he was exiled from Apple. He did not rest, however, and was enormously successful, founding NeXT computer company and the computer animation outfit of Pixar. When a struggling Apple purchased NeXT in 1996, in order to use the computer operating system it had developed, Jobs returned to the company. Initially named informal adviser to Apple CEO Gil Amelio, in 1997 Jobs ousted Amelio and himself became "interim CEO." The glory years were about to begin and Apple began its comeback with the famous "Think different" marketing campaign launched in 1997 on television and in print ads.

PRODUCT TESTER FOCUSED ON SIMPLICITY

For achieving excellence, Jobs emphasized the importance of focus and simplicity. At Apple he fixed his attention on what he called the "forward-looking stuff." His executive team—and in particular his ultimate successor Tim

THE IPRODUCTS THAT TOOK THE WORLD BY STORM

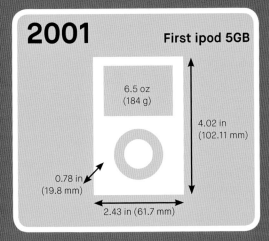

2001   First ipod 5GB

6.5 oz (184 g)

4.02 in (102.11 mm)

0.78 in (19.8 mm)

2.43 in (61.7 mm)

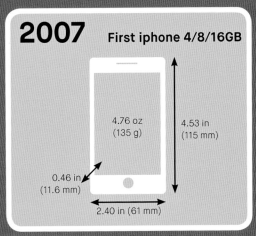

2007   First iphone 4/8/16GB

4.76 oz (135 g)

4.53 in (115 mm)

0.46 in (11.6 mm)

2.40 in (61 mm)

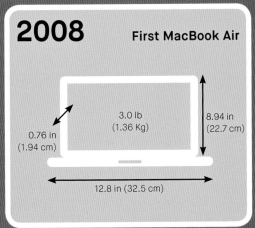

2008   First MacBook Air

3.0 lb (1.36 Kg)

8.94 in (22.7 cm)

0.76 in (1.94 cm)

12.8 in (32.5 cm)

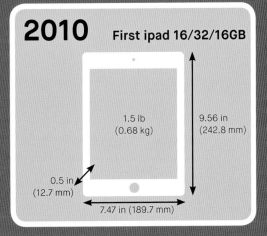

2010   First ipad 16/32/16GB

1.5 lb (0.68 kg)

9.56 in (242.8 mm)

0.5 in (12.7 mm)

7.47 in (189.7 mm)

Cook—carried most of the weight of work normally done by a chief executive officer. Jobs said simplicity was key. "Simple can be harder than complex" he explained, "You have to work hard to get your thinking clean to make it simple. But it's worth it in the end because once you get there, you can move mountains."

Jobs concentrated his efforts particularly on product design, recruitment, and marketing. He was intimately involved with the design of Apple's products. Often in the company's industrial design laboratory, he personally carried out an exhaustive testing of all the items in development, feeding back detailed responses to the designers. He cast himself as Apple's end-user and applied the highest standards. He was never afraid to give negative feedback: "My best contribution is not settling for anything but really good stuff, in all the details. That's my job—to make sure everything is great."

RECRUITER OF TALENT

Jobs strongly believed in the importance of high-quality people and took an active role in recruitment. He believed in the effectiveness of small- and medium-sized teams, with the leaders of these groups coordinating with one another. With such a model, he said, "you can collectively do things that are very impressive." Small teams of extraordinary people could "run circles around large teams of normal people." So recruitment was key: "My number one job here at Apple is to make sure that the top 100 people are A-plus players. And everything else will take care of itself."

MARKETING MAN

Jobs had a particular gift for marketing and closely managed the way in which the Apple brand was presented. He held weekly meetings with the Apple marketing team and advertising agency and personally approved new ads and commercials. He was a consummate showman, and carefully rehearsed the apparently effortless promotional performances he gave at launches and other events.

On top of this, he was also an extremely tough negotiator. He achieved number-crunching deals that were key to the success of Apple, notably in coming to agreements with mobile telephone companies before launching the iPhone and with record labels before unveiling the iTunes music platform. Perhaps his greatest asset was his almost visionary gift for understanding and plotting technological changes. He knew that you had to be ahead of popular taste: "You can't just ask customers what they want and then try to give that to them ... By the time you get it built, they'll want something new."

INNER VOICE

In 2005 Jobs delivered a commencement speech to students at Stanford University. He told them that dropping out of college was the best thing he ever did and paved the way for his later success. He said: "Your time is limited, so don't waste it living someone else's life. Don't be trapped by dogma—which is living with the results of other people's thinking." He emphasized the importance of listening to your inner voice for guidance: "Don't let the noise of others' opinions drown out your own inner voice. And most important, have the courage to follow your heart and intuition." Leaders willing to trust their intuition have an edge over rivals who don't: Less likely to be trapped by received wisdom, they have the benefit of being difficult to predict—and are often energized because they powerfully believe in what they choose to do.

LASTING IMPACT

In addition to the key designs of the iPod, the iPhone, and the iPad, which together formed the backbone of Apple's technological offering, the company also released in 2008 the ultra-thin and very light MacBook Air, a bold and widely acclaimed new step in laptop computers. Jobs also revolutionized computer animation as CEO of Pixar, the computer animation film company that racked up a string of box office triumphs and movie awards from Toy Story (1995) onward.

Tirelessly creative and always striving for perfection, at Apple Jobs

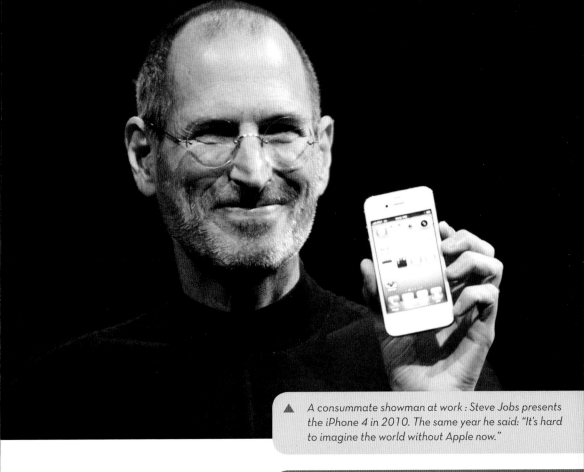

A consummate showman at work : Steve Jobs presents the iPhone 4 in 2010. The same year he said: "It's hard to imagine the world without Apple now."

succeeded in building a bridge between super-complicated technology and the ordinary person: No matter how complex the product, Apple would ensure that it would be easy to handle and operate. Jobs led the way in the personal computer revolution, transformed the way people bought and owned music, changed the face of animated film, and created the demand for smart phones. He will be remembered above all as the man whose company made once-forbidding computer technology user-friendly—a pleasure to use. He famously said, "I want to put a ding in the universe." He certainly made his mark.

LEADERSHIP ANALYSIS

LEADER TYPE: *Innovator*
KEY QUALITIES: *Focused innovator, dedicated to simplicity*
LIKEMINDED LEADERS: *Pablo Picasso*
FACT: *Jobs believed recruitment decisions were ultimately based on gut decisions. He asked every candidate: "Why are you here?"*

INDEX

ACKNOWLEDGMENTS

Quantum Books would like to thank the following for supplying images for inclusion in this book:

Corbis
Leemage 71; Brian A. Vikander 119; Bettmann 131

Getty Images
Giovanni Antonio Pellegrini 29; Print Collector/Contributor 55; Heritage Images/Contributor 59; Popperfoto/Contributor 93; MPI/Stringer 113; Universal History Archive/Contributor 143; Universal History Archive/Contributor 147; William A. Atkins/Stringer 171; Robert Riger 181; Keystone-France/Contributor 193; UniversalImagesGroup/Contributor 203

Prints & Photographs Division, Library of Congress
LC-DIG-ppmsca-19305 2; LC-DIG-ppmsca-15711 90; LC-DIG-ppmsca-08351 105; LC-DIG-ppmsca-19305 109; LC-DIG-ggbain-13889 135; LC-USW33-019093-C 141; LC-USZ62-137196 149; LC-USZ62-139361 151; LC-USZ62-15185 159; LC-USZ62-11988 165; LC-USZ62-134157 185; LC-USZ62-111157 207; LC-U9-10364-25 211; LC-USZ62-120210 211

Shutterstock.com
Jule_Berlin 7; Georgios Kollidas 15; AISA – Everett 35; Claudio Divizia 39; Stocksnapper 75; Georgios Kollidas 77; AISA – Everett 81; AISA – Everett 87; ASIA – Everett 97

Wiki Art
Ivan Kramskoy, public domain 13; Antoine Pesne, Public domain 83; Adolph Menzel, Public domain 85; Franz Xaver Winterhalter, Public domain 126

Wikimedia Commons
By Purshi, CC BY-SA 3.0 21; Placido Costanzi, Public domain 23; CC BY-DA 2.5 25; By Gun Powder Ma, CC-BY-SA-3.0 31; By Meister des Registrum Gregorii, Trier, Stadtbibliothek, Hs. 171/1626, Public domain 45; By Basil D Soufi, CC-BY-SA-3.0 47; Raphael, photo by Jebulon, Public domain 51; James William Edmund Doyle, Public domain 57; Caravaggio, The Ella Gallup Sumner and Mary Catlin Sumner Collection Fund, CC-BY-2.0 65; Titian, Public domain 67; Jyothis, CC-BY-SA-3.0 103; Bundesarchiv, Bild 146-1990-023-06A / CC-BY-SA 115; Frederick Hollyer, Public domain 129; By Jack Downey, US Office of War Information,

Public Domain 173; By Office of War Information, Overseas Picture Division, Public domain 175; By US Information Service (India), photograph JK-000256, Public domain 187; CC-BY-SA 3.0 200; Matthew Yohe, CC-BY-SA-3.0 219

Other sources
W. and D. Downey/Library and Archives Canada/C-019313 125; Tim Graham/Alamy 177; NMF/Benny Gool 191; MTF, Thatcher MSS, White House photos 197; Luis Castilla/WEDO 213

All infographics have been created by Quantum Books, information sources:
Encyclopaedia Britannica.com and Ancient History Encyclopedia.eu 17; University of Oregon, Kelly-RE-Caesar map and Van Roseen Classical Studies, Roman Expansion Map 27; www.cia.gov, The World Factbook 33; english.alarabiya.net, "The Journey of Hajj: Islam's sacred pilgrimage," 2013 49; Lake Superior State University, Charles the Great map 53; Encyclopaedia Britannica, "Genghis Khan: Mongol Empire" 61; The Third Order, Society of St. Francis, Province of the Americas 63; MIT Libraries Dome, Süleymaniye Mosque 69; Folger Shakespeare Library 75; Royal Museums Greenwich, "Peter the Great" 79; Encyclopaedia Britannica, "Founding Fathers" 95; BBC, Italy Before Unification 1796 107; Civil War Trust 111; The Cambridge Illustrated History of the British Empire, ed. P.J. Marshall, pp. 113-121 123; Baseball Hall.org 137; BBC, "Sir Winston Churchill: The Greatest Briton?" 139; United States History.com, "Unemployment Statistics During the Great Depression" and Visualizing Economics.com 161; BBC, "About the BBC: What We Do," 169; Pro-Football-Reference.com 183; Stanford.edu, "The History of Apartheid in South Africa," Figure 1: Disproportionate Treatment circa 1978 and History.com, "Apartheid" 189; Ipsos-mori, Conservative leader image 199

While every effort has been made to credit contributors, Quantum Books would like to apologize should there have been any omissions or errors and would be pleased to make the appropriate correction to future editions of the book.